The Cessna 150 & 152

2nd Edition

Bill Clarke

TAB Books

Division of McGraw-Hill, Inc.

New York   San Francisco   Washington, D.C.   Auckland   Bogotá
Caracas   Lisbon   London   Madrid   Mexico City   Milan
Montreal   New Delhi   San Juan   Singapore
Sydney   Tokyo   Toronto

To my wife,
for without her keeping me on target,
this book would not exist.

© 1993 by **TAB Books**.
TAB Books is a division of McGraw-Hill, Inc.

Printed in the United States of America. All rights reserved. The publisher takes no responsibility for the use of any of the materials or methods described in this book, nor for the products thereof.

pbk   2 3 4 5 6 7 8 9 10 11   FGR/FGR   9 9 8 7 6 5

Library of Congress Cataloging-in-Publication Data

Clarke, Bill (Charles W.)
    The Cessna 150 & 152/ by Bill Clarke. — 2nd ed.
        p.   cm.
    Includes index.
    ISBN 0-8306-4293-5 (paper)
    1. Cessna 150 (Private planes)—Handbooks, manuals, etc.
    2. Cessna 152 (Private planes)—Handbooks, manuals, etc. I. Title.
    II. Title: Cessna 150 and 152.
    TL686.C4C55 1993
    629.133'343—dc20   92-35194
                                                                         CIP

Acquisitions Editor: Jeff Worsinger
Director of Production: Katherine G. Brown
Book Design: Jaclyn J. Boone
Cover design: Cindy Staub, Hanover, Pa.   AV1

Contents

4 Cessna 152 specifications   65

5 Engines   81

6 ADs and other problems   95

7 Buying a used airplane   100

Acknowledgments

THIS BOOK WAS made possible by the kind assistance and contributions of:

Dean Humphrey, Lorretta Kelly, and Alice Helson of Cessna Aircraft Company.

Smithsonian Institution

Skip Carden of the Cessna 150/152 Club.

And many other wonderful airplane people who provided me with photographs, descriptions, advice, hardware, and friendship.

A special thanks to the research librarians at the Voorheesville Public Library, of Voorheesville, New York—the finest small-town library a writer could ask for.

Introduction

THE CESSNA 150/152 airplanes are the most popular two-place airplanes ever produced. This book was written to assist you—the pilot, the owner, the would-be owner, or the aviation buff—in gaining a complete understanding of these airplanes. Here, you will learn all about the various years and models and their differences, read about problems and how to fix the problems, and learn about modifications that can be made to improve performance and comfort.

If you're thinking of purchasing a used 150/152, you will discover where and how to locate a good one. Although the prospective buyer might have a basic idea of what an advertised airplane looks like, the buyer should have a source to review for further information about the airplane, its equipment, and its value. This book is just such a source. A price guide, based on the current used airplane market, is found at the back of the book. A walk-through of all the purchase paperwork is performed, including examples of the forms to be filled out.

Read about how to care for your plane, and learn what preventive maintenance you may legally perform. See what an annual is all about. An avionics section is included to help you make practical and economical decisions when you decide to upgrade avionics.

Hangar-fly the 150/152 and see what the pilots of these planes have to say. Hear from the mechanics who service the aircraft. Read what the National Transportation Safety Board has to say about this Cessna model compared to other small airplanes.

In summary, this book was written to provide the Cessna 150 and 152 owner/pilot with as much background material as possible in one reference guide.

1

Company history

ON A JUNE DAY IN 1911, Clyde Cessna started the engine of his homemade wood-and-fabric airplane and made his first successful flight; thus, a 31-year-old farmer and mechanic from Rago, Kansas, became the first person to build and fly an airplane west of the Mississippi River and east of the Rocky Mountains. Clyde Cessna had laid the cornerstone of today's Cessna Aircraft Company, a world leader in general aviation production and sales (Fig. 1-1).

From that time until America's entry into World War I curtailed civilian flying, Clyde Cessna designed and built one airplane each year. He improved and refined his basic design every year, then flew each on exhibition flights.

EARLY DAYS

In the winter of 1916–17, Cessna accepted an invitation from the Jones Motor Car Company to build his newest airplane in their plant in Wichita, Kansas; thus, he pioneered the manufacture of powered aircraft in Wichita. Wichita is still home for the Cessna Aircraft Company.

On July 5, 1917, Cessna set a notable speed record of 124.62 mph on a cross-country flight from Blackwell, Oklahoma, to Wichita. This record was only the first of many racing and competition triumphs to be scored by Cessna airplanes.

In 1925, with a total of six successful airplane designs to his credit, Cessna joined Walter Beech and Lloyd Stearman in establishing the Travel Air Manufacturing Company at Wichita, and became its president. Cessna remained with Travel Air until 1927, when he sold his share to Beech. He then built his first production model airplane, the four-place full-cantilever high-winged Comet monoplane.

On December 31, 1927, the Cessna Aircraft Company officially came into being. Cessna placed the A series on the market in 1928, the year that a Cessna AW won the Class A Transcontinental Air Derby from New York to Los Angeles. By 1929, the Cessna Aircraft Company had built a new factory southwest of Wichita on about 80 acres of land. During the Depression, Cessna built the CG-2 Glider. The CG indicated "Cessna glider" and the 2 designation indicated model number two.

Fig. 1-1. Clyde Cessna (right) started Cessna Aircraft. His nephew Dwane Wallace (left) became president of Cessna in 1936 and directed the company to its position of leadership in the general aviation industry. In 1985, Cessna became a subsidiary of General Dynamics Corporation and in 1992 was sold to Textron, Incorporated.

Cessna's AW won two more trophies in 1931 for the Detroit News Trophy Race and the "World's Most Efficient Airplane" award. Always moving forward, Cessna built the first retractable landing gear airplane, the CR-2 Racer, in 1933. An updated version, the CR-3 Racer, flew at the American Air Races and set a world speed record—242.35 mph—for airplanes with engines having fewer than 500 cubic inches of displacement. The Model C-34 won the Detroit News Trophy Race and "World's Most Efficient Airplane" award in 1935 and 1936.

Airmaster production started in 1937 with the C-37 and continued with the C-146 and C-165 from 1938–40.

WORLD WAR II

Cessna introduced the Model T-50 Bobcat in 1940 for World War II. More than 5400 of these airplanes were produced. This was Cessna's first twin-engine airplane and the first low-wing design by the company. The T-50 is sometimes referred to as the Bamboo Bomber, and officially known as the UC-78. Other names that should not be repeated have also been used to identify it, no doubt due to its tube-and-fabric design and unexceptional flying characteristics. The T-50 was made famous to a nation of young television watchers as the original *Songbird* flown by Kirby Grant in the TV series "Sky King" of the early 1950s.

During the war period, Cessna, like all the other aviation manufacturers, had grown. The Wichita-based company constructed a new production plant in 1942 in nearby Hutchinson, Kansas.

POSTWAR

In the postwar period, starting in 1946, Cessna returned to commercial production with the Models 120 and 140 airplanes. They were the first Cessna airplanes with spring-steel landing gear, which became a hallmark of the Cessna fixed-gear airplanes and was not improved upon for nearly 25 years. Just after introducing the two-place models to the postwar flying public, Cessna started production of the five-place Models 190 and 195. The 190 and 195 planes were Cessna's first all-metal airplanes.

Vying with the other postwar airplane manufacturers, Cessna introduced the Model 170, a four-place version of the 120/140 series airplanes. Introduced in 1948, the first 170s had metal fuselages and fabric-covered wings. Of course, all Cessna airplanes had conventional landing gear (tailwheels), as did most airplanes of that era.

In 1949, the 120/140 and 170 models were updated, and became all-metal airplanes. Gone were the rag-covered wings, ending the fabric-covered airplane era for Cessna.

Cessna reentered the military market in 1950 with the Bird Dog (L-19). This was the first production model Cessna airplane to incorporate high-lift wing flaps. The flaps, then called Para-Lift flaps, were introduced on the Model 170B in 1952. Since that time, Cessna airplanes have always been known for the wonderful barn door-sized flaps.

In 1953, the Model 180 entered production, and has since become one of the most respected heavy-hauling single-engine airplanes ever built. Its most important hauling roles are in Alaska and Canada, where it can be found on wheels, skis, or floats.

Cessna also took another giant step forward in 1953 by producing its first jet airplane, the XT-37A. Later models of this airplane would provide flight training for U.S. Air Force pilots well into the 1980s, and used many years later for pilot proficiency flying in Air National Guard units. Cessna also built its first turboprop airplane (XL-19B) in 1953 and set a world altitude record of 37,063 feet on July 16, 1953.

Cessna began production of the Model 310 in 1954. It was the first all-metal production twin-engine airplane by Cessna and its appearance was miles ahead of the competition. The older Model 310s still look as modern as today. In 1955, Cessna started production of the T-37A trainer. The first production models of the U.S. Marines' OE-2 were also built that year.

BIRTH OF THE MODERN CESSNAS

Modernization in 1956 resulted in introduction of the Model 172 and 182 airplanes. Both were tricycle landing-gear craft, displaying only minor differences from their predecessors, the 170s and 180s. New sales phrases heralded these trigeared planes and would be heard for many years, for instance "Land-O-Matic," referring to the tricycle landing gear, driving the airplane into the air and back onto the ground.

Sales of the conventional-geared Model 170 lagged in 1957 and production was halted. The average flying family man wanted an easy-to-handle airplane, and the trigeared 172 was the answer. This was not the case for the 180 because it found a niche with heavy hauling duties as a bushplane.

The popular Model 310 was given a U.S. Air Force designation, the U-3 (Utility 3), and in 1957 USAF deliveries began. The U-3s were used to transport VIPs, documents, and medical patients on short flights. The T-37A was phased out in 1959 with the introduction of the T-37B jet trainer. Cessna also reentered the two-place airplane market in 1959 with the Model 150. The 150 series was destined to become the most popular line of trainers ever built.

In 1960, all Cessna production airplanes adopted swept tails except the Models 150 and 180. The 150 would later have a swept tail. The 180 never would. Also, in 1960 Cessna entered the class of sleek, fast retractables with the Model 210. The 210 was unique in its field, however, because it had a high wing, unlike the low wings of the competition (Piper's Comanche). Also in 1960, Cessna purchased 49 percent interest in Reims Aviation, Reims, France. This is interesting to note because Reims produces Cessna airplanes in France that are identical to the Wichita Cessnas. Cessna also purchased McCauley Industrial Corporation (makers of propellers) as a wholly owned subsidiary.

Production of the Skyknight, Cessna's first supercharged twin-engine airplane, started in 1961. The Skyknight was an outgrowth of the Model 310, with similar sleek lines.

To better serve the users of the Model 180, Cessna introduced the Skywagon. An upgraded 180, the 185 carries more than its own weight in cargo. Many Skywagons can be found in Alaska and Canada doing bush flying. Others are in the outback of Australia and even in the African jungles.

In 1962, Cessna began updating some production models to Omni-Vision (wraparound windshields and rear windows). Models 210 and 182 were the first to be changed. The famous L-19 was redesignated the O-1 and production restarted in 1962. The O-1 saw extensive duty in Vietnam. Cessna also introduced the six-place trigear Model 205 in 1962. Omni-Vision was introduced on the 172 in 1963, and Cessna manufactured its 50,000th airplane—a Skyhawk (172).

In 1964, Cessna received a contract to manufacture 170 Model T-41A aircraft, a modified 172, for the U.S. Air Force. The T-41A became the Air Force's standard primary flight trainer. Also in 1964, Cessna started production of the Model 411 twin- engine airplane. The 411 was the first cabin-class airplane built by Cessna.

By 1965, Cessna production had reached the milestone of one airplane every 23 minutes during the eight-hour working day. This year also saw the delivery of the 10,000th Model 172 to a flying club in Elaine, Arkansas.

Cessna took a big step in 1966 to broaden the base of the private aircraft market by launching a worldwide learn-to-fly campaign. Production of the 1966 Model 150 two-place trainer increased to 3000 (Fig. 1-2) units and the price was reduced more than 10 percent; thus, making the 150 more readily available. Cessna

Fig. 1-2. Cessna was proud when the 3,000th 150 rolled out the door. Who would have dreamed that only 20 years later the entire light airplane industry would die?

also delivered its 60,000th airplane to an Oklahoma supermarket manager in 1966 and struck an agreement with the Argentine government allowing Cessna to manufacture certain models in Argentina. Cessna's Reims Aviation in France began production of the Model 150 in 1966.

By 1967, the T-41A had proven its worth as an Air Force trainer and additional models of the T-41 were developed to satisfy the needs of the U.S. Army and the Air Force Academy. Cessna also delivered its 75,000th airplane in 1967. The year also marked the first time since the 1930s that a U.S. manufacturer had built a combat-designated airplane. This new aircraft, designated the A-37 (A- for attack), was a highly modified and heavily armored version of the T-37.

Milestones in 1968 included deliveries of the 10,000th Model 150, 10,000th Model 182/Skylane, and 1000th T-37 jet trainer. From 1969 until 1975 the production marks continued to rise, and in 1975 Cessna passed the 110,000th airplane mark in total production.

By 1978, the Cessna pilot training center program, which had started in 1966, had expanded into 33 countries worldwide. Cessna's the total yearly production reached a record 9197 airplanes in 1978.

CLOUDS OF DESPAIR

The year 1980 was the silver anniversary of the Model 172 airplane. More than 31,000 had been delivered, but clouds were forming on the horizon of general aviation, and Cessna felt the first effects of the brewing storm when it was forced to lay off 750 workers in anticipation of a reduced demand for single-engine airplanes. These storm clouds continued to build and in 1983 Cessna posted the first yearly loss in the company's 55-year history. In 1984, Cessna entered the black hole of zero production on some models. Sales lagged as prices rose above what prospective purchasers were willing to pay.

Several factors caused the sharp price increases of Cessna airplanes, as well as other aircraft manufacturer's airplanes: increased labor costs, rising materials costs, soaring engine prices, and product liability expenses. The first three items causing price increases can really be attributed to inflation, but the last cannot. Product liability continues to be a very serious threat to all of general aviation manufacturing.

A prime example of a product liability claim is the infamous failure of the Cessna Model 172 seat tracks. Many such failures have resulted in crashes, extensive property damage, personal injuries, and deaths. The manufacturer, in this case Cessna, was successfully sued in a product liability claim for having built a defective product. The fact that the airplane was more than 25 years old, and the fact that the FARs very specifically lay airworthiness at the pilot's feet, appears to have little bearing on such claims.

Cessna is by no means alone in defending itself from these legal actions. All general aviation aircraft manufacturers are facing similar battles—most involving alleged manufacturing or design defects. Cessna and other manufacturers state that the cost of protection—insurance—from product liability suits represents 25 percent, or more, of the price of a new airplane.

CESSNA IN THE 1990s

General Dynamics sold Cessna to Textron, Inc. and the Wichita company said it continues to "support all of the roughly 130,000 Cessna airplanes that are still in operation around the world." In spite of the rumors that persist about Textron, Inc., also the owner of Lycoming, Cessna states, as noted above, that due to the product liability problem they have no plans to start building more light aircraft.

2

History of the Cessna 150/152

CESSNA AIRCRAFT COMPANY RETURNED to commercial airplane production in 1946 by introducing a new two-place metal fuselage airplane series, the Models 120 and 140. They had the spring steel landing gear that was to become the strength and simplicity standard of the lightplane industry. These airplanes would become the design base for the Model 150 a decade later.

THE 120/140 AIRPLANES

The 120 and 140 had the same basic aircraft structure (Fig. 2-1). The 140 was a metal-fuselage craft with fabric-covered high wings. Naturally, it was a taildragger. The

Fig. 2-1. The Cessna 140 was the deluxe version of the 120/140 models. Early models had a metal fuselage, fabric-covered wings, and dual wing struts.

seating, as in all the Cessna two-placers, was side-by-side. Control wheels graced the instrument panel. It had an electrical system, flaps, and a well-appointed cabin.

The Model 120 was a plain version of the 140 without an electrical system or flaps and a plain cabin. Many Model 120s have been updated to look like 140s by the addition of extra side windows and electrical systems.

The 140A was a much improved version of the 140—all metal (no fabric-covered wings) and a Continental C-90 engine. About 500 140As were built (Fig. 2-2). It's interesting to note that the 140A airplane sold new for $3695 and now commands a price more than four times that. Production ceased in 1950 after more than 7000 120/140/140As had been manufactured.

Cessna Aircraft Company

Fig. 2-2. The Cessna 140A was the last of the two-seat Cessnas for nearly a decade. It was all-metal and had a single strut for each wing.

Specifications

Model: 120/140
Engine
    Make: Continental
    Model: C-85
    hp: 85
    TBO: 1800
Seats: two side-by-side
Speed
    Max: 125 mph
    Cruise: 105 mph
    Stall: 49 mph (w/o flaps)
    Stall: 45 mph (with flaps)
Fuel Capacity: 25 gal
Rate of Climb: 640 fpm
Transitions
    Takeoff over 50-ft obs: 1850 ft
    Ground run: 650 ft

Landing over 50-ft obs: 1530 ft
    Ground roll: 460 ft
Weights
    Gross: 1450 lbs
    Empty: 800 lbs
Dimensions
    Length: 20 ft 9 in
    Height: 6 ft 3 in
    Span: 32 ft 8 in (120)
    Span: 33 ft 3 in (140)

Model: 140A
Engine
    Make: Continental
    Model: C-90
    hp: 90
    TBO: 1800
Seats: two side-by-side
Speed
    Max: 125 mph
    Cruise: 105 mph
    Stall: 45 mph
Fuel Capacity: 25 gal
Rate of Climb: 640 fpm
Transitions
    Takeoff over 50-ft obs: 1850 ft
    Ground run: 680 ft
    Landing over 50-ft obs: 1530 ft
    Ground roll: 460 ft
Weights
    Gross: 1500 lbs
    Empty: 850 lbs
Dimensions
    Length: 20 ft 9 in
    Height: 6 ft 3 in
    Span: 33 ft 3 in

Support for older models

Cessna still produces parts for these airplanes; however, the company admits that delays will often be encountered when ordering. Many other part suppliers advertise in *Trade-A-Plane*. Many Model 150 parts fit the 120/140s.

Some of these two-placers have been modified by a change to the Continental O-200 engine, which is a bolt-in job, requiring few conversion modifications. Also, Cessna 150 seats have found new homes in some 120/140 planes.

Several enthusiasts clubs support the 120/140 aircraft. These clubs provide a backbone of information for the owner with fly-ins, newsletters, and the like. For more information, contact the appropriate club:

Cessna Owner Organizations
P.O. Box 337
Iola, WI 54945
(800) 331-0038

International Cessna 120/140 Association
Box 830092
Richardson, TX 75083
(817) 497-4757

THE 150

In late 1958, after a period of almost 10 years, Cessna once again saw the need for a two-place trainer airplane. Because the 120/140 series had been such a success, Cessna felt that an updated version of these little airplanes would fill the bill for a new trainer.

The new airplane was given the tricycle landing gear that had proved so popular on the Model 172, and a new engine, the Continental O-200 rated at 100 hp. This new all-metal airplane was called the Model 150 (Fig. 2-3).

Smithsonian Institute photo No. 85-7396

Fig. 2-3. The early Cessna 150 airplanes are called fastbacks due to the lack of rear windows.

In a news release, Cessna Aircraft Company announced the complete performance and specifications for the new Model 150, which was scheduled for an October 1958 release. For historical interest, the Cessna news release that heralded the 150's arrival is reprinted here:

The new model is a two-place, high-wing, all-metal, single-engine airplane equipped with 'Land-O-Matic' landing gear.

Cessna designed the new model to fill the increasing needs for a modern two-place trainer, charter, pleasure and inter-city airplane.

Powered with a four-cylinder Continental O-200-A engine, the 150 has a maximum speed of 124 mph at sea level and a maximum recommended cruising speed of 121 mph utilizing 70 percent power at 9,000 ft. Range at maximum cruise is 520 miles or 4.3 hours. Maximum range at economy cruise or 43 percent power at 10,000 ft. is 630 miles or 6.6 hours with a true airspeed of 95 mph.

Exceptional performance features of the 150 are the rate of climb and service ceiling. Rate of climb is 740 feet per minute, while service ceiling is 15,300 ft. Gross weight of the 150 is 1,500 lbs. Empty weight is 962 lbs.

The Model 150 will be available in three different versions starting with the Standard at $6,995. Equipment on the Standard model will include all items listed under standard equipment. The Trainer is priced at $7,940 and will be equipped with a Narco Superhomer with nine crystals or a Sunair for export airplanes, microphone and cabin speaker, turn and bank indicator, rate of climb, outside air temperature gauges, dual controls, landing lights, sensitive altimeter, clock, sun visors, control lock and cigarette lighter. Cessna officials said the Trainer carries all the equipment necessary to accomplish a modern training mission for daytime and night flying.

The 'Inter-City' Commuter will sell for $8,545, which includes directional and horizon gyros with engine-driven vacuum system and a fin-mounted rotating beacon. Both the Trainer and Inter-City models have all standard equipment included in the Standard model. The Inter-City model also has all standard equipment included on the Trainer except dual controls.

A special patroller wing with an additional fuel capacity, for pipeline or special patrol duty where additional range is required, will be available as optional equipment in the near future. Other optional equipment items include shoulder harness kit, children's seat kit, winterization kit, tow bar, oil filter, fire extinguisher, stainless steel control cables, corrosion proofing, high intensity fluorescent paint, speed fairings, dual controls, and bullet-styled propeller spinner.

The Continental O-200-A engine is rated at 100 hp at 2750 rpm. Recommended overhaul time is set initially at 600 hours. Basic dry weight of the engine is 189.69 lbs. or 220 lbs. with accessories. Displacement is 200.91 cubic inches with a 7:1 compression ratio.

The engine is bolted to the engine mounts through resilient rubber cushions, providing complete separation between the engine and airframe, allowing vibration to dissipate before reaching the fuselage. This suspension system, combined with the newly designed Cessna mufflers, provides quiet and comfortable flight.

The propeller of the 150 is an all-metal Sensenich M69CK-52 with a ground clearance of 10 inches.

Oil capacity is five quarts. Operating oil weights are SAE 30 for temperatures below 40 degrees and SAE 50 for temperatures above 40 degrees. Fuel requirements are 80/87 octane.

Model 150 fuel tanks are of all-metal construction with total capacity of 26 gallons, of which 22-½ gallons are usable under all flight conditions, and 24.4 gallons are usable under level flight conditions. The anti-ice fuel vent is located in a protected area behind the strut on the left wing.

The airplane is equipped with large 'Para-Lift' flaps which have an area of 17.24 square feet or 2472 square inches. Flaps are manually operated by a lever between the two front seats in the cabin. The ailerons are large (2575 square inches) and give good positive control. Ailerons are effective throughout the entire stall. Control surfaces are mounted on friction-free compression-molded oilyte bearings.

The 150 landing gear is the same 'Land-O-Matic' design Cessna has used on the 172, 175, and 182. The chrome vanadium steel gear has been used on thousands of Cessna airplanes since it was first introduced. It is strong, durable, and constructed to withstand the shocks of rough field operation. Tread width between the two main gears is 77 inches, which gives exceptionally good ground handling characteristics in crosswinds. The tread width allows good positive steering. New 'gear-toothed' Goodyear individually operated hydraulic toe brakes permit the pilot to turn the airplane in the radius of the wingspan. The new gear-toothed brakes have been incorporated on the main gears which offer positive braking action. Matched gears and teeth around the perimeter of the disc and the inside of the wheel castings have been used to replace keys and clips previously used to hold the discs in place.

Cessna has scored a first in the use of nylon tubeless tires on the 150. The tubeless tires are blowout resistant and will stand rugged shocks. Tire size (5:00 × 5) is the same for all three wheels.

The cabin area, which has excellent head and leg room, is tastefully decorated. Interiors are available in a choice of Cherokee Red or Amazon Blue. Headliners in both interiors will be ivory-colored and side panels are of ivory royalite.

The top and bottom of the seat back is adjustable both forward and aft. The top of the seat also folds forward to provide easy access to the baggage compartment, which has an 80 pound capacity. A utility shelf above the baggage area may be used for small articles that can be kept within easy reach of the pilot or passenger during a flight. A children's seat of sufficient size to accommodate two small youngsters will be available in kit form from the factory as optional equipment.

The windshield of the 150 is free blown and free floating. It is designed with no center strip and provides unrestricted forward visibility. Ground visibility is exceptionally good from the airplane.

The shock-mounted instrument panel is clean, neat, and functional. Space has been maintained for installation of additional instruments, even with a full panel in the Inter-City Commuter. Arrangement of the instruments makes them clearly visible from either side. On the Inter-City Commuter, the radio is mounted directly in front of the pilot at the lower left of the panel for easy tuning. Engine controls and switches are grouped on the lower center of the panel.

The master switch, key ignition, and starter handle are located for ease of operation with the left hand while the right hand is free to operate the mixture control, primer and throttle. These switches and controls are all within easy reach of either hand, eliminating any cross-arm operation when starting.

A map case and glove compartment is located at the lower right side of the panel. Manually controlled ventilators are positioned on each side of the cabin above the windshield.

A positive control lock is standard equipment on the Trainer and Inter-City Commuter. The upper end of the lock passes through the control shaft and collar while the lower end fastens over the starter handle. The starter cannot be engaged until the control lock has been removed.

The tail group on the airplane incorporates compression-molded oilyte bearings for frictionless control movement. The massive dorsal fin provides good directional control as well as an added touch to styling.

The exterior of the Model 150 is available in a choice of three colors—Forest Green, Damask Red, Colonial Blue. Special high intensity fluorescent paint is also available at additional cost.

Equipment lists

Cessna was proud of the new Model 150s and how they had been equipped. The following lists indicate the various equipment and appointments found on each of the models:

Standard Model (base price $6,995)
All-metal fixed-pitch propeller
Starter
Generator (20 amp)
Navigational lights
Dome light
Tachometer (recording)
Altimeter (standard)
Oil pressure
Oil temperature
Two electric fuel gauges
Mixture control with safety lock
Instrument panel lights
Carburetor heater
Gravity fuel system
Shock-mounted instrument panel
Stall warning indicator
Airspeed indicator
Compass
Cabin heat control
Parking brake
Hydraulic individually toe-operated brakes (pilot side only)
Steerable nosewheel
Para-Lift flaps
Tiedown rings
Engine mufflers, stainless steel
Map compartment
12-volt electrical system
Outside access step
Key-operated ignition
Generator indicator light

Adjustable seat backs
Individual ashtrays
Carburetor air filter
Two fresh-air vents
Key-operated door lock
Engine shielding
Dual magnetos
Landing light wiring and brackets
Attachment for sun visors and shoulder harness
Side-filling tubeless nylon tires
Non-sag seat springs
Propeller spinner

Trainer Model (base price $7,940)
All of the equipment on the Standard Model
Narco Superhomer (9 crystals)
Dual controls
Dual brakes
Turn and bank indicator
Rate of climb
Landing lights
Outside air temperature gauge
Control lock
Sensitive altimeter
Clock
Cigarette lighter
Sun visors
Microphone and cabin speaker

Inter-City Commuter (base price $8,545)
All of the equipment on the Standard Model and Trainer Model
Engine-driven vacuum system
Horizon gyro
Directional gyro
Rotating fin-mounted beacon light

THE AEROBAT

In 1970, Cessna introduced the Aerobat, which is properly referred to as the Model A150. It is a structurally beefed-up adaptation of the 150 (Fig. 2-4 and Fig. 2-5). Cessna called the Aerobat a fun plane, stating that the A150 met the requirements for acrobatic maneuvers of 6 Gs positive and 3 Gs negative load and was certified for barrel rolls, aileron rolls, snap rolls, spins, chandelles, lazy eights, Immelmanns, vertical reversements, and Cuban eights.

The Aerobat was equipped with quick-release door mechanisms, seats with removable cushions to accommodate parachutes, quick-release lap belts and shoul-

Fig. 2-4. Aerobat version of the 150/152 series is stressed for aerobatics and has a distinctive paint scheme.

Fig. 2-5. Popularity of the 150 encouraged Cessna to build the Aerobat as an ideal transitional airplane into aerobatics.

der harnesses, skylights in the ceiling, and a G-meter. The Aerobats have very distinctive paint schemes—as compared to standard 150s—and matching interiors.

THE 152

In April 1977, Cessna announced and began delivering, the Model 152. The new plane, although very similar in appearance, was a complete revision of the Model 150 (Fig. 2-6). The 152 was destined to be the last of the metal two-place Cessna airplanes, dating back to 1946; however, this was not known in 1977, when the following Cessna news release announced the new Model 152:

Cessna Aircraft Company has introduced a new training airplane, with deliveries of the 1978 Model 152 scheduled to begin in May.

Heading the list of new features engineered into the Model 152 is a 100 octane-burning Lycoming O-235-L2C engine rated at 110 horsepower.

Other all-new features include:

—An exclusive McCauley 'Gull Wing' propeller, with redesigned spinner.

—An easily removable and replaceable one-piece cowling, held in place by quarter-turn, quick-release fasteners, for easy access to the engine.

—A 28-volt electrical system that provides more starting power and allows more avionics options.

—Redesigned fuel tanks that reduce unusable fuel to only 1.5 gallons.

—An oil cooler as standard equipment.

The new Lycoming Blue Streak engine achieves its 110 horsepower at a low 2550 rpm. As a result, the derated powerplant reduces external and internal sound levels and puts the Model 152 five decibels below allowable FAA and ICAO maximums that will go into effect in 1980.

The 152 takes off in 725 feet, climbs at 715 feet per minute, and cruises at 107 knots (123 mph). Maximum range is 350 nautical miles at 75 percent power.

The maximum useful load of Cessna's new trainer is 589 pounds. With full fuel, the 152 has 433 pounds of payload for people, baggage, and/or acces-

Cessna Aircraft Company

Fig. 2-6. This 1978 model 152, actually introduced in 1977, replaced the 150.

sories. Contributing to the impressive useful load is an unusable fuel quantity of only 1.5 gallons.

The Lycoming engine delivers improved specific fuel consumption and allows 2000 hours of operation between overhauls. The high compression ratio powerplant and slower-turning prop combine to provide significant fuel efficiency in flight training operations. A dynafocal engine mount has been added to reduce vibration and engine noise and a new exhaust system with a single muffler reduces exhaust sound levels and contributes to engine efficiency. The new muffler uses a single exhaust on the right side of the lower cowl.

A new engine cooling system, paired with an oil cooler that is standard equipment, reduces engine operating temperatures in the hottest weather conditions.

The 28-volt electrical system produces more power for quicker cold starts and the frequent engine starts required in an active training environment. A heavy-duty voltage regulator and starter clutch are included in the system. The 152 will also accept 28-volt avionics and such items as bulbs, regulators, and other parts now standard across the Cessna line.

Engine starting characteristics of the new model will also be enhanced by a cylinder-direct primer system that will inject fuel directly into three cylinders, assuring even distribution and reliable cold weather starts.

The upper cowl on the 152 is a new design, with the engine baffling attached at the cowl instead of the engine for improved cooling and easier maintenance.

A one-piece upper cowl skin attached with quarter-turn, quick removal fasteners is easily removed to place all engine components and accessories within easy reach.

The (cowling) nose cap is a one-piece unit designed to accept a single or dual landing light installation.

Cessna's new, 69-inch, fixed-pitch propeller teams with the derated engine to produce more efficient climb and cruise performance at a reduced rpm, resulting in quieter operation. The new prop design also eliminates the need for an attached spacer between the propeller and engine.

Electrically operated 'Para-Lift' flaps with 30-degree extension on the 152 provide better performance during a balked landing. During go-around, with full 30 degree flap extension, the airplane will climb at 450 feet per minute.

In the cabin, a new recessed window latch allows positive locking, tighter seal, and increased shoulder room.

Options on the airplane include a padded headset with attached microphone that can be operated by pressing a button on the control wheel. Rudder pedal extensions for shorter pilots are also optional.

A 152 Aerobat will also be available. It meets the requirements for acrobatic maneuvers of 6Gs positive and 3Gs negative load and is certified for barrel rolls, aileron rolls, snap rolls, spins, chandelles, lazy eights, Immelmanns, vertical reversements and Cuban eights.

The Model 152 will replace the Cessna's venerable Model 150 in the company's product line, ending a 19-year production run of almost 24,000 that began in 1958. More 150s have been sold than all other two-place training airplanes combined.

"We feel the 152 is the airplane that will replace the world's training fleets with modern, up-to-date equipment designed and engineered for the training environment of the 1980s," said Cessna Senior Vice President Bob Lair.

"Operators of the 150 told us they wanted a training airplane that would burn 100 octane fuel while producing lower sound levels inside and out, better fuel consumption, and more payload," Lair said. "These performance features are all found in the 152."

Suggested list prices of the 152 models, f.a.f. (fly away factory), Wichita, Kansas are: Model 152, $14,950; Model 152 II, $17,995; Model 152 with Nav Pac, $20,635; and Model 152 Aerobat, $19,500.

CHRONOLOGY

Each year of production of the Model 150/152s saw changes to the airplane. Some changes were major, other changes were merely cosmetic. The yearly changes were:

1959. The initial TBO of the Continental O-200 engine is raised from 600 to 1,800 hours.

1960. A 35-amp generator becomes standard on the Commuter, and is optional on other models. The Patroller package with 35-gallon fuel tanks (maximum range of 980 miles) and plexiglass doors is offered as an option (Fig. 2-7).

Fig. 2-7. The Patroller doors offered the pilot good vision below for pipeline and powerline observation. Larger fuel tanks were part of the Patroller package.

1961. The main gear is moved two inches aft to eliminate the problem of a nosewheel that was too light. Cockpit glass (rear side windows) area is increased 15 percent and adjustable seats are offered as an option.

1962. A new propeller airfoil is introduced that increases the cruise speed by 2 knots. Optional family seat becomes available (Fig. 2-8).

Fig. 2-8. Child seats installed in the baggage area permit carriage of extra passengers up to a total 120 pounds. These seats are no longer in production, and are much sought after by 150 owners.

1963. Larger tires (6.00 × 6) are offered as an option. Quick-drain fuel strainers are introduced.

1964. Omni-Vision is added to the Model 150 airplanes giving 360-degree vision (Fig. 2-9). Gross weight is increased by 50 lbs to 1,600 lbs and the baggage load is increased from 80 lbs to 120 lbs.

1965. Improved seats, similar to those in the 172, are installed for pilot comfort.

1966. The swept fin is added (Fig. 2-10). Wider cabin doors, which are 23 percent larger, become standard. New brakes and a change to the 6.00 x 6 tire is made. Electric flaps replace manually operated flaps and a pneumatic-reed stall warning system is installed. The baggage compartment size is increased by 50 percent (Fig. 2-11).

1967. The fuselage is widened at the shoulder level to give 3 inches additional spread. A short-stroke nose gear is introduced to reduce drag. A 60-amp gear-driven alternator replaces the generator. For the first time, the 150 is float-certified (Fig. 2-12).

1968. A restyled center console gives slightly more leg room for the pilot and passenger. A revised flap control system allows for hands-off operation.

Fig. 2-9. The second generation 150s have vertical tails, but were built after the introduction of Omni-Vision.

Fig. 2-10. The 1967 Model 150 has the swept tail and Omni-Vision, as do all succeeding models.

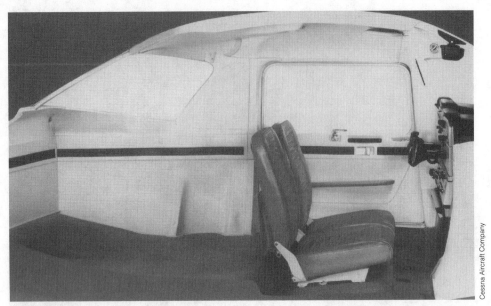

Fig. 2-11. Interior of a 150. Notice the large baggage space behind the seats. Unfortunately, it is very easy to overload this area.

Fig. 2-12. Few Cessna 150s are on floats—probably due to the high cost of installation and the poor performance returns.

1969. A key starter replaces the old pull-type and a ground service plug becomes optional. Improved rocker-type electrical switches replace the older style toggle switches.

1970. The Aerobat version is introduced. Conical cambered wingtips are added for better slow flight control (Figs. 2-13, 2-14).

Fig. 2-13. This wingtip style was found on 150s until 1969.

Fig. 2-14. The improved conical cambered tips appeared in 1970. The conical tips provided for better slow-speed handling characteristics.

1971. Tubular main gear legs replace the flat steel type (Figs. 2-15, 2-16) and the tread width is increased by 16 percent for better ground handling. The landing lights are moved from the wing to the engine cowl.

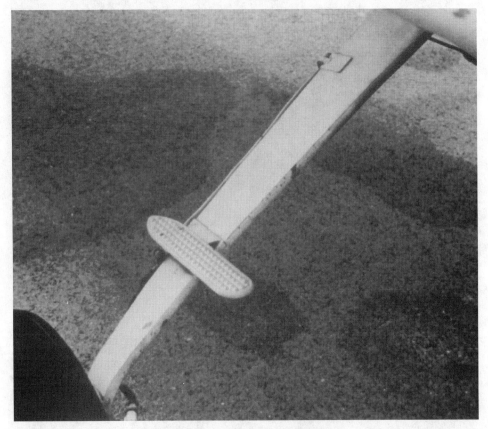

Fig. 2-15. Spring landing gear installed on 1970 and earlier 150s.

1972. Improved fuel filler caps are installed to prevent water from entering the fuel tanks. A more versatile seat and seat track are installed.

1973. The seats are lowered to give increased headroom in the cabin.

1974. The Clark Y airfoil propeller is installed on the Aerobat for improved cruise (4 mph increase).

1975. The Commuter II is introduced with a special package of avionics. The fin is increased in size by 6 inches. Inertial-reel shoulder harness/lap belts become an option.

1976. Circuit breakers replace the fuses. Fully articulated seats are installed.

1977. Preselectable flap settings with detents are installed. This is the last year of the 150 and in May, the 1978 Model 152 is introduced (Fig. 2-17).

1978. No significant changes from the 152 first introduced in 1977.

Fig. 2-16. Tubular landing gear found on later 150s and all 152s.

Cessna Aircraft Company

Fig. 2-17. Cessna ceased production of the 150 in 1977 and introduced this new 152 as a 1978 model.

1979. Dual impulse coupling is installed to increase the voltage to the magnetos and four-cylinder direct fuel priming makes starting easier. Seat padding is increased for comfort.

1980. An accelerator pump is installed to inject fuel directly into the throat of the carburetor, while a slower turning starter provides better starting performance. Dual windshield defrosters become standard.

1981. A hot microphone intercom becomes standard on the Trainer and optional on other models. Quick oil drain becomes available as an option.

1982. A third quick-drain fuel valve is installed for easier contamination checks.

1983. The Lycoming O-235-N2C rated at 108 hp is installed to reduce the 100LL fuel problems.

1984. Landing and taxiing lights are moved back to the left wing, where they were on models prior to 1971 (Figs. 2-18, 2-19).

Fig. 2-18. In the beginning, Cessna 150s had leading-edge landing lights. This was changed in 1971, but returned in 1984.

1985. List prices were:

- Model 152II: $36,400 (factory standard)
- Model 152II: $41,935 (average equipped airplane)
- Aerobat: $39,350 (factory standard)
- Aerobat: $46,720 (average equipped airplane)

These prices were so high that sales dropped to near zero. The average FBO could no longer afford the cost of a new Cessna two-seat airplane—more than $40,000—for training and rental; hence, few were sold. The end of the line arrived when Cessna announced May 31 that they were shutting down all production of the Cessna 152. (Fig. 2-20 through Fig. 2-24).

Fig. 2-19. The improved cowl-mounted landing lights utilized during the '70s and early '80s.

Fig. 2-20. The final version of the Cessna 152, just prior to the end of 152 production.

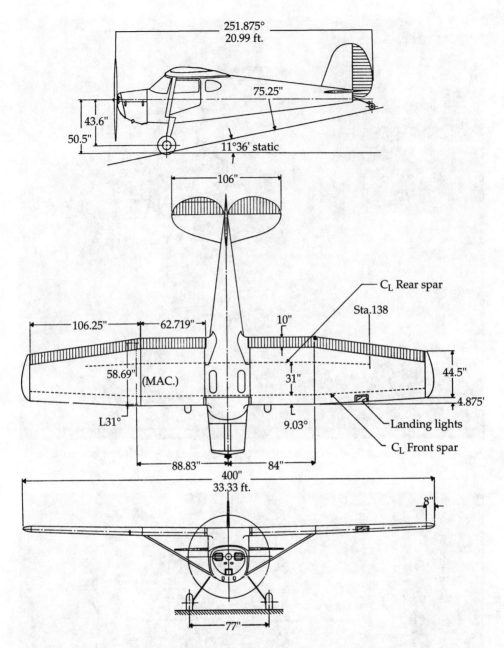

Fig. 2-21. A Cessna 140A reveals a resemblance to the 150. Cessna Aircraft Company

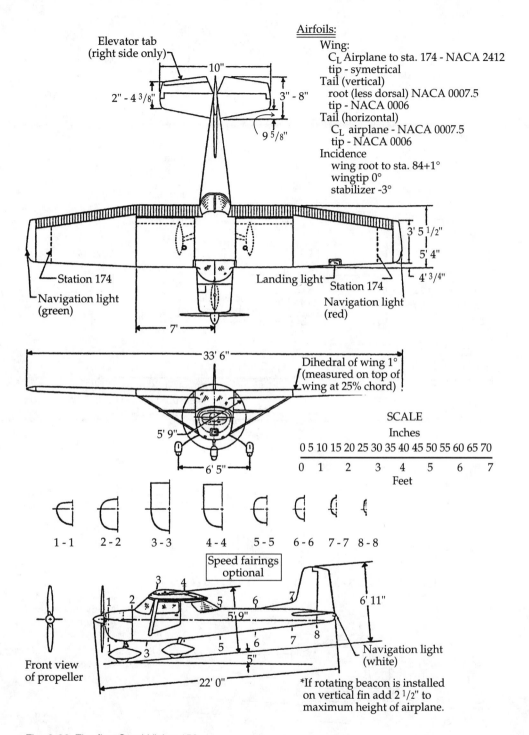

Elevator tab
(right side only)

10"

2" - 4 3/8"

3" - 8"

9 5/8"

Airfoils:
Wing:
C_L Airplane to sta. 174 - NACA 2412
tip - symetrical
Tail (vertical)
root (less dorsal) NACA 0007.5
tip - NACA 0006
Tail (horizontal)
C_L airplane - NACA 0007.5
tip - NACA 0006
Incidence
wing root to sta. 84+1°
wingtip 0°
stabilizer -3°

3' 5 1/2"
5' 4"
4' 3/4"

Station 174

Navigation light
(green)

Landing light — Station 174

Navigation light
(red)

7'

33' 6"

Dihedral of wing 1°
(measured on top of
wing at 25% chord)

5' 9"

6' 5"

SCALE
Inches
0 5 10 15 20 25 30 35 40 45 50 55 60 65 70

0   1   2   3   4   5   6   7
Feet

1 - 1   2 - 2   3 - 3   4 - 4   5 - 5   6 - 6   7 - 7   8 - 8

Speed fairings
optional

3   4

1   2   5   6   7

6' 11"

5' 9"

5   6   7   8

Navigation light
(white)

5"

Front view
of propeller

22' 0"

*If rotating beacon is installed
on vertical fin add 2 1/2" to
maximum height of airplane.

Fig. 2-22. The first Omni-Vision 150. Cessna Aircraft Company

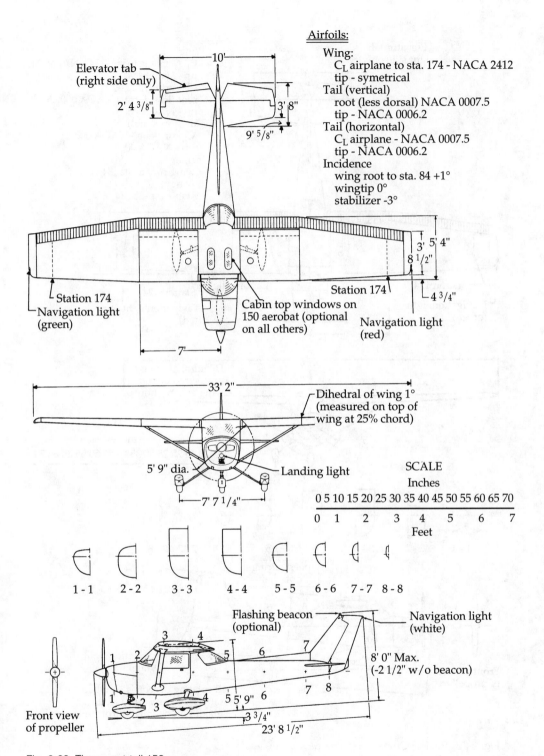

Airfoils:
Wing:
C_L airplane to sta. 174 - NACA 2412
tip - symetrical
Tail (vertical)
root (less dorsal) NACA 0007.5
tip - NACA 0006.2
Tail (horizontal)
C_L airplane - NACA 0007.5
tip - NACA 0006.2
Incidence
wing root to sta. 84 +1°
wingtip 0°
stabilizer -3°

Elevator tab (right side only)

10'

2' 4 3/8"

3' 8"

9' 5/8"

Station 174
Navigation light (green)

Cabin top windows on 150 aerobat (optional on all others)

Station 174

Navigation light (red)

3' 5' 4"

8 1/2"

4 3/4"

7'

33' 2"

Dihedral of wing 1° (measured on top of wing at 25% chord)

5' 9" dia.

Landing light

7' 7 1/4"

SCALE
Inches
0 5 10 15 20 25 30 35 40 45 50 55 60 65 70
0   1   2   3   4   5   6   7
Feet

1 - 1   2 - 2   3 - 3   4 - 4   5 - 5   6 - 6   7 - 7   8 - 8

Flashing beacon (optional)

Navigation light (white)

8' 0" Max.
(-2 1/2" w/o beacon)

Front view of propeller

5' 9"

3 3/4"

23' 8 1/2"

Fig. 2-23. The swept-tail 150. Cessna Aircraft Company

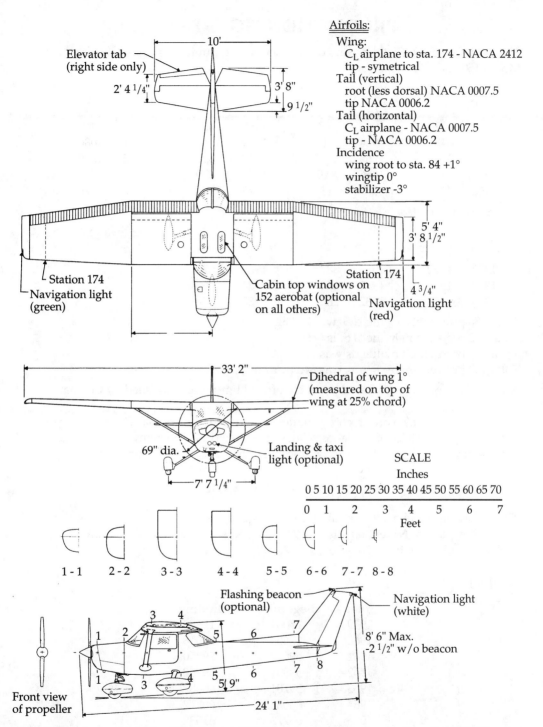

Airfoils:
Wing:
C_L airplane to sta. 174 - NACA 2412
tip - symetrical
Tail (vertical)
root (less dorsal) NACA 0007.5
tip NACA 0006.2
Tail (horizontal)
C_L airplane - NACA 0007.5
tip - NACA 0006.2
Incidence
wing root to sta. 84 +1°
wingtip 0°
stabilizer -3°

Elevator tab
(right side only)

10'

2' 4 1/4"

3' 8"

9 1/2"

Station 174
Navigation light
(green)

Cabin top windows on
152 aerobat (optional
on all others)

Station 174

5' 4"
3' 8 1/2"

4 3/4"

Navigation light
(red)

33' 2"

Dihedral of wing 1°
(measured on top of
wing at 25% chord)

69" dia.

Landing & taxi
light (optional)

7' 7 1/4"

SCALE

Inches

0 5 10 15 20 25 30 35 40 45 50 55 60 65 70

0   1   2   3   4   5   6   7

Feet

1 - 1   2 - 2   3 - 3   4 - 4   5 - 5   6 - 6   7 - 7   8 - 8

Flashing beacon
(optional)

Navigation light
(white)

8' 6" Max.
-2 1/2" w/o beacon

Front view
of propeller

5' 9"

24' 1"

Fig. 2-24. Scale-drawing of the 1983 Cessna 152. When compared to its ancestors, the 120/140 series and the 150, there is little difference in performance. Cessna Aircraft Company

PRODUCTION FIGURES

The following charts list the years of production and number of units built for the Model 150 and 152 airplanes:

150

1958	122*	1963	472	1968	2007	1973	1460
1959	648	1964	804	1969	1714	1974	1080
1960	354	1965	1637	1970	832	1975	1269
1961	344	1966	3087	1971	879	1976	1399
1962	331	1967	2114	1972	1100	1977	429

* Sold as 1959 models.

152

1977	1522	1980	887	1983	167
1978	1918	1981	634	1984	86
1979	1268	1982	265	1985	113

Total 150 production in the U.S. was 22,082.
Total 152 production in the U.S. is 6860.
Total 150 production by Reims was 1758.
Total 152 production by Reims was 640 (through 1987).

Note: This information is based upon the official figures as published by Cessna.

These are not the world-record production figures of the Cessna 172, but the figures still represent a lot of airplanes. With so many sold, and so many pilots trained in these airplanes, it is certainly easy to see why they are called "Little Wonders."

SERIAL NUMBERS

The following list gives the serial number ranges for all years and models of the 150/152 airplanes. **Note:** Starting in 1961, Cessna serial numbers were prefixed with the model number (150, A150, 152, A152).

150

Year	Beginning	Ending
1959	17001	17683
1960	17684	59018
1961	59019	59350
1962	59351	59700
1963	59701	60087
1964	60088	60772
1965	60773	61532
1966	61533	64532
1967	64533	67198

150 (continued)

Year	Beginning	Ending
1968	67199	69308
1969	69309	71128
1970	71129	72003
1971	72004	72628
1972	72629	73658
1973	73659	74850
1974	74851	75781
1975	75782	77005
1976	77006	78505
1977	78506	79405

A150 (Aerobat)

Year	Beginning	Ending
1970	0001	0226
1971	0227	0276
1972	0277	0342
1973	0343	0429
1974	0430	0523
1975	0524	0609
1976	0610	0684
1977	0685	0734

152

Year	Beginning	Ending
1978	79406	82031
1979	82032	83591
1980	83592	84541
1981	84542	85161
1982	85162	85594
1983	85595	85833
1984	85834	85939
1985	85940	86033

A152 (Aerobat)

Year	Beginning	Ending
1978	0735	0808
1979	0809	0878
1980	0879	0943
1981	0944	0983
1982	0984	1014
1983	1015	1025
1984	1026	1927
1985	1028	1049

3

Cessna 150 specifications

WHEN STUDYING THE SPECIFICATIONS of the Cessna 150 airplanes, it is important to note that specific model differences between some years were very slight, while other models vary greatly from preceding models. Certain model and year changes included drastic dimensional changes, significant changes in cruising range and/or speed, or only a Cessna rehash of the previous year's figures. All yearly specifications are an important part of the history of these airplanes and are included for historical purposes, even those that reflect minor yearly changes.

The following specifications are those issued by Cessna Aircraft Company and may be considered official. The specifications given are for the Commuter Models. Also available were Trainer and Standard Models. The differences between the Commuter and the Trainer are speed and empty weight. The Commuter is 2 mph faster than the Trainer and, due to the additional standard avionics in the Commuter, the Commuter's empty weight exceeds that of the Trainer by 50–90 pounds. The Standard Model was so bare of instruments, options, and the like, that its sales were almost nonexistent. Specification differences reflect the same cruise speeds as the Trainer, but a reduced empty weight due to the lack of installed equipment.

1959

Model: 150

Speed
     Top Speed at Sea Level: 124 mph
     Cruise (70% at 9000 ft): 121 mph
Range
     Cruise (no allowance): 520 mi - 4.3 hrs at 121 mph
     Maximum Range at 10,000 ft: 630 mi - 6.3 hrs at 95 mph
Performance
     Rate of Climb at Sea Level: 740 fpm
     Service Ceiling: 15,300 ft
Baggage: 80 lbs

Fuel Capacity
   Standard: 26 gal
Engine
   Make: Continental O-200A
   TBO: 1800 hrs
   Power: 100 hp
Dimensions
   Wingspan: 33 ft 4 in
   Wing Area (sq ft): 160
   Length: 21 ft
   Height: 6 ft 11 in
Loading
   Wing Loading (lbs/sq ft): 9.4
   Power Loading (lbs/hp): 15.0
Weight
   Gross Weight: 1500 lbs
   Empty Weight: 962 lbs
   Useful Load: 538 lbs

1960

Model: 150

Speed
   Maximum at Sea Level: 124 mph
   Cruise (70% at 9000 ft): 121 mph
Range
   Maximum (70% at 9000 ft): 520 mi - 4.3 hrs at 121 mph
   Maximum Range at 10,000 ft: 630 mi - 6.6 hrs at 95 mph
   Patroller version maximum: 980 mi - 10.3 hrs
Performance
   Rate of Climb at Sea Level: 740 fpm
   Service Ceiling: 15,300 ft
   Takeoff
      Ground run: 680 ft
      Over 50-ft obstacle: 1205 ft
   Landing
      Landing roll: 360 ft
      Over 50-ft obstacle: 1055 ft
Fuel Capacity
   Standard: 26 gal
   Patroller: 38 gal
Engine
   Make: Continental O-200A
   TBO: 1800 hrs
   Power: 100 hp

Oil capacity: 5 qts
Propeller: Sensenich M69CK52
Dimensions
Wingspan: 33 ft 4 in
Wing Area (sq ft): 160
Length: 21 ft 6 in
Height: 6 ft 11 in
Loading
Wing Loading (lbs/sq ft): 9.4
Power Loading (lbs/hp): 15.0
Weight
Gross: 1500 lbs
Empty: 946 lbs
Baggage: 80 lbs

1961

Model: 150A

Speed
Maximum at Sea Level: 124 mph
Cruise (70% at 9000 ft): 121 mph
Range
Maximum (70% at 9000 ft): 520 mi - 4.3 hrs at 121 mph
Maximum Range at 10,000 ft: 630 mi - 6.6 hrs at 95 mph
Patroller version maximum: 980 mi - 10.3 hrs
Performance
Rate of Climb at Sea Level: 740 fpm
Service Ceiling: 15,300 ft
Takeoff
Ground run: 680 ft
Over 50-ft obstacle: 1205 ft
Landing
Landing roll: 360 ft
Over 50-ft obstacle: 1055 ft
Fuel capacity
Standard: 26 gal
Patroller: 38 gal
Engine
Make: Continental O-200A
TBO: 1800 hrs
Power: 100 hp
Oil capacity: 5 qts
Propeller: Sensenich M69CK52
Dimensions
Wingspan: 33 ft 4 in
Wing Area(sq ft): 160

Length: 21 ft 6 in
Height: 6 ft 11 in
Loading
Wing Loading (lbs/sq ft): 9.4
Power Loading (lbs/hp): 15.0
Weight
Gross: 1500 lbs
Empty: 950 lbs
Baggage: 80 lbs

1962

Model: 150B

Speed
Maximum at Sea Level: 127 mph
Cruise (75% at 7500 ft): 125 mph
Range
Maximum (75% at 7500 ft): 500 mi - 4.0 hrs at 125 mph
Optimum range at 10,000 ft: 610 mi - 5.9 hrs at 104 mph
Patroller version maximum: 945 mi - 9.1 hrs
Performance
Rate of Climb at Sea Level: 760 fpm
Service Ceiling: 15,600 ft
Takeoff
Ground run: 680 ft
Over 50-ft obstacle: 1205 ft
Landing
Landing roll: 360 ft
Over 50-ft obstacle: 1055 ft
Fuel capacity
Standard: 26 gal
Patroller: 38 gal
Engine
Make: Continental O-200A
TBO: 1800 hrs
Power: 100 hp
Oil capacity: 6 qts
Propeller: Metal, diameter: 69 in
Dimensions
Wingspan: 33 ft 4 in
Wing Area (sq ft): 160
Length: 21 ft 6 in
Height: 6 ft 11 in
Loading
Wing Loading (lbs/sq ft): 9.4
Power Loading (lbs/hp): 15.0

Weight
    Gross: 1500 lbs
    Empty: 950 lbs
    Baggage: 80 lbs

1963

Model: 150C

Speed
    Maximum at Sea Level: 127 mph
    Cruise (75% at 7500 ft): 125 mph
Range
    Maximum (75% at 7500 ft): 500 mi - 4.0 hrs at 125 mph
    Optimum range at 10,000 ft: 610 mi - 5.9 hrs at 104 mph
    Patroller version maximum: 945 mi - 9.1 hrs
Performance
    Rate of Climb at Sea Level: 760 fpm
    Service Ceiling: 15,600 ft
    Takeoff
        Ground run: 680 ft
        Over 50-ft obstacle: 1205 ft
    Landing
        Landing roll: 360 ft
        Over 50-ft obstacle: 1055 ft
Fuel capacity
    Standard: 26 gal
    Patroller: 38 gal
Engine
    Make: Continental O-200A
    TBO: 1800 hrs
    Power: 100 hp
    Oil capacity: 6 qts
    Propeller: Metal, diameter: 69 in
Dimensions
    Wingspan: 33 ft 4 in
    Wing Area (sq ft): 160
    Length: 21 ft 6 in
    Height: 6 ft 11 in
Loading
    Wing Loading (lbs/sq ft): 9.4
    Power Loading (lbs/hp): 15.0
Weight
    Gross: 1500 lbs

Empty: 950 lbs
Baggage: 80 lbs

1964

Model: 150D

Speed
    Maximum at Sea Level: 125 mph
    Cruise (75% at 7500 ft): 122 mph
Range
    Maximum (75% at 7500 ft): 490 mi - 4.0 hrs at 122 mph
    Optimum range at 10,000 ft: 565 mi - 5.7 hrs at 99 mph
    Patroller version maximum: 885 mi - 8.9 hrs
Performance
    Rate of Climb at Sea Level: 670 fpm
    Service Ceiling: 12,650 ft
    Takeoff
        Ground run: 735 ft
        Over 50-ft obstacle: 1385 ft
    Landing
        Landing roll: 445 ft
        Over 50-ft obstacle: 1075 ft
Fuel capacity
    Standard: 26 gal
    Patroller: 38 gal
Engine
    Make: Continental O-200A
    TBO: 1800 hrs
    Power: 100 hp
    Oil capacity: 6 qts
    Propeller: Metal, diameter: 69 in
Dimensions
    Wingspan: 33 ft 6 in
    Wing Area (sq ft): 160
    Length: 21 ft 7 in
    Height: 7 ft 10 in
Loading
    Wing Loading (lbs/sq ft): 10.0
    Power Loading (lbs/hp): 16.0
Weight
    Gross: 1600 lbs
    Empty: 970 lbs
    Baggage: 120 lbs

1965

Model: 150E

Speed
 Maximum at Sea Level: 125 mph
 Cruise (75% at 7500 ft): 122 mph
Range
 Maximum (75% at 7500 ft): 490 mi - 4.0 hrs at 122 mph
 Optimum range at 10,000 ft: 565 mi - 5.7 hrs at 99 mph
 Patroller version maximum: 885 mi - 8.9 hrs
Performance
 Rate of Climb at Sea Level: 670 fpm
 Service Ceiling: 12,650 ft
 Takeoff
  Ground run: 735 ft
  Over 50-ft obstacle: 1385 ft
 Landing
  Landing roll: 445 ft
  Over 50-ft obstacle: 1075 ft
Fuel Capacity
 Standard: 26 gal
 Patroller: 38 gal
Engine
 Make: Continental O-200A
 TBO: 1800 hrs
 Power: 100 hp
 Oil Capacity: 6 qts
 Propeller: Metal, diameter: 69 in
Dimensions
 Wingspan: 33 ft 6 in
 Wing Area (sq ft): 160
 Length: 21 ft 7 in
 Height: 7 ft 10 in
Loading
 Wing Loading (lbs/sq ft): 10.0
 Power Loading (lbs/hp): 16.0
Weight
 Gross: 1600 lbs
 Empty: 1010 lbs
 Baggage: 120 lbs

1966

Model: 150F

Speed
 Maximum at Sea Level: 125 mph

Cruise (75% at 7500 ft): 122 mph

Range

    Maximum (75% at 7500 ft): 490 mi - 4.0 hrs at 122 mph

    Optimum range at 10,000 ft: 565 mi - 5.7 hrs at 99 mph

    Long range version maximum: 885 mi - 8.9 hrs

Performance

    Rate of Climb at Sea Level: 670 fpm

    Service Ceiling: 12,650 ft

    Takeoff

        Ground run: 735 ft

        Over 50-ft obstacle: 1385 ft

    Landing

        Landing roll: 445 ft

        Over 50-ft obstacle: 1075 ft

Fuel Capacity

    Standard: 26 gal

    Patroller: 38 gal

Engine

    Make: Continental O-200A

    TBO: 1800 hrs

    Power: 100 hp

    Oil capacity: 6 qts

    Propeller: metal, diameter: 69 in

Dimensions

    Wingspan: 32 ft 8 in

    Wing Area (sq ft): 157

    Length: 23 ft 9 in

    Height: 8 ft 9 in

Loading

    Wing Loading (lbs/sq ft): 10.2

    Power Loading (lbs/hp): 16.0

Weight

    Gross: 1600 lbs

    Empty: 1060 lbs

    Baggage: 120 lbs

1967

Model: 150G

Speed

    Maximum at Sea Level: 125 mph

    Cruise (75% at 7500 ft): 122 mph

Range

    Maximum (75% at 7500 ft): 490 mi - 4.0 hrs at 122 mph

    Optimum range at 10,000 ft: 565 mi - 5.7 hrs at 99 mph

    Long-range version maximum: 880 mi - 8.9 hrs

Performance
    Rate of Climb at Sea Level: 670 fpm
    Service Ceiling: 12,650 ft
    Takeoff
    Ground run: 735 ft
        Over 50-ft obstacle: 1385 ft
        Landing
        Landing roll: 445 ft
        Over 50-ft obstacle: 1075 ft
Fuel Capacity
    Standard: 26 gal
    Patroller: 38 gal
Engine
    Make: Continental O-200A
    TBO: 1800 hrs
    Power: 100 hp
    Oil capacity: 6 qts
    Propeller: Metal, diameter: 69 in
Dimensions
    Wingspan: 32 ft 8 in
    Wing Area (sq ft): 157
    Length: 23 ft 9 in
    Height: 8 ft 7 in
Loading
    Wing Loading (lbs/sq ft): 10.2
    Power Loading (lbs/hp): 16.0
Weight
    Gross: 1600 lbs
    Empty: 1060 lbs
    Baggage: 120 lbs

Model: 150G Floatplane

Speed
    Maximum at Sea Level: 103 mph
    Cruise (75% at 7000 ft): 98 mph
Range
    Maximum (75% at 7000 ft): 380 mi - 3.9 hrs at 98 mph
    Optimum range at 10,000 ft: 425 mi - 5.5 hrs at 78 mph
    Long-range version maximum: 670 mi - 8.6 hrs
Performance
    Rate of Climb at Sea Level: 560 fpm
    Service Ceiling: 10,700 ft
    Takeoff
        Water run: 1310 ft
        Over 50-ft obstacle: 2075 ft

Landing
Water run: 415 ft
Over 50-ft obstacle: 850 ft
Fuel Capacity
Standard: 26 gal
Patroller: 38 gal
Engine
Make: Continental O-200A
TBO: 1800 hrs
Power: 100 hp
Oil capacity: 6 qts
Propeller: Metal, diameter: 75 in
Dimensions
Wingspan: 32 ft 8 in
Wing Area (sq ft): 157
Length: 24 ft 1 in
Height: 9 ft 1 in
Loading
Wing Loading (lbs/sq ft): 10.5
Power Loading (lbs/hp): 16.5
Weight
Gross: 1650 lbs
Empty: 1135 lbs
Baggage: 120 lbs

1968

Model: 150H

Speed
Maximum at Sea Level: 122 mph
Cruise (75% at 7000 ft): 117 mph
Range
Maximum (75% at 7000 ft): 475 mi - 4.0 hrs at 117 mph
Optimum range at 10,000 ft: 565 mi - 6.1 hrs at 93 mph
Long-range version maximum: 880 mi - 9.4 hrs
Performance
Rate of Climb at Sea Level: 670 fpm
Service Ceiling: 12,650 ft
Takeoff
Ground run: 735 ft
Over 50-ft obstacle: 1385 ft
Landing
Landing roll: 445 ft
Over 50-ft obstacle: 1075 ft

Fuel Capacity
  Standard: 26 gal
  Patroller: 38 gal
Engine
  Make: Continental O-200A
  TBO: 1800 hrs
  Power: 100 hp
  Oil capacity: 6 qts
  Propeller: Metal, diameter: 69 in
Dimensions
  Wingspan: 32 ft 8 in
  Wing Area (sq ft): 157
  Length: 23 ft 9 in
  Height: 8 ft 7 in
Loading
  Wing Loading (lbs/sq ft): 10.2
  Power Loading (lbs/hp): 16.0
Weight
  Gross: 1600 lbs
  Empty: 1060 lbs
  Baggage: 120 lbs

Model: 150H Floatplane

Speed
  Maximum at Sea Level: 103 mph
  Cruise (75% at 7000 ft): 98 mph
Range
  Maximum (75% at 7000 ft): 380 mi - 3.9 hrs at 98 mph
  Optimum range at 10,000 ft: 425 mi - 5.5 hrs at 78 mph
  Long-range version maximum: 670 mi - 8.6 hrs
Performance
  Rate of Climb at Sea Level: 560 fpm
  Service Ceiling: 10,700 ft
  Takeoff
    Water run: 1310 ft
    Over 50-ft obstacle: 2075 ft
  Landing
    Water run: 415 ft
    Over 50-ft obstacle: 850 ft
Fuel Capacity
  Standard: 26 gal
  Patroller: 38 gal
Engine
  Make: Continental O-200A
  TBO: 1800 hrs

Power: 100 hp
Oil capacity: 6 qts
Propeller: Metal, diameter: 75 in
Dimensions
Wingspan: 32 ft 8 in
Wing Area (sq ft): 157
Length: 24 ft 1 in
Height: 9 ft 1 in
Loading
Wing Loading (lbs/sq ft): 10.5
Power Loading (lbs/hp): 16.5
Weight
Gross: 1650 lbs
Empty: 1135 lbs
Baggage: 120 lbs

1969

Model: 150J

Speed
Maximum at Sea Level: 122 mph
Cruise (75% at 7000 ft): 117 mph
Range
Maximum (75% at 7000 ft): 475 mi - 4.0 hrs at 117 mph
Optimum range at 10,000 ft: 565 mi - 6.1 hrs at 93 mph
Long-range version maximum: 880 mi - 9.4 hrs
Performance
Rate of Climb at Sea Level: 670 fpm
Service Ceiling: 12,650 ft
Takeoff
Ground run: 735 ft
Over 50-ft obstacle: 1385 ft
Landing
Landing roll: 445 ft
Over 50-ft obstacle: 1075 ft
Fuel Capacity
Standard: 26 gal
Patroller: 38 gal
Engine
Make: Continental O-200A
TBO: 1800 hrs
Power: 100 hp
Oil capacity: 6 qts
Propeller: Metal, diameter: 69 in

Dimensions
    Wingspan: 32 ft 8 in
    Wing Area (sq ft): 157
    Length: 23 ft 9 in
    Height: 8 ft 7 in
Loading
    Wing Loading (lbs/sq ft): 10.2
    Power Loading (lbs/hp): 16.0
Weight
    Gross: 1600 lbs
    Empty: 1060 lbs
    Baggage: 120 lbs

Model: 150J Floatplane

Speed
    Maximum at Sea Level: 103 mph
    Cruise (75% at 7000 ft): 98 mph
Range
    Maximum (75% at 7000 ft): 380 mi - 3.9 hrs at 98 mph
    Optimum range at 10,000 ft: 425 mi - 5.5 hrs at 78 mph
    Long-range version maximum: 670 mi - 8.6 hrs
Performance
    Rate of Climb at Sea Level: 560 fpm
    Service Ceiling: 10,700 ft
    Takeoff
        Water run: 1310 ft
        Over 50-ft obstacle: 2075 ft
    Landing
        Water run: 415 ft
        Over 50-ft obstacle: 850 ft
Fuel Capacity
    Standard: 26 gal
    Patroller: 38 gal
Engine
    Make: Continental O-200A
    TBO: 1800 hrs
    Power: 100 hp
    Oil capacity: 6 qts
    Propeller: Metal, diameter: 75 in
Dimensions
    Wingspan: 32 ft 8 in
    Wing Area (sq ft): 157
    Length: 24 ft 1 in
    Height: 9 ft 1 in

Loading
> Wing Loading (lbs/sq ft): 10.5
> Power Loading (lbs/hp): 16.5

Weight
> Gross: 1650 lbs
> Empty: 1135 lbs
> Baggage: 120 lbs

1970

Model: 150K

Speed
> Maximum at Sea Level: 122 mph
> Cruise (75% at 7000 ft): 117 mph

Range
> Cruise (75% at 7000 ft): 475 mi - (26 gallons fuel) 4.1 hrs at 117 mph
> Cruise (75% at 7000 ft): 725 mi - (38 gallons fuel) 6.2 hrs at 117 mph
> Optimum range at 10,000 ft: 565 mi - (26 gallons fuel) 6.1 hrs at 93 mph
> Optimum range at 10,000 ft: 880 mi - (38 gallons fuel) 9.4 hrs at 93 mph

Performance
> Rate of Climb at Sea Level: 670 fpm
> Service Ceiling: 12650 ft
> Takeoff
>> Ground run: 735 ft
>> Over 50-ft obstacle: 1385 ft
> Landing
>> Landing roll: 445 ft
>> Over 50-ft obstacle: 1075 ft

Stall Speed
> Flaps up, power off: 55 mph
> Flaps down, power off: 48 mph

Fuel Capacity
> Standard: 26 gal
> Optional: 38 gal

Engine
> Make: Continental O-200A
> TBO: 1800 hrs
> Power: 100 hp
> Oil capacity: 6 qts
> Propeller: Metal, diameter: 69 in

Dimensions
> Wingspan: 33 ft 2 in
> Wing Area (sq ft): 159.5
> Length: 23 ft 9 in
> Height: 8 ft 7 in

Loading
> Wing Loading (lbs/sq ft): 10.2
> Power Loading (lbs/hp): 16.0

Weight
> Gross: 1600 lbs
> Empty: 1060 lbs
> Baggage: 120 lbs

Model: 150K Aerobat

Speed
> Maximum at Sea Level: 120 mph
> Cruise (75% at 7000 ft): 115 mph

Range
> Cruise (75% at 7000 ft): 470 mi - (26 gallons fuel) 4.1 hrs at 115 mph
> Cruise (75% at 7000 ft): 715 mi - (38 gallons fuel) 6.2 hrs at 115 mph
> Optimum range at 10,000 ft: 555 mi - (26 gallons fuel) 6.1 hrs at 91 mph
> Optimum range at 10,000 ft: 885 mi - (38 gallons fuel) 9.4 hrs at 91 mph

Performance
> Rate of Climb at Sea Level: 670 fpm
> Service Ceiling: 12650 ft
> Takeoff
>> Ground run: 735 ft
>> Over 50-ft obstacle: 1385 ft
> Landing
>> Landing roll: 445 ft
>> Over 50-ft obstacle: 1075 ft

Stall Speed
> Flaps up, power off: 55 mph
> Flaps down, power off: 48 mph

Fuel Capacity
> Standard: 26 gal
> Optional: 38 gal

Engine
> Make: Continental O-200A
> TBO: 1800 hrs
> Power: 100 hp
> Oil capacity: 6 qts
> Propeller: Metal, diameter: 69 in

Dimensions
> Wingspan: 33 ft 2 in
> Wing Area (sq ft): 157
> Length: 23 ft 7 in
> Height: 8 ft 7 in

Loading
> Wing Loading (lbs/sq ft): 10.2

Power Loading (lbs/hp): 16.0

Weight
    Gross: 1600 lbs
    Empty: 1020 lbs
    Baggage: 120 lbs

Model: 150K Floatplane

Speed
    Maximum at Sea Level: 103 mph
    Cruise (75% at 7000 ft): 98 mph

Range
    Cruise (75% at 7000 ft): 380 mi - (26 gallons fuel) 3.9 hrs at 98 mph
    Cruise (75% at 7000 ft): 590 mi - (38 gallons fuel) 6.0 hrs at 98 mph
    Optimum range at 10,000 ft: 425 mi - (26 gallons fuel) 5.5 hrs at 78 mph
    Optimum range at 10,000 ft: 670 mi - (38 gallons fuel) 8.6 hrs at 78 mph

Performance
    Rate of Climb at Sea Level: 560 fpm
    Service Ceiling: 10,700 ft
    Takeoff
        Water run: 1310 ft
        Over 50-ft obstacle: 2075 ft
    Landing
        Water run: 415 ft
        Over 50-ft obstacle: 850 ft

Stall Speed
    Flaps up, power off: 54 mph
    Flaps down, power off: 48 mph

Fuel Capacity
    Standard: 26 gal
    Optional: 38 gal

Engine
    Make: Continental O-200A
    TBO: 1800 hrs
    Power: 100 hp
    Oil capacity: 6 qts
    Propeller: Metal, diameter: 75 in

Dimensions
    Wingspan: 33 ft 2 in
    Wing Area (sq ft): 157
    Length: 24 ft 1 in
    Height: 9 ft 1 in

Loading
    Wing Loading (lbs/sq ft): 10.5
    Power Loading (lbs/hp): 16.5

Weight
    Gross: 1650 lbs
    Empty: 1135 lbs
    Baggage: 120 lbs

1971

Model: 150L

Speed
    Maximum at Sea Level: 122 mph
    Cruise (75% at 7000 ft): 117 mph
Range
    Cruise (75% at 7000 ft): 475 mi - (26 gallons fuel) 4.1 hrs at 117 mph
    Cruise (75% at 7000 ft): 725 mi - (38 gallons fuel) 6.2 hrs at 117 mph
    Optimum range at 10,000 ft: 565 mi - (26 gallons fuel) 6.1 hrs at 93 mph
    Optimum range at 10,000 ft: 880 mi - (38 gallons fuel) 9.4 hrs at 93 mph
Performance
    Rate of Climb at Sea Level: 670 fpm
    Service Ceiling: 12650 ft
    Takeoff
        Ground run: 735 ft
        Over 50-ft obstacle: 1385 ft
    Landing
        Landing roll: 445 ft
        Over 50-ft obstacle: 1075 ft
Stall Speed
  Flaps up, power off: 55 mph
  Flaps down, power off: 48 mph
Fuel Capacity
    Standard: 26 gal
    Optional: 38 gal
Engine
    Make: Continental O-200A
    TBO: 1800 hrs
    Power: 100 hp
    Oil capacity: 6 qts
Propeller: Metal, diameter: 69 in
Dimensions
    Wingspan: 32 ft 8 in
    Wing Area (sq ft): 159.5
    Length: 23 ft 9 in
    Height: 8 ft 7 in
Loading
    Wing Loading (lbs/sq ft): 10.2
    Power Loading (lbs/hp): 16.0

Weight
>   Gross: 1600 lbs
>   Empty: 1070 lbs
>   Baggage: 120 lbs

Model: 150L Aerobat

Speed
>   Maximum at Sea Level: 120 mph
>   Cruise (75% at 7000 ft): 115 mph

Range
>   Cruise (75% at 7000 ft): 470 mi - (26 gallons fuel) 4.1 hrs at 115 mph
>   Cruise (75% at 7000 ft): 715 mi - (38 gallons fuel) 6.2 hrs at 115 mph
>   Optimum range at 10,000 ft: 555 mi - (26 gallons fuel) 6.1 hrs at 91 mph
>   Optimum range at 10,000 ft: 885 mi - (38 gallons fuel) 9.4 hrs at 91 mph

Performance
>   Rate of Climb at Sea Level: 670 fpm
>   Service Ceiling: 12650 ft
>   Takeoff
>>   Ground run: 735 ft
>>   Over 50-ft obstacle: 1385 ft
>   Landing
>>   Landing roll: 445 ft
>>   Over 50-ft obstacle: 1075 ft

Stall Speed
>   Flaps up, power off: 55 mph
>   Flaps down, power off: 48 mph

Fuel Capacity
>   Standard: 26 gal
>   Optional: 38 gal

Engine
>   Make: Continental O-200A
>   TBO: 1800 hrs
>   Power: 100 hp
>   Oil capacity: 6 qts
>   Propeller: Metal, diameter: 69 in

Dimensions
>   Wingspan: 32 ft 8 in
>   Wing Area (sq ft): 157
>   Length: 23 ft 9 in
>   Height: 8 ft 7 in

Loading
>   Wing Loading (lbs/sq ft): 10.2
>   Power Loading (lbs/hp): 16.0

Weight
>   Gross: 1600 lbs

Empty: 1030 lbs
Baggage: 120 lbs

1972

Model: 150L

Speed
    Maximum at Sea Level: 122 mph
    Cruise (75% at 7000 ft): 117 mph
Range
    Cruise (75% at 7000 ft): 475 mi - (26 gallons fuel) 4.1 hrs at 117 mph
    Cruise (75% at 7000 ft): 725 mi - (38 gallons fuel) 6.2 hrs at 117 mph
    Optimum range at 10,000 ft: 565 mi - (26 gallons fuel) 6.1 hrs at 93 mph
    Optimum range at 10,000 ft: 880 mi - (38 gallons fuel) 9.4 hrs at 93 mph
Performance
    Rate of Climb at Sea Level: 670 fpm
    Service Ceiling: 12650 ft
    Takeoff
        Ground run: 735 ft
        Over 50-ft obstacle: 1385 ft
    Landing
        Landing roll: 445 ft
        Over 50-ft obstacle: 1075 ft
Stall Speed
    Flaps up, power off: 55 mph
    Flaps down, power off: 48 mph
Fuel Capacity
    Standard: 26 gal
    Optional: 38 gal
Engine
    Make: Continental O-200A
    TBO: 1800 hrs
    Power: 100 hp
    Oil capacity: 6 qts
    Propeller: Metal, diameter: 69 in
Dimensions
    Wingspan
        Trainer: 32 ft 8 in
        Commuter: 33 ft 1 in
    Wing Area (sq ft): 157
    Length: 23 ft 9 in
    Height: 8 ft
Loading
    Wing Loading (lbs/sq ft): 10.2
    Power Loading (lbs/hp): 16.0

Weight
    Gross: 1600 lbs
    Empty: 1065 lbs
    Baggage: 120 lbs

Model: 150L Aerobat

Speed
    Maximum at Sea Level: 120 mph
    Cruise (75% at 7000 ft): 115 mph
Range
    Cruise (75% at 7000 ft): 470 mi - (26 gallons fuel) 4.1 hrs at 115 mph
    Cruise (75% at 7000 ft): 715 mi - (38 gallons fuel) 6.2 hrs at 115 mph
    Optimum range at 10,000 ft: 555 mi - (26 gallons fuel) 6.1 hrs at 91 mph
    Optimum range at 10,000 ft: 855 mi - (38 gallons fuel) 9.4 hrs at 91 mph
Performance
    Rate of Climb at Sea Level: 670 fpm
    Service Ceiling: 12,650 ft
    Takeoff
        Ground run: 735 ft
        Over 50-ft obstacle: 1385 ft
    Landing
        Landing roll: 445 ft
        Over 50-ft obstacle: 1075 ft
Stall Speed
    Flags up, power off: 55 mph
    Flaps down, power off: 48 mph
Fuel Capacity
    Standard: 26 gal
    Optional: 38 gal
Engine
    Make: Continental O-200A
    TBO: 1800 hrs
    Power: 100 hp
    Oil capacity: 6 qts
    Propeller: Metal, diameter: 69 in
Dimensions
    Wingspan: 32 ft 8 in
    Wing Area (sq ft): 157
    Length: 23 ft 9 in
    Height: 8 ft
Loading
    Wing Loading (lbs/sq ft): 10.2
    Power Loading (lbs/hp): 16.0
Weight
    Gross: 1600 lbs

Empty: 1035 lbs
Baggage: 120 lbs

1973

Model: 150L

Speed
  Maximum at Sea Level: 122 mph
  Cruise (75% at 7000 ft): 117 mph
Range
  Cruise (75% at 7000 ft): 475 mi - (26 gallons fuel) 4.1 hrs at 117 mph
  Cruise (75% at 7000 ft): 725 mi - (38 gallons fuel) 6.2 hrs at 117 mph
  Optimum range at 10,000 ft: 565 mi - (26 gallons fuel) 6.1 hrs at 93 mph
  Optimum range at 10,000 ft: 880 mi - (38 gallons fuel) 9.4 hrs at 93 mph
Performance
  Rate of Climb at Sea Level: 670 fpm
  Service Ceiling: 12650 ft
  Takeoff
    Ground run: 735 ft
    Over 50-ft obstacle: 1385 ft
  Landing
    Landing roll: 445 ft
    Over 50-ft obstacle: 1075 ft
Stall Speed
  Flaps up, power off: 55 mph
  Flaps down, power off: 48 mph
Fuel Capacity
  Standard: 26 gal
  Optional: 38 gal
Engine
  Make: Continental O-200A
  TBO: 1800 hrs
  Power: 100 hp
  Oil capacity: 6 qts
  Propeller: Metal, diameter: 69 in
Dimensions
  Wingspan
    Trainer: 32 ft 8 in
    Commuter: 33 ft 2 in
  Wing Area (sq ft)
    Trainer: 157
    Commuter: 159.5
  Length: 23 ft 9 in
  Height: 8 ft

Loading
    Wing Loading (lbs/sq ft)
        Trainer: 10.2
        Commuter: 10.0
    Power Loading (lbs/hp): 16.0
Weight
    Gross: 1600 lbs
    Empty: 1060 lbs
    Baggage: 120 lbs

Model: 150L Aerobat

Speed
    Maximum at Sea Level: 120 mph
    Cruise (75% at 7000 ft): 115 mph
Range
    Cruise (75% at 7000 ft): 470 mi - (26 gallons fuel) 4.1 hrs at 115 mph
    Cruise (75% at 7000 ft): 715 mi - (38 gallons fuel) 6.2 hrs at 115 mph
    Optimum range at 10,000 ft: 555 mi - (26 gallons fuel) 6.1 hrs at 91 mph
    Optimum range at 10,000 ft: 855 mi - (38 gallons fuel) 9.4 hrs at 91 mph
Performance
    Rate of Climb at Sea Level: 670 fpm
    Service Ceiling: 12650 ft
    Takeoff
        Ground run: 735 ft
        Over 50-ft obstacle: 1385 ft
    Landing
        Landing roll: 445 ft
        Over 50-ft obstacle: 1075 ft
Stall speed
    Flaps up, power off: 55 mph
    Flaps down, power off: 48 mph
Fuel Capacity
    Standard: 26 gal
    Optional: 38 gal
Engine
    Make: Continental O-200A
    TBO: 1800 hrs
    Power: 100 hp
    Oil capacity: 6 qts
    Propeller: Metal, diameter: 69 in
Dimensions
    Wingspan: 32 ft 8 in
    Wing Area (sq ft): 157
    Length: 23 ft 9 in
    Height: 8 ft

Loading
　　Wing Loading (lbs/sq ft): 10.2
　　Power Loading (lbs/hp): 16.0
Weight
　　Gross: 1600 lbs
　　Empty: 1040 lbs
　　Baggage: 120 lbs

1974

Model: 150L

Speed
　　Maximum at Sea Level: 122 mph
　　Cruise (75% at 7000 ft): 117 mph
Range
　　Cruise (75% at 7000 ft): 475 mi - (26 gallons fuel) 4.1 hrs at 117 mph
　　Cruise (75% at 7000 ft): 725 mi - (38 gallons fuel) 6.2 hrs at 117 mph
　　Optimum range at 10,000 ft: 565 mi - (26 gallons fuel) 6.1 hrs at 93 mph
　　Optimum range at 10,000 ft: 880 mi - (38 gallons fuel) 9.4 hrs at 93 mph
Performance
　　Rate of Climb at Sea Level: 670 fpm
　　Service Ceiling: 12650 ft
　　Takeoff
　　　　Ground run: 735 ft
　　　　Over 50-ft obstacle: 1385 ft
　　Landing
　　　　Landing roll: 445 ft
　　　　Over 50-ft obstacle: 1075 ft
Stall Speed
　　Flaps up, power off: 55 mph
　　Flaps down, power off: 48 mph
Fuel Capacity
　　Standard: 26 gal
　　Optional: 38 gal
Engine
　　Make: Continental O-200A
　　TBO: 1800 hrs
　　Power: 100 hp
　　Oil capacity: 6 qts
　　Propeller: Metal, diameter: 69 in
Dimensions
　　Wingspan
　　　　Trainer: 32 ft 8 in
　　　　Commuter: 33 ft 2 in
　　Wing Area (sq ft)

Trainer: 157
Commuter: 159.5
Length: 23 ft 9 in
Height: 8 ft
Loading
Wing Loading (lbs/sq ft)
Trainer: 10.2
Commuter: 10.0
Power Loading (lbs/hp): 16.0
Weight
Gross: 1600 lbs
Empty: 1060 lbs
Baggage: 120 lbs

Model: 150L Aerobat

Speed
Maximum at Sea Level: 124 mph
Cruise (75% at 7000 ft): 119 mph
Range
Cruise (75% at 7000 ft): 485 mi - (26 gallons fuel) 4.1 hrs at 119 mph
Cruise (75% at 7000 ft): 735 mi - (38 gallons fuel) 6.2 hrs at 119 mph
Optimum range at 10,000 ft: 580 mi - (26 gallons fuel) 6.1 hrs at 96 mph
Optimum range at 10,000 ft: 900 mi - (38 gallons fuel) 9.4 hrs at 96 mph
Performance
Rate of Climb at Sea Level: 670 fpm
Service Ceiling: 14000 ft
Takeoff
Ground run: 735 ft
Over 50-ft obstacle: 1385 ft
Landing
Landing roll: 445 ft
Over 50-ft obstacle: 1075 ft
Stall Speed
Flaps up, power off: 55 mph
Flaps down, power off: 48 mph
Fuel Capacity
Standard: 26 gal
Optional: 38 gal
Engine
Make: Continental O-200A
TBO: 1800 hrs
Power: 100 hp
Oil capacity: 6 qts
Propeller: Metal, diameter: 69 in

Dimensions
   Wingspan: 32 ft 8 in
   Wing Area (sq ft): 157
   Length: 23 ft 9 in
   Height: 8 ft
Loading
   Wing Loading (lbs/sq ft): 10.2
   Power Loading (lbs/hp): 16.0
Weight
   Gross: 1600 lbs
   Empty: 1040 lbs
   Baggage: 120 lbs

1975

Model: 150M

Speed
   Maximum at Sea Level: 125 mph
   Cruise (75% at 7000 ft): 122 mph
Range
   Cruise (75% at 7000 ft): 500 mi - (26 gallons fuel) 4.1 hrs at 122 mph
   Cruise (75% at 7000 ft): 755 mi - (38 gallons fuel) 6.2 hrs at 122 mph
   Optimum range at 10,000 ft: 660 mi - (26 gallons fuel) 6.9 hrs at 95 mph
   Optimum range at 10,000 ft: 1025 mi - (38 gallons fuel) 10.8 hrs at 95 mph
Performance
   Rate of Climb at Sea Level: 670 fpm
   Service Ceiling: 14000 ft
   Takeoff
      Ground run: 735 ft
      Over 50-ft obstacle: 1385 ft
   Landing
      Landing roll: 445 ft
      Over 50-ft obstacle: 1075 ft
Stall Speed
   Flaps up, power off: 55 mph
   Flaps down, power off: 48 mph
Fuel Capacity
   Standard: 26 gal
   Optional: 38 gal
Engine
   Make: Continental O-200A
   TBO: 1800 hrs
   Power: 100 hp
   Oil capacity: 6 qts
   Propeller: Metal, diameter: 69 in

Dimensions
    Wingspan: 33 ft 2 in
    Wing Area (sq ft): 159.5
    Length: 23 ft 11 in
    Height: 8 ft 6 in
Loading
    Wing Loading (lbs/sq ft): 10.0
    Power Loading (lbs/hp): 16.0
Weight
    Gross: 1600 lbs
    Empty: 1040 lbs
        Commuter: 1065 lbs
        Commuter II: 1085 lbs
    Baggage: 120 lbs

Model: 150M Aerobat

Speed
    Maximum at Sea Level: 124 mph
    Cruise (75% at 7000 ft): 121 mph
Range
    Cruise (75% at 7000 ft): 495 mi - (26 gallons fuel) 4.1 hrs at 121 mph
    Cruise (75% at 7000 ft): 750 mi - (38 gallons fuel) 6.2 hrs at 121 mph
    Optimum range at 10,000 ft: 650 mi - (26 gallons fuel) 6.9 hrs at 94 mph
    Optimum range at 10,000 ft: 1010 mi - (38 gallons fuel) 10.8 hrs at 94 mph
Performance
    Rate of Climb at Sea Level: 670 fpm
    Service Ceiling: 14000 ft
    Takeoff
        Ground run: 735 ft
        Over 50-ft obstacle: 1385 ft
    Landing
        Landing roll: 445 ft
        Over 50-ft obstacle: 1075 ft
Stall Speed
    Flaps up, power off: 55 mph
    Flaps down, power off: 48 mph
Fuel Capacity
    Standard: 26 gal
    Optional: 38 gal
Engine
    Make: Continental O-200A
    TBO: 1800 hrs
    Power: 100 hp
    Oil capacity: 6 qts
    Propeller: Metal, diameter: 69 in

Dimensions
    Wingspan: 32 ft 8 in
    Wing Area (sq ft): 157
    Length: 23 ft 11 in
    Height: 8 ft 6 in
Loading
    Wing Loading (lbs/sq ft): 10.2
    Power Loading (lbs/hp): 16.0
Weight
    Gross: 1600 lbs
    Empty: 1040 lbs
    Baggage: 120 lbs

1976

Model: 150M

Speed
    Maximum at Sea Level: 125 mph
    Cruise (75% at 7000 ft): 122 mph
Range
    Cruise (75% at 7000 ft): 500 mi - (26 gallons fuel) 4.1 hrs at 122 mph
    Cruise (75% at 7000 ft): 755 mi - (38 gallons fuel) 6.2 hrs at 122 mph
    Optimum range at 10,000 ft: 660 mi - (26 gallons fuel) 6.9 hrs at 95 mph
    Optimum range at 10,000 ft: 1025 mi - (38 gallons fuel) 10.8 hrs at 95 mph
Performance
    Rate of Climb at Sea Level: 670 fpm
    Service Ceiling: 14,000 ft
    Takeoff
        Ground run: 735 ft
        Over 50-ft obstacle: 1385 ft
    Landing
        Landing roll: 445 ft
        Over 50-ft obstacle: 1075 ft
Stall Speed
    Flaps up, power off: 55 mph
    Flaps down, power off: 48 mph
Fuel Capacity
    Standard: 26 gal
    Optional: 38 gal
Engine
    Make: Continental O-200A
    TBO: 1800 hrs
    Power: 100 hp
    Oil capacity: 6 qts
    Propeller: Metal, diameter: 69 in

Dimensions
  Wingspan: 33 ft 2 in
  Wing Area (sq ft): 159.5
  Length: 23 ft 11 in
  Height: 8 ft 6 in
Loading
  Wing Loading (lbs/sq ft): 10.0
  Power Loading (lbs/hp): 16.0
Weight
  Gross: 1600 lbs
  Empty
    Commuter: 1065 lbs
    Commuter II: 1085 lbs
  Baggage: 120 lbs

Model: 150M Aerobat

Speed
  Maximum at Sea Level: 124 mph
  Cruise (75% at 7000 ft): 121 mph
Range
  Cruise (75% 7000 ft): 495 mi - (26 gallons fuel) 4.1 hrs at 121 mph
  Cruise (75% 7000 ft): 750 mi - (38 gallons fuel) 6.2 hrs at 121 mph
  Optimum range at 10,000 ft: 650 mi - (26 gallons fuel) 6.9 hrs at 94 mph
  Optimum range at 10,000 ft: 1010 mi - (38 gallons fuel) 10.8 hrs at 94 mph
Performance
  Rate of Climb at Sea Level: 670 fpm
  Service Ceiling: 14,000 ft
  Takeoff
    Ground run: 735 ft
    Over 50-ft obstacle: 1385 ft
  Landing
    Landing roll: 445 ft
    Over 50-ft obstacle: 1075 ft
Stall Speed
  Flaps up, power off: 55 mph
  Flaps down, power off: 48 mph
Fuel Capacity
  Standard: 26 gal
  Optional: 38 gal
Engine
  Make: Continental O-200A
  TBO: 1800 hrs
  Power: 100 hp
  Oil capacity: 6 qts
  Propeller: Metal, diameter: 69 in

Dimensions
   Wingspan: 32 ft 8 in
   Wing Area (sq ft): 157
   Length: 23 ft 11 in
   Height: 8 ft 6 in
Loading
   Wing Loading (lbs/sq ft): 10.2
   Power Loading (lbs/hp): 16.0
Weight
   Gross: 1600 lbs
   Empty: 1040 lbs
   Baggage: 120 lbs

1977

Model: 150M

Speed
   Maximum at Sea Level: 109 kts
   Cruise (75% at 7000 ft): 106 kts
Range
   Cruise (75% at 7000 ft): 340 nm - (22.5 gallons usable fuel) 3.3 hrs
   Cruise (75% at 7000 ft): 580 nm - (35 gallons usable fuel) 5.5 hrs
   Maximum Range at 10,000 ft: 420 nm - (22.5 gallons usable fuel) 4.9 hrs
   Maximum Range at 10,000 ft: 735 nm - (35 gallons usable fuel) 8.5 hrs
Performance
   Rate of Climb at Sea Level: 670 fpm
      Service Ceiling: 14,000 ft
   Takeoff
      Ground run: 735 ft
      Over 50-ft obstacle: 1385 ft
   Landing
      Landing roll: 445 ft
      Over 50-ft obstacle: 1075 ft
Stall Speed
   Flaps up, power off: 48 kts
   Flaps down, power off: 42 kts
Fuel Capacity
   Standard: 26 gal
   Long-range: 38 gal
Engine
   Make: Continental O-200A
   TBO: 1800 hrs
   Power: 100 hp
   Oil capacity: 6 qts
   Propeller: Metal, diameter: 69 in

Dimensions
    Wingspan: 33 ft 2 in
    Wing Area (sq ft): 159.5
    Length: 23 ft 11 in
    Height: 8 ft 6 in
Loading
    Wing Loading (lbs/sq ft): 10.0
    Power Loading (lbs/hp): 16.0
Weight
    Gross: 1600 lbs
    Empty
        Commuter: 1111 lbs
        Commuter II: 1129 lbs
    Baggage: 120 lbs

Model: 150M Aerobat

Speed
    Maximum at Sea Level: 108 kts
    Cruise (75% at 7000 ft): 105 kts
Range
    Cruise (75% at 7000 ft): 335 nm - (22.5 gallons usable fuel) 3.3 hrs
    Cruise (75% at 7000 ft): 570 nm - (35 gallons usable fuel) 5.5 hrs
    Maximum Range at 10,000 ft: 415 nm - (22.5 gallons usable fuel) 4.9 hrs
    Maximum Range at 10,000 ft: 725 nm - (35 gallons usable fuel) 8.5 hrs
Performance
    Rate of Climb at Sea Level: 670 fpm
        Service Ceiling: 14,000 ft
    Takeoff
        Ground run: 735 ft
        Over 50-ft obstacle: 1385 ft
    Landing
        Landing roll: 445 ft
        Over 50-ft obstacle: 1075 ft
Stall Speed
    Flaps up, power off: 48 kts
    Flaps down, power off: 42 kts
Fuel Capacity
    Standard: 26 gal
    Long-range: 38 gal
Engine
    Make: Continental O-200A
    TBO: 1800 hrs
    Power: 100 hp
    Oil capacity: 6 qts
    Propeller: Metal, diameter 69 in

Dimensions
    Wingspan: 32 ft 8 in
    Wing Area (sq ft): 157
    Length: 23 ft 11 in
    Height: 8 ft 6 in
Loading
    Wing Loading (lbs/sq ft): 10.2
    Power Loading (lbs/hp): 16.0
Weight
    Gross: 1600 lbs
    Empty: 1093 lbs
    Baggage: 120 lbs

4

Cessna 152 specifications

CESSNA'S MODEL 152 WAS INTRODUCED IN 1978. As with the Model 150 airplanes, some of the specification changes from one year to the next are minimal; however, for historical purposes, all changes are included. The wing area and wingspan specifications shown are for an airplane equipped with the optional modified conical wingtips. For an airplane equipped with standard wingtips, the wing area is 157 square feet and the wingspan is 32 feet 8.5 inches.

The speed performance specifications are for an airplane equipped with the optional speed fairings, which increase the speed by approximately 2 knots. A corresponding difference applies to the range. All other performance figures remain unchanged when speed fairings are installed. Empty weight of the 152 and 152 II is different—the II is 40 pounds heavier with additional avionics equipment. Specifications are for the 152.

1978

Model: 152

Speed
    Maximum at Sea Level: 110 kts
    Cruise (75% at 8000 ft): 107 kts
Range
    Cruise (75% at 8000 ft): 350 nm - (24.5 gallons usable fuel) 3.4 hrs
    Cruise (75% at 8000 ft): 580 nm - (37.5 gallons usable fuel) 5.5 hrs
    Maximum Range at 10,000 ft: 415 nm - (24.5 gallons usable fuel) 5.2 hrs
    Maximum Range at 10,000 ft: 690 nm - (37.5 gallons usable fuel) 8.7 hrs
Performance
    Rate of Climb at Sea Level: 715 fpm
    Service Ceiling: 14,700 ft
    Takeoff
        Ground run: 725 ft
        Over 50-ft obstacle: 1340 ft

Landing
Landing roll: 475 ft
Over 50-ft obstacle: 1200 ft
Stall Speed
Flaps up, power off: 48 kts
Flaps down, power off: 43 kts
Fuel Capacity
Standard: 26 gal
Long-range: 39 gal
Engine
Make: AVCO Lycoming O-235-L2C
TBO: 2000 hrs
Power: 110 hp
Oil capacity: 6 qts
Propeller: Metal, diameter: 69 in
Dimensions
Wingspan: 33 ft 2 in
Wing Area (sq ft): 159.5
Length: 24 ft 1 in
Height: 8 ft 6 in
Loading
Wing Loading (lbs/sq ft): 10.5
Power Loading (lbs/hp): 15.2
Weight
Gross: 1670 lbs
Empty: 1081 lbs
Baggage: 120 lbs

Model: 152 Aerobat

Speed
Maximum at Sea Level: 109 kts
Cruise (75% at 8000 ft): 106 kts Range
Cruise (75% at 8000 ft): 345 nm - (24.5 gallons usable fuel) 3.4 hrs
Cruise (75% at 8000 ft): 575 nm - (37.5 gallons usable fuel) 5.5 hrs
Maximum Range at 10,000 ft: 410 nm - (24.5 gallons usable fuel) 5.2 hrs
Maximum Range at 10,000 ft: 685 nm - (37.5 gallons usable fuel) 8.7 hrs
Performance
Rate of Climb at Sea Level: 715 fpm
Service Ceiling: 14,700 ft
Takeoff
Ground run: 725 ft
Over 50-ft obstacle: 1340 ft
Landing
Landing roll: 475 ft
Over 50-ft obstacle: 1200 ft

Stall Speed
    Flaps up, power off: 48 kts
    Flaps down, power off: 43 kts
Fuel Capacity
    Standard: 26 gal
    Long-range: 39 gal
Engine
    Make: AVCO Lycoming O-235-L2C
    TBO: 2000 hrs
    Power: 110 hp
    Oil capacity: 6 qts
    Propeller: Metal, diameter: 69 in
Dimensions
    Wingspan: 33 ft 2 in
    Wing Area (sq ft): 159.5
    Length: 24 ft 1 in
    Height: 8 ft 6 in
Loading
    Wing Loading (lbs/sq ft): 10.5
    Power Loading (lbs/hp): 15.2
Weight
    Gross: 1670 lbs
    Empty: 1125 lbs
    Baggage: 120 lbs

1979

Model: 152

Speed
    Maximum at Sea Level: 110 kts
    Cruise (75% at 8000 ft): 107 kts
Range
    Cruise (75% at 8000 ft): 350 nm - (24.5 gallons usable fuel) 3.4 hrs
    Cruise (75% at 8000 ft): 580 nm - (37.5 gallons usable fuel) 5.5 hrs
    Maximum Range at 10,000 ft: 415 nm - (24.5 gallons usable fuel) 5.2 hrs
    Maximum Range at 10,000 ft: 690 nm - (37.5 gallons usable fuel) 8.7 hrs
Performance
    Rate of Climb at Sea Level: 715 fpm
    Service Ceiling: 14,700 ft
    Takeoff
        Ground run: 725 ft
        Over 50-ft obstacle: 1340 ft
    Landing
        Landing roll: 475 ft
        Over 50-ft obstacle: 1200 ft

Stall Speed
    Flaps up, power off: 48 kts
    Flaps down, power off: 43 kts
Fuel Capacity
    Standard: 26 gal
    Long-range: 39 gal
Engine
    Make: AVCO Lycoming O-235-L2C
    TBO: 2000 hrs
    Power: 110 hp
    Oil capacity: 6 qts
    Propeller: Metal, diameter: 69 in
Dimensions
    Wingspan: 33 ft 2 in
    Wing Area (sq ft): 159.5
    Length: 24 ft 1 in
    Height: 8 ft 6 in
Loading
    Wing Loading (lbs/sq ft): 10.5
    Power Loading (lbs/hp): 15.2
Weight
    Gross: 1670 lbs
    Empty: 1101 lbs
    Baggage: 120 lbs

Model: 152 Aerobat

Speed
    Maximum at Sea Level: 109 kts
    Cruise (75% at 8000 ft): 106 kts
Range
    Cruise (75% at 8000 ft): 345 nm - (24.5 gallons usable fuel) 3.4 hrs
    Cruise (75% at 8000 ft): 575 nm - (37.5 gallons usable fuel) 5.5 hrs
    Maximum Range at 10,000 ft: 410 nm - (24.5 gallons usable fuel) 5.2 hrs
    Maximum Range at 10,000 ft: 685 nm - (37.5 gallons usable fuel) 8.7 hrs
Performance
    Rate of Climb at Sea Level: 715 fpm
    Service Ceiling: 14,700 ft
    Takeoff
        Ground run: 725 ft
        Over 50-ft obstacle: 1340 ft
    Landing
        Landing roll: 475 ft
        Over 50-ft obstacle: 1200 ft
Stall Speed
    Flaps up, power off: 48 kts
    Flaps down, power off: 43 kts

Fuel Capacity
    Standard: 26 gal
    Long-range: 39 gal
Engine
    Make: AVCO Lycoming O-235-L2C
    TBO: 2000 hrs
    Power: 110 hp
    Oil capacity: 6 qts
    Propeller: Metal, diameter: 69 in
Dimensions
    Wingspan: 33 ft 2 in
    Wing Area (sq ft): 159.5
    Length: 24 ft 1 in
    Height: 8 ft 6 in
Loading
    Wing Loading (lbs/sq ft): 10.5
    Power Loading (lbs/hp): 15.2
Weight
    Gross: 1670 lbs
    Empty: 1132 lbs
    Baggage: 120 lbs

1980

Model: 152

Speed
    Maximum at Sea Level: 110 kts
    Cruise (75% at 8000 ft): 107 kts
Range
    Cruise (75% at 8000 ft): 320 nm - (24.5 gallons usable fuel) 3.1 hrs
    Cruise (75% at 8000 ft): 545 nm - (37.5 gallons usable fuel) 5.2 hrs
    Maximum Range at 10,000 ft: 415 nm - (24.5 gallons usable fuel) 5.2 hrs
    Maximum Range at 10,000 ft: 690 nm - (37.5 gallons usable fuel) 8.7 hrs
Performance
    Rate of Climb at Sea Level: 715 fpm
    Service Ceiling: 14,700 ft
    Takeoff
        Ground run: 725 ft
        Over 50-ft obstacle: 1340 ft
    Landing
        Landing roll: 475 ft
        Over 50-ft obstacle: 1200 ft
Stall Speed
    Flaps up, power off: 48 kts
    Flaps down, power off: 43 kts

Fuel Capacity
    Standard: 26 gal
    Long-range: 39 gal
Engine
    Make: AVCO Lycoming O-235-L2C
    TBO: 2000 hrs
    Power: 110 hp
    Oil capacity: 6 qts
    Propeller: Metal, diameter: 69 in
Dimensions
    Wingspan: 33 ft 2 in
    Wing Area (sq ft): 159.5
    Length: 24 ft 1 in
    Height: 8 ft 6 in
Loading
    Wing Loading (lbs/sq ft): 10.5
    Power Loading (lbs/hp): 15.2
Weight
    Gross: 1670 lbs
    Empty: 1109 lbs
    Baggage: 120 lbs

Model: 152 Aerobat

Speed
    Maximum at Sea Level: 109 kts
    Cruise (75% at 8000 ft): 106 kts
Range
    Cruise (75% at 8000 ft): 315 nm - (24.5 gallons usable fuel) 3.1 hrs
    Cruise (75% at 8000 ft): 540 nm - (37.5 gallons usable fuel) 5.2 hrs
    Maximum Range at 10,000 ft: 410 nm - (24.5 gallons usable fuel) 5.2 hrs
    Maximum Range at 10,000 ft: 680 nm - (37.5 gallons usable fuel) 8.7 hrs
Performance
    Rate of Climb at Sea Level: 715 fpm
    Service Ceiling: 14,700 ft
    Takeoff
        Ground run: 725 ft
        Over 50-ft obstacle: 1340 ft
    Landing
        Landing roll: 475 ft
        Over 50-ft obstacle: 1200 ft
Stall Speed
    Flaps up, power off: 48 kts
    Flaps down, power off: 43 kts
Fuel Capacity
    Standard: 26 gal
    Long-range: 39 gal

Engine
    Make: AVCO Lycoming O-235-L2C
    TBO: 2000 hrs
    Power: 110 hp
    Oil capacity: 6 qts
    Propeller: Metal, diameter: 69 in
Dimensions
    Wingspan: 33 ft 2 in
    Wing Area (sq ft): 159.5
    Length: 24 ft 1 in
    Height: 8 ft 6 in
Loading
    Wing Loading (lbs/sq ft): 10.5
    Power Loading (lbs/hp): 15.2
Weight
    Gross: 1670 lbs
    Empty: 1135 lbs
    Baggage: 120 lbs

1981

Model: 152

Speed
    Maximum at Sea Level: 110 kts
    Cruise (75% at 8000 ft): 107 kts
Range
    Cruise (75% at 8000 ft): 320 nm - (24.5 gallons usable fuel) 3.1 hrs
    Cruise (75% at 8000 ft): 545 nm - (37.5 gallons usable fuel) 5.2 hrs
    Maximum Range at 10,000 ft: 415 nm - (24.5 gallons usable fuel) 5.2 hrs
    Maximum Range at 10,000 ft: 690 nm - (37.5 gallons usable fuel) 8.7 hrs
Performance
    Rate of Climb at Sea Level: 715 fpm
    Service Ceiling: 14,700 ft
    Takeoff
        Ground run: 725 ft
        Over 50-ft obstacle: 1340 ft
    Landing
        Landing roll: 475 ft
        Over 50-ft obstacle: 1200 ft
Stall Speed
    Flaps up, power off: 48 kts
    Flaps down, power off: 43 kts
Fuel Capacity
    Standard: 26 gal
    Long-range: 39 gal

Engine
    Make: AVCO Lycoming O-235-L2C
    TBO: 2000 hrs
    Power: 110 hp
    Oil capacity: 7 qts
    Propeller: Metal, diameter: 69 in
Dimensions
    Wingspan: 33 ft 2 in
    Wing Area (sq ft): 159.5
    Length: 24 ft 1 in
    Height: 8 ft 6 in
Loading
    Wing Loading (lbs/sq ft): 10.5
    Power Loading (lbs/hp): 15.2
Weight
    Gross: 1670 lbs
    Empty: 1104 lbs
    Baggage: 120 lbs

Model: 152 Aerobat

Speed
    Maximum at Sea Level: 109 kts
    Cruise (75% at 8000 ft): 106 kts
Range
    Cruise (75% at 8000 ft): 315 nm - (24.5 gallons usable fuel) 3.1 hrs
    Cruise (75% at 8000 ft): 540 nm - (37.5 gallons usable fuel) 5.2 hrs
    Maximum Range at 10,000 ft: 410 nm - (24.5 gallons usable fuel) 5.2 hrs
    Maximum Range at 10,000 ft: 680 nm - (37.5 gallons usable fuel) 8.7 hrs
Performance
    Rate of Climb at Sea Level: 715 fpm
    Service Ceiling: 14,700 ft
    Takeoff
        Ground run: 725 ft
        Over 50-ft obstacle: 1340 ft
    Landing
        Landing roll: 475 ft
        Over 50-ft obstacle: 1200 ft
Stall Speed
    Flaps up, power off: 48 kts
    Flaps down, power off: 43 kts
Fuel Capacity
    Standard: 26 gal
    Long-range: 39 gal
Engine
    Make: AVCO Lycoming O-235-L2C

TBO: 2000 hrs
Power: 110 hp
Oil capacity: 7 qts
Propeller: Metal, diameter: 69 in
Dimensions
Wingspan: 33 ft 2 in
Wing Area (sq ft): 159.5
Length: 24 ft 1 in
Height: 8 ft 6 in
Loading
Wing Loading (lbs/sq ft): 10.5
Power Loading (lbs/hp): 15.2
Weight
Gross: 1670 lbs
Empty: 1129 lbs
Baggage: 120 lbs

1982

Model: 152

Speed
Maximum at Sea Level: 110 kts
Cruise (75% at 8000 ft): 107 kts
Range
Cruise (75% at 8000 ft): 320 nm - (24.5 gallons usable fuel) 3.1 hrs
Cruise (75% at 8000 ft): 545 nm - (37.5 gallons usable fuel) 5.2 hrs
Maximum Range at 10,000 ft: 415 nm - (24.5 gallons usable fuel) 5.2 hrs
Maximum Range at 10,000 ft: 690 nm - (37.5 gallons usable fuel) 8.7 hrs
Performance
Rate of Climb at Sea Level: 715 fpm
Service Ceiling: 14,700 ft
Takeoff
Ground run: 725 ft
Over 50-ft obstacle: 1340 ft
Landing
Landing roll: 475 ft
Over 50-ft obstacle: 1200 ft
Stall Speed
Flaps up, power off: 48 kts
Flaps down, power off: 43 kts
Fuel Capacity
Standard: 26 gal
Long-range: 39 gal
Engine
Make: AVCO Lycoming O-235-L2C

TBO: 2000 hrs
Power: 110 hp
Oil capacity: 7 qts
Propeller: Metal, diameter: 69 in
Dimensions
Wingspan: 33 ft 2 in
Wing Area (sq ft): 159.5
Length: 24 ft 1 in
Height: 8 ft 6 in
Loading
Wing Loading (lbs/sq ft): 10.5
Power Loading (lbs/hp): 15.2
Weight
Gross: 1670 lbs
Empty: 1112 lbs
Baggage: 120 lbs

Model: 152 Aerobat

Speed
Maximum at Sea Level: 109 kts
Cruise (75% at 8000 ft): 106 kts
Range
Cruise (75% at 8000 ft): 315 nm - (24.5 gallons usable fuel) 3.1 hrs
Cruise (75% at 8000 ft): 540 nm - (37.5 gallons usable fuel) 5.2 hrs
Maximum Range at 10,000 ft: 410 nm - (24.5 gallons usable fuel) 5.2 hrs
Maximum Range at 10,000 ft: 680 nm - (37.5 gallons usable fuel) 8.7 hrs
Performance
Rate of Climb at Sea Level: 715 fpm
Service Ceiling: 14,700 ft
Takeoff
Ground run: 725 ft
Over 50-ft obstacle: 1340 ft
Landing
Landing roll: 475 ft
Over 50-ft obstacle: 1200 ft
Stall Speed
Flaps up, power off: 48 kts
Flaps down, power off: 43 kts
Fuel Capacity
Standard: 26 gal
Long-range: 39 gal
Engine
Make: AVCO Lycoming O-235-L2C
TBO: 2000 hrs
Power: 110 hp

Oil capacity: 7 qts
Propeller: Metal, diameter: 69 in
Dimensions
Wingspan: 33 ft 2 in
Wing Area (sq ft): 159.5
Length: 24 ft 1 in
Height: 8 ft 6 in
Loading
Wing Loading (lbs/sq ft): 10.5
Power Loading (lbs/hp): 15.2
Weight
Gross: 1670 lbs
Empty: 1133 lbs
Baggage: 120 lbs

1983

Model: 152

Speed
Maximum at Sea Level: 109 kts
Cruise (75% at 8000 ft): 106 kts
Range
Cruise (75% at 8000 ft): 315 nm - (24.5 gallons usable fuel) 3.0 hrs
Cruise (75% at 8000 ft): 540 nm - (37.5 gallons usable fuel) 5.2 hrs
Maximum Range at 10,000 ft: 370 nm - (24.5 gallons usable fuel) 4.1 hrs
Maximum Range at 10,000 ft: 625 nm - (37.5 gallons usable fuel) 6.9 hrs
Performance
Rate of Climb at Sea Level: 715 fpm
Service Ceiling: 14,700 ft
Takeoff
Ground run: 725 ft
Over 50-ft obstacle: 1340 ft
Landing
Landing roll: 475 ft
Over 50-ft obstacle: 1200 ft
Stall Speed
Flaps up, power off: 48 kts
Flaps down, power off: 43 kts
Fuel Capacity
Standard: 26 gal
Long-range: 39 gal
Engine
Make: AVCO Lycoming O-235-N2C
TBO: 2000 hrs
Power: 108 hp

Oil capacity: 7 qts
Propeller: Metal, diameter: 69 in
Dimensions
Wingspan: 33 ft 2 in
Wing Area (sq ft): 159.5
Length: 24 ft 1 in
Height: 8 ft 6 in
Loading
Wing Loading (lbs/sq ft): 10.5
Power Loading (lbs/hp): 15.2
Weight
Gross: 1670 lbs
Empty: 1104 lbs
Baggage: 120 lbs

Model: 152 Aerobat

Speed
Maximum at Sea Level: 108 kts
Cruise (75% at 8000 ft): 105 kts
Range
Cruise (75% at 8000 ft): 310 nm - (24.5 gallons usable fuel) 3.0 hrs
Cruise (75% at 8000 ft): 530 nm - (37.5 gallons usable fuel) 5.2 hrs
Maximum Range at 10,000 ft: 365 nm - (24.5 gallons usable fuel) 4.1 hrs
Maximum Range at 10,000 ft: 615 nm - (37.5 gallons usable fuel) 6.9 hrs
Performance
Rate of Climb at Sea Level: 715 fpm
Service Ceiling: 14,700 ft
Takeoff
Ground run: 725 ft
Over 50-ft obstacle: 1340 ft
Landing
Landing roll: 475 ft
Over 50-ft obstacle: 1200 ft
Stall Speed
Flaps up, power off: 48 kts
Flaps down, power off: 43 kts
Fuel Capacity
Standard: 26 gal
Long-range: 39 gal
Engine
Make: AVCO Lycoming O-235-N2C
TBO: 2000 hrs
Power: 108 hp
Oil capacity: 7 qts
Propeller: Metal, diameter: 69 in

Dimensions
    Wingspan: 33 ft 2 in
    Wing Area (sq ft): 159.5
    Length: 24 ft 1 in
    Height: 8 ft 6 in
Loading
    Wing Loading (lbs/sq ft): 10.5
    Power Loading (lbs/hp): 15.2
Weight
    Gross: 1670 lbs
    Empty: 1131 lbs
    Baggage: 120 lbs

1984

Model: 152

Speed
    Maximum at Sea Level: 109 kts
    Cruise (75% at 8000 ft): 106 kts
Range
    Cruise (75% at 8000 ft): 315 nm - (24.5 gallons usable fuel) 3.0 hrs
    Cruise (75% at 8000 ft): 540 nm - (37.5 gallons usable fuel) 5.2 hrs
    Maximum Range at 10,000 ft: 370 nm - (24.5 gallons usable fuel) 4.1 hrs
    Maximum Range at 10,000 ft: 625 nm - (37.5 gallons usable fuel) 6.9 hrs
Performance
    Rate of Climb at Sea Level: 715 fpm
    Service Ceiling: 14,700 ft
    Takeoff
        Ground run: 725 ft
        Over 50-ft obstacle: 1340 ft
    Landing
        Landing roll: 475 ft
        Over 50-ft obstacle: 1200 ft
Stall Speed
    Flaps up, power off: 48 kts
    Flaps down, power off: 43 kts
Fuel Capacity
    Standard: 26 gal
    Long-range: 39 gal
Engine
    Make: AVCO Lycoming O-235-N2C
    TBO: 2000 hrs
    Power: 108 hp
    Oil capacity: 7 qts
    Propeller: Metal, diameter: 69 in

Dimensions
  Wingspan: 33 ft 2 in
  Wing Area (sq ft): 159.5
  Length: 24 ft 1 in
  Height: 8 ft 6 in
Loading
  Wing Loading (lbs/sq ft): 10.5
  Power Loading (lbs/hp): 15.2
Weight
  Gross: 1670 lbs
  Empty: 1104 lbs
  Baggage: 120 lbs

Model: 152 Aerobat

Speed
  Maximum at Sea Level: 108 kts
  Cruise (75% at 8000 ft): 105 kts
Range
  Cruise (75% at 8000 ft): 310 nm - (24.5 gallons usable fuel) 3.0 hrs
  Cruise (75% at 8000 ft): 530 nm - (37.5 gallons usable fuel) 5.2 hrs
  Maximum Range at 10,000 ft: 365 nm - (24.5 gallons usable fuel) 4.1 hrs
  Maximum Range at 10,000 ft: 615 nm - (37.5 gallons usable fuel) 6.9 hrs
Performance
  Rate of Climb at Sea Level: 715 fpm
  Service Ceiling: 14,700 ft
  Takeoff
    Ground run: 725 ft
    Over 50-ft obstacle: 1340 ft
  Landing
    Landing roll: 475 ft
    Over 50-ft obstacle: 1200 ft
Stall Speed
  Flaps up, power off: 48 kts
  Flaps down, power off: 43 kts
Fuel Capacity
  Standard: 26 gal
  Long-range: 39 gal
Engine
  Make: AVCO Lycoming O-235-N2C
  TBO: 2000 hrs
  Power: 108 hp
  Oil capacity: 7 qts
  Propeller: Metal, diameter: 69 in
Dimensions
  Wingspan: 33 ft 2 in

Wing Area (sq ft): 159.5
Length: 24 ft 1 in
Height: 8 ft 6 in
Loading
Wing Loading (lbs/sq ft): 10.5
Power Loading (lbs/hp): 15.2
Weight
Gross: 1670 lbs
Empty: 1131 lbs
Baggage: 120 lbs

1985

Model: 152

Speed
Maximum at Sea Level: 109 kts
Cruise (75% at 8000 ft): 106 kts
Range
Cruise (75% at 8000 ft): 315 nm - (24.5 gallons usable fuel) 3.0 hrs
Cruise (75% at 8000 ft): 540 nm - (37.5 gallons usable fuel) 5.2 hrs
Maximum Range at 10,000 ft: 370 nm - (24.5 gallons usable fuel) 4.1 hrs
Maximum Range at 10,000 ft: 625 nm - (37.5 gallons usable fuel) 6.9 hrs
Performance
Rate of Climb at Sea Level: 715 fpm
Service Ceiling: 14,700 ft
Takeoff
Ground run: 725 ft
Over 50-ft obstacle: 1340 ft
Landing
Landing roll: 475 ft
Over 50-ft obstacle: 1200 ft
Stall Speed
Flaps up, power off: 48 kts
Flaps down, power off: 43 kts
Fuel Capacity
Standard: 26 gal
Long-range: 39 gal
Engine
Make: AVCO Lycoming O-235-N2C
TBO: 2000 hrs
Power: 108 hp
Oil capacity: 7 qts
Propeller: Metal, diameter: 69 in
Dimensions
Wingspan: 33 ft 2 in

Wing Area (sq ft): 159.5
Length: 24 ft 1 in
Height: 8 ft 6 in
Loading
Wing Loading (lbs/sq ft): 10.5
Power Loading (lbs/hp): 15.2
Weight
Gross: 1670 lbs
Empty: 1104 lbs
Baggage: 120 lbs

5

Engines

ONLY TWO BASIC ENGINES have been utilized in the Cessna 150/152 series airplanes. The Continental O-200 engines (Fig. 5-1) are found in all 150s and the Lycoming O-235 engines are found in the 152s (Fig. 5-2).

Fig. 5-1. The Continental O-200 engine powers all Cessna 150 airplanes.

Avco Lycoming

Fig. 5-2. The Avco Lycoming O-235 engine powers the Cessna 152s. This -L2C version is found on airplanes built before the 1984 model year.

CONTINENTAL ENGINES

The Continental engines used in the 150s are out of production. This does not mean they are poor quality engines, just that they are no longer made. The Continental O-200 engines were designed to operate on 80/87 octane fuel, which, for a number of reasons, is in short supply; hence, there is no longer a market for engines using 80/87. This should be a consideration when making a purchase because no factory production means dwindling parts, supplies, and higher costs for repairs. Actually, the O-200 engines are very similar to the O-300s found in the early Cessna Model 172s, just two fewer cylinders. Many small parts are interchangeable between the O-200 and O-300 engines.

Continental O-200-A

Horsepower: 100 at 2750 rpm
Number of Cylinders: 4 horizontally opposed
Displacement: 200.91 cu in
    Bore: 4.0625 in
    Stroke: 3.875 in
    Compression Ratio: 7.0:1

Magnetos: Slick 4001
  Right: Fires 28 degrees BTC upper
  Left: Fires 28 degrees BTC lower
Firing Order: 1-3-2-4
Spark Plugs: SH15
  Gap: .018 to .022 in
  Torque: 330 lbs-in
Carburetor: Marvel-Schebler MA-3-SPA
Alternator: 14 volts at 60 amps
Starter: Automatic engagement
Tachometer: Mechanical
Oil Capacity: 6 qts (7 qts with external oil filter)
Oil Pressure
  Minimum at idle: 10 psi.
  Normal: 30–60 psi.
Oil Temperature, Red Line: 225 Degrees F
Propeller Rotation: Clockwise (view from rear)
Dry Weight: 200 lbs

LYCOMING ENGINES

Cessna used two versions of the Lycoming O-235 in the 152. First was the -L2C, introduced with the 1978 model and remaining through 1982. The O-235-L2C was designed to operate on 100LL avgas, but the new Lycoming suffered from lead fouling problems, although to a lesser extent than did the Continental O-200 engines.

In 1983, the O-235-L2C was replaced with the O-235-N2C. The -N2C has lead gathering pockets inside the combustion chamber. Spark plug life is a good indicator of reduced lead fouling: The plug life for the -N2C appears to be about three times greater than the -L2C, which also means fewer valve problems, which ultimately means the -N2C is a better engine.

Lycoming O-235-L2C and -N2C

Horsepower: (L2C) 110 at 2250 rpm
(N2C) 108 at 2250 rpm
Number of Cylinders: 4 horizontally opposed
Displacement: 233.3 cu in
  Bore: 4.375 in
  Stroke: 3.875 in
Compression Ratio:
  (L2C) 8.5:1
  (N2C) 8.1:1
Magnetos
  Bendix S4LN-20 or S4LN-204 (right) S4LN-21 (left)
  Slick 4250 (right) 4281 or 4252 (left)
Firing Order: 1-3-2-4

Carburetor: Marvel-Schebler MA-3 or MA-3PA
Alternator: 28 volts after 1977
Starter: Automatic engagement
Tachometer: Mechanical
Oil Capacity: 6 qts
Propeller Rotation: Clockwise (view from rear)
Dry Weight: 252 lbs

ENGINE TALK

Engines are the lifeblood of powered flight and the more you know about them, the better. Here are a few definitions to help you understand and discuss airplane engines:

TBO. The time between overhauls recommended by the manufacturer as the maximum engine life. It has no legal bearing on airplanes not used in commercial service; it's only an indicator. Many well-cared-for engines last hundreds of hours beyond TBO, but not all.

Overhaul. Disassembly, repair, inspection, cleaning, and reassembly of an engine. There is no FAR standard; therefore, the work may be done to new limits or to service limits.

Rebuild. Disassembly, repair, alteration, inspection, cleaning and reassembly of an engine, including bringing all specifications back to factory-new limits. In accordance with the FARs, only the engine's manufacturer can rebuild an engine. When rebuilt, the engine is zero timed and comes with a new logbook.

Remanufactured. A term having no official validity, but often used by engine overhaul shops. The term generally equates to an overhaul to new limits.

Top overhaul. Rebuilding of the head assemblies, but not of the entire engine. In other words, the case of the engine is not split, only the cylinders are pulled. Top overhaul is utilized to bring engines that burn oil or have low compressions within specifications. It is a method of stretching the life of an otherwise sound engine. A top overhaul can include such work as valve replacement or grinding, cylinder replacement or repair, piston and ring replacement, and the like. It is not necessarily an indicator of a poor engine. The need for a top overhaul might have been brought on by such things as pilot abuse, lack of care, lack of use, or abuse (hard climbs and fast let-downs). Note that the term top overhaul does not indicate the extent of the rebuilt job—number of cylinders rebuilt or the completeness of the job.

New limits. Dimensions and specifications used when constructing a new engine. Parts meeting new limits will normally reach TBO with no further attention, save for routine maintenance.

Service limits. Dimensions and specifications below which use is forbidden. Many used engine parts will fit into this category; however, they are unlikely to last the full TBO, as they are already partially worn.

Magnaflux and magnaglow. Methods of detecting invisible defects (cracks) in ferrous metals. Parts normally magnafluxed or magnaglowed are crankshafts, camshafts, piston pins, rocker arms, and the like. Magnaflux and magnaglow inspections are routinely done during remanufacture and overhaul.

Nitriding. A means of hardening cylinder barrels and crankshafts. The purpose is to create a hard surface that resists wear, thereby extending the useful life of the part.

Chromeplating. Used to bring the internal dimensions of the cylinders back to specifications. The plating produces a hard, machinable, and long-lasting surface. The major drawback of chromeplating is a longer break-in time; however, an advantage of the chromeplating is a resistance to destructive oxidation (rust) within combustion chambers.

Cermicrome. Trademarked process of chromeplating combined with an oil wettable silicon carbide impregnated coating.

Used engines

Many airplane ads proudly state the hours on the engine (716 SMOH). Basically, this means that there have been 716 hours of operation since the engine was overhauled. Not stated is how it was used, or how completely it was overhauled. The time on an engine, since new or overhaul, is an important factor when placing a value on an airplane. The recommended TBO, less the hours currently on the engine, is the time remaining. The difference between these times is the expected remaining life of the engine.

Three basic terms are normally used when referring to the time on an airplane engine:

- Low time—first ⅓ of TBO
- Mid time—second ⅓ of TBO
- High time—last ⅓ of TBO

Naturally, other variables come into play when referring to TBO:

- Are the hours on the engine since new, remanufacture, or overhaul?
- What type of flying has the engine seen?
- Was it flown on a regular basis?
- What kind of maintenance did the engine get?

The engine logbook will indicate whether the engine is operating on time since new, remanufacture, or overhaul. The logs should also be of some help in determining questions about engine maintenance. Preventive maintenance should have been accomplished and logged throughout the engine's life (oil changes, plug changes, and the like). In accordance with FARs, all maintenance must be logged.

Airplanes that have not been flown on a regular basis—and maintained in a similar fashion—will never reach full TBO. Manufacturers refer to regular usage —40 hours monthly: however, there are few privately owned airplanes meeting the upper limits of this requirement. Most pilots don't have the time or money required for such constant use. Logging 20-to-40 hours monthly equates to 240 to 480 hours yearly. When an engine isn't run, acids and moisture in the oil will oxidize engine components. In addition, the lack of lubricant movement will cause the seals to dry out. Left long enough, the engine will seize and no longer be operable.

Just as hard on engines as no use is abuse. Hard climbs and fast descents, causing abnormal heating and cooling conditions, are extremely destructive to aircooled engines. Training aircraft often exhibit this trait due to their usage (takeoff and landing practice).

Overhauled engines

Beware of the engine that has just a few hours on it since an overhaul. Perhaps something is not right with the overhaul, or it was a very cheap job, just to make the plane more salable.

When it comes to overhauls, I always recommend the large shops that specialize in aircraft engine rebuilding. I'm not saying that the local FBO can't do a good job; I just feel that the large organizations specializing in this work have more experience and equipment to work with. In addition, they have reputations to live up to, and most will back you in the event of difficulties.

Engines are expensive to rebuild/overhaul. Here are some typical costs for a complete overhaul (1993 pricing): O-200, $8,500; O-235, $8,900. If Lycoming does the work at its factory, a zero-time engine (factory rebuild) could cost more than $15,000. A new engine is in excess of $25,000.

Cylinder color codes

When looking at the engine of an airplane you can sometimes see a little of the past work done on it. You will notice that some of the cylinders (often referred to as *jugs*) might be painted or banded. The colors of the paint or band tell you about the physical properties of the individual cylinder:

- Orange indicates a chromeplated cylinder barrel
- Blue indicates a nitrided cylinder barrel
- Green indicates internal cylinder dimension is .010 oversize
- Yellow indicates .020 oversize

AVIATION FUELS AND RELATED PROBLEMS

Airplane owners have recently been voicing many questions and concerns about the limited availability of 80/87 grade fuel, and the use of higher leaded fuel in engines rated for grade 80/87 fuel.

A quick look around the country indicates that fuel suppliers are not making 80/87 grade aviation fuel available. The suppliers claim there is too little profit in 80/87 manufacture and supply. They also state that the new 100LL avgas is a replacement for the 80/87. The trend is toward a complete phaseout of 80/87-grade aviation fuel.

Avgas color coding

Avgas is color-coded to prevent incorrect refueling:

- Red is 80 octane containing .50 ml lead/gal
- Blue is 100 octane containing 2 ml lead/gal
- Green is 100 octane containing 3 ml lead/gal

It's interesting to note that the Blue 100, also referred to as 100LL (LL for low lead), contains four times the amount of lead as did the 80/87 octane fuel. This low-lead fuel will gradually become the only fuel available for small piston airplane engines. It must be used as a replacement fuel whenever 80/87 is not available. Continuous use of the 100LL fuel as a replacement for 80/87 will result in increased engine deposits in the combustion chamber and in the engine oil, and subsequent increased spark plug maintenance and more frequent oil changes. The frequency of spark plug maintenance and oil drain periods may be controlled to some extent by the type of operation.

Reducing 100LL problems

The following instructions are directed toward the operators of Continental O-200 engines; however, operators of Lycoming O-235 engines might also realize engine maintenance benefit. Operation at full-rich mixture requires more frequent maintenance; therefore, it is very important to learn, and use, proper leaning techniques.

To keep engine deposits at a minimum when using the higher leaded 100LL avgas blue, it is essential that the following four conditions of operation and maintenance be met:

- Proper fuel management
- Proper shutdown technique
- Frequent oil changes
- Additional spark plug maintenance

Proper fuel management. The use of economy cruise engine leaning will keeps deposits to a minimum, and, as a side benefit, reduce the direct operating (fuel) costs. Never lean the mixture from full-rich during takeoff, climb, or high-performance cruise operation. (Exception: During takeoff from high elevation airports or during climb at higher altitudes, leaning might be required to eliminate roughness or reduced power that might occur at full-rich mixtures. In such instances, the mixture should be adjusted only enough to obtain smooth engine operation.) Careful observation of temperature instruments should be practiced. Always return the mixture to full-rich before increasing power settings. During the approach and landing sequence, the mixture should be placed in the full rich position unless landing at high elevation fields where leaning might be necessary.

Lean the engine with RPM or airspeed. The engine tachometer and/or the airspeed indicator may be used to approximate the maximum power and best economy mixture ranges. Set the controls for the desired cruise power as shown in the owner's manual, then gradually lean the mixture from full-rich until either the tachometer or the airspeed indicator reach their highest readings. At peak indication, the engine is operating at maximum power.

Where best economy operation is desired, the mixture is first leaned from full-rich to maximum power, then gradually leaned until engine power is rapidly diminishing as noted by a decrease in airspeed. When this reduction occurs, enrich the mixture sufficiently to regain most of the lost airspeed or engine rpm. Some slight engine power and airspeed must be sacrificed to gain best economy mixture setting.

An alternate method of leaning at altitude is to lean the mixture until engine operation becomes slightly rough, then enrichen the mixture until the engine is again evenly firing. Remember: Proper leaning will not only result in fewer engine deposits and reduced maintenance cost, but will provide more economical operation and fuel saving.

Proper shutdown. The deposit formation rate can be greatly reduced by controlling ground operations to minimize the separation of nonvolatile components of the higher leaded aviation fuels. The formation rate is accelerated by low fuel/mixture temperatures caused by the rich fuel and air mixtures associated with idling and taxiing operations.

To reduce the effects of excessive deposit formation, it is important that engine idling speed be set in the 600–650 rpm range with the idle mixture adjusted properly to provide smooth idling operation. Additionally, engine speed should be increased to 1200 rpm for one minute prior to shutdown. This will increase the combustion chamber temperature and allow the deposits to dissipate. After one minute, slow the engine down and lean until operation ceases.

Frequent oil changes. Many of the engine deposits formed by the use of the higher leaded 100LL fuel are in suspension within the engine oil, yet are not removed by a full-flow filter. When large amounts of these contaminants in the oil reach a high temperature area of the engine, the contaminants can be baked out. This baking out, and the subsequent deposits left in such areas as the exhaust valve guides, can cause sticking valves. Left unattended, sticking valves can cause extensive engine damage. Extensive may be alternately spelled e-x-p-e-n-s-i-v-e.

When using the higher leaded fuels (100LL), the recommended oil drain period of 50 hours should not be extended, and if valve sticking is noted, all valve guides should be reamed and the oil drain period reduced. It is not uncommon for oil changes to be made on a 25-hour basis.

Additional spark plug maintenance. Spark plugs should be rotated from the top cylinder position to the bottom position on a 50-hour basis, and should be cleaned, inspected, and gapped on a 100-hour basis. Depending upon the lead content of the fuel and the type of operation, more frequent cleaning of the spark plugs might be necessary.

If excessive spark plug lead fouling occurs, the selection of a hotter plug might be necessary; however, depending upon the type of lead deposit formed, a colder plug might better resolve the problem. When the engine is operated primarily at a low power setting, such as patrolling, a hotter plug would be advantageous. Conversely, when operating at a high cruise power setting, a colder plug is recommended. If in doubt as to the plug temperature range that is proper for your particular circumstance, pay a visit to a friendly mechanic for some advice.

A word from the FAA

In April 1977, the use of tricresyl phosphate (TCP) was approved for use in Lycoming and Continental engines without turbosuperchargers. TCP is a fuel additive that prevents lead fouling. It is available from most FBOs and

Alcor, Inc.
10130 Jones-Maltsberger Rd.
Box 32516
San Antonio, TX 78216
(800) 354-7233
(512) 349-3771

Sticking valves

The following is based on an article that appeared in the *Cessna 150-152 News* (courtesy of the AVCO Lycoming *Flyer*) about sticking valves:

> An aircraft had been purchased recently and the owner flew it to altitude in the vicinity of his home airport to satisfy himself of the aircraft's capability to fly over mountainous terrain during a planned vacation trip. Content that the aircraft and engine were capable of meeting his requirements, the vacation trip was undertaken. All went smoothly on the first 300-mile leg of the trip, which ended with a planned overnight stop.
>
> When the engine was started the next day, it was very, very rough, but smoothed out and ran normally after a short time. With the engine running smoothly, the vacation trip continued to its destination. The aircraft was then tied down and not operated until it was time for the return trip . . . a period of about a week.
>
> As the engine was started for the return trip, it again gave indications that a valve was momentarily sticking . . . it ran very rough for several seconds, but then smoothed out. With the engine running smoothly again, the return trip was started. After one to two hours of flight at altitude, over mountainous terrain, the engine ran very rough again for a short period of time, and then smoothed out. The pilot decided to land at the nearest airport.
>
> Examination of the engine revealed a considerable amount of oil leakage. The cause . . . a valve which had stuck solidly and caused the pushrod to bend. This bending ruptured the pushrod shroud tube and allowed oil to escape. This is a classic example of the damage which sticking valves can cause.
>
> The lesson to be learned is quite simple: Do not neglect the warning signs. Perhaps the experience related here will allow others to recognize a rough-running engine at start-up as a possible indication of sticking valves. The next step is to take immediate action to prevent damage.

Although there might be occasional exceptions, it is almost always an exhaust valve which sticks. To prevent further valve sticking and to reduce the possibility of damage, all exhaust valve guides should be cleaned of any carbon, varnish, or other contamination buildup. This is accomplished by reaming the guides to their original size as specified by the manufacturer.

AUTO FUELS

As a result of the scarcity of 80/87 avgas, there has been considerable controversy and discussion about the use of auto fuels (sometimes referred to as mogas) in certified aircraft engines. This would be in lieu of the 100LL products.

Why use mogas?

The use of auto fuels has many pros and cons. This debate has been going on for several years, and will probably continue until piston airplane engines are no longer used. It is up to the individual pilot to make a choice about the use of non-aviation fuels in an airplane with an STC to do so. To aid in this decision-making, consider the following:

- Unleaded auto fuel is certainly less expensive than 100LL.
- Auto fuel does appear to operate well in the older engines that require 80 octane fuel.
- If you have a private gas tank and pump, it might be advantageous to utilize auto fuel. It'll be far easier to locate an auto fuel supplier willing to keep your tank filled than it will be to find an avgas supplier willing to make small deliveries. This could be the determining factor at a small private strip.
- There is a decided lack of consistency among the various brands of auto fuels (gasolines) and their additives. In particular, many low-lead auto fuels have alcohol in them. Alcohol is destructive to some parts of the typical aircraft fuel system.
- The engine manufacturers claim the use of auto fuels will void warranty service. This is not really important unless you have a new or factory remanufactured engine.
- Many FBOs are reluctant to make auto fuels available for reasons such as product liability and less profit.
- The FAA states that auto fuels might reduce maintenance costs (FAA AC 91-33).

However, just to fuel the fire even further, here is a partial reprint of Advisory Circular #AC 150/5190-A, dated April 4, 1972. (Be familiar with this because you will see it again and you might someday need to quote from it to stand up for your rights.):

Restrictions on self-service. Any unreasonable restriction imposed on the owners and operators of aircraft regarding the servicing of their own aircraft and equipment may be considered as a violation of agency policy. The owner of an aircraft should be permitted to fuel, wash, repair, paint, and otherwise take care of his own aircraft, provided there is no attempt to perform such services for others. Restrictions which have the effect of diverting activity of this type to a commercial enterprise amount to an exclusive right contrary to law.

Mogas standards

If you decide that mogas is to be your fuel of choice, be sure your fuel complies with Specification D-439 and D-4814 by ASTM (American Society for Testing Materials). For environmental reasons it is possible that new legislation will require 10 percent oxygenates (alcohol) in auto fuels to reduce air pollution. This could have an adverse affect upon the STCs for auto fuels because new auto fuel formulas might not meet the requirements of D-439. **Caution:** The FAA warns against use of any auto fuel containing ethanol or methanol (IAW AC 23.1521); information relative to alcohol in fuel may be found in AC 91-40. Beyond the alcohol concerns, compliance should be no problem if you select a major brand. Lesser brands, doing business in the 17 states not requiring compliance with the above standards, should be checked before use. States not requiring compliance with the ATSM standards are:

Alaska	New York
Kentucky	Ohio
Maine	Oregon
Massachusetts	Pennsylvania
Michigan	Texas
Missouri	Vermont
Nebraska	Washington
New Hampshire	West Virginia
New Jersey	

STC sources

Warning: Prior to purchasing the auto fuel STC, check with your insurance carrier and get their approval in writing for the use of auto fuel. Some aviation insurance companies are not keen on the use of mogas, and if you don't comply with their wishes, they could deny a claim.

STCs for mogas are available for the Cessna 150/152 airplanes from:

Petersen Aviation, Inc.
Auto Fuel STCs
RR #1 Box 18
Minden, NE 68959
(308) 237-9338

Petersen Aviation, Inc., provides auto fuel STCs for the Cessna 150 and 152 (limited to models using the O-235-L2C engine). The Petersen STCs allow for the use of leaded and unleaded auto fuels.

Experimental Aircraft Association
Wittman Field
Oshkosh, WI 54903
(414) 426-4800

The EAA's STCs (unleaded auto fuel only) are available for all Cessna 150 airplanes and a limited number of Model 152s.

ENGINE MONITORING

Various gauges and instruments are available to monitor what is going on inside the engine. Most, such as the tachometer, oil temperature, and oil pressure gauges are all familiar and found on the typical instrument panel. Other instruments will aid the pilot in closely monitoring engine operation:

EGT. The exhaust gas temperature gauge measures the temperature of the exhaust gases as they enter the exhaust manifold. This instrument is extremely valuable for monitoring leaning procedures.

CHT. The cylinder head temperature gauge indicates the temperature of the cylinder heads. Problems such as inadequate engine cooling can be detected by its use.

Carburetor ice detector. The carburetor ice detector is designed to actually detect ice, not just low temperature in the carburetor throat. Because ice is a product of temperature and humidity, mere temperature indication is not satisfactory because temperature alone does not relate the whole picture. The detector utilizes an optical probe in the carburetor throat and is so sensitive that it can detect frost up to five minutes before ice begins to form, allowing the pilot plenty of time to take corrective action (Fig. 5-3).

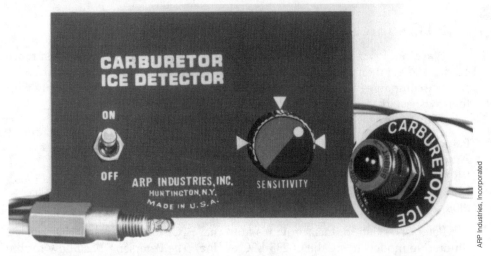

Fig. 5-3. An ice detector could save your life by indicating ice forming inside the carburetor.

PROPELLERS

Many pilots might not give much thought to the metal propeller. They should. Even though a high margin of safety is built into the design of metal propeller blades, failures do occur. Most propeller blade failures occur because of fatigue cracks that started as dents, cuts, scars, scratches, nicks, or leading edge pits. Only in rare instances have failures been caused by material defects or surface disconti- nuities that existed before the blades were placed in service.

Improperly performed repairs can also lead to failure. Fatigue failures of blades have occurred at the place where previous damage has been repaired. This might be due to the failure having actually started prior to the repair, and the re- pair merely amplifying the problem. Too much flexing of the blade—blade- straightening or blade-pitching—can overstress the metal, causing it to fail.

Metal propeller blade failure might also occur in areas seldom inspected, such as underneath leading edge abrasion boots and underneath propeller blade decals. It is advisable to inspect these hidden areas when the propeller is serviced/repaired.

Another cause of metal propeller blade failure (though less frequent) is *flutter*, a vibration that causes the ends of the blade to twist back and forth at a high fre- quency around an axis perpendicular to the crankshaft. At certain engine speeds, this vibration can become critical and, if the propeller is allowed to operate in this range, propeller blade failure might occur. At the very least, metal fatigue will re- sult. It is for this reason that tachometer accuracy is so very important. Periodic tachometer accuracy checks should be made using reliable testing instruments. Then, by referencing your tachometer, you avoid propeller speeds that can be damaging. These speeds are indicated as red arcs on the tachometer, and listed in the operations manual.

Many stresses are on a propeller. The propeller is at the end of the energy chain, and is responsible for efficiently converting engine power into thrust. Dur- ing normal operation, four separate stresses are imposed on a propeller:

- Thrust
- Torque
- Centrifugal force
- Aerodynamic force

The stresses that normally occur in the propeller blades may be viewed as par- allel lines of force that run within the blade approximately parallel to the surface. Additional stresses can be imposed by vibration caused by fluttering or uneven tracking of the blades.

When a defect occurs (scratch, nick, dent) these lines of force will be squeezed together, concentrating the stress. The increase in stress can be sufficient to cause a crack to start, which results in a greater stress concentration. This greater stress concentration causes the crack to enlarge until the inevitable blade failure.

Most blade failures occur within a few inches of the blade tip; however, fail- ures can occur in other portions of the blade when dents, cuts, scratches, or nicks are ignored. No damage should be overlooked or allowed to go without repair. When performing preflight inspection of the propeller, inspect not only the leading edge but the entire blade for erosion, scratches, nicks, and cracks. Regardless of how small any surface irregularities might appear, consider each as a stress point subject to fatigue failure.

The following tips will help you care for your propeller, and provide for its long life:

- Keep the blades clean because complete inspections cannot be made if the blades are covered with dirt, oil, or other foreign matter.

- Avoid engine runup areas containing loose sand, stones, gravel, or broken asphalt. These particles can result in nicks to the propeller if sucked toward the blades during run-up.

- Propeller blades are not designed to be used as handles for moving an airplane.

- During the normal 100-hour or annual inspection, the engine tachometer should be checked for accuracy to preclude operation in any restricted rpm range.

6

ADs and other problems

UNFORTUNATELY, AIRPLANES ARE NOT PERFECT in design or manufacture and will from time to time require inspection and repairs or service as a result of unforeseen problems. These problems generally affect numerous makes and models due to parts interchangeability. The required procedures are set forth in *airworthiness directives* (ADs) that are described in FAR Part 39 and must be complied with. The AD might be a simple one-time inspection, a periodic inspection (every 50 hours of operation, for instance), or a major modification to the airframe or engine. The records of AD compliance become a part of the aircraft's logbooks. When looking at an airplane with a purchase in mind, check for AD compliance.

Notice of an AD is placed in the *Federal Register* and sent by mail to registered owners of the aircraft concerned. In an emergency, the information will be sent by telegram to registered owners. Either way, the AD's purpose is to assure the integrity of an aircraft and the safety of those onboard.

Some ADs are relatively inexpensive to comply with because they are basically inspections; other ADs can be very expensive, involving extensive engine or airframe modifications or repairs. ADs are not normally handled like automobile recalls, where the manufacturer is responsible for the costs involved. Sometimes the airplane manufacturer will offer the parts and labor free of charge, but don't count on it. Even though ADs correct deficient design or poor quality control of parts or workmanship, AD compliance is usually paid for by the individual airplane owner.

AD LIST

The 150/152 airplanes are relatively AD-free; however, there are some. The following AD list should not be considered a last end word. The list is only an abbreviated guide to help anyone checking for AD compliance. Not all ADs listed affect all 150/152 airplanes.

For a complete check of ADs on an airplane, see your mechanic, or contact the AOPA (Aircraft Owners and Pilots Association):

AOPA
421 Aviation Way
Frederick, MD 21701
(301) 695-2000

AOPA will provide a list of ADs for a particular aircraft (by serial number) for a small fee. This type of search is highly accurate, and well worth the money spent.

Many of the following ADs are old and should have previously been complied with, however, you should still check: (**Warning:** This AD list is for reference purposes only and must not be used for certifying AD compliance.)

Model 150

62-22-1: Reinstall the vacuum pump on all O-200A engines.

67-3-1: Modify the cabin heat unit on SN 15017001 through 15061328.

67-31-4: Modify the glove compartment on G and H models.

68-17-4: Test and rework as needed stall warning system on all models.

71-22-2: Inspect and replace as needed the nose gear fork after 1000 hours of operation.

72-3-3: Each 100 hours of operation, inspect the flap screw jack.

73-23-7: Replace the wing attachment fittings.

74-24-13: Replace altimeter if part no. 5932 or 5934.

74-26-9: Inspect Bendix magnetos for solid steel drive shaft bushing. Replace as necessary.

75-15-8: Rework the Beryl oil filter.

76-1-1: Placard speeds in the Aerobat if Flint long-range fuel tanks are installed.

77-2-9: Replace the flap actuator ball nut assembly on some models.

77-13-3: Reset the magnetic timing on the O-200 engine.

78-25-7: Replace the vertical fin brackets on some Aerobats.

79-8-3: Remove and/or modify the cigarette lighter wiring harness.

79-10-14: Install a vented fuel cap, and placard same.

79-13-8: Replace the Airborne dry air pump, if installed after 5-15-79.

79-18-5: Replace LiS02 ELT batteries.

80-6-3: Install a new flap cable clamp.

80-6-5: Test the magnetic impulse coupling.

80-11-4: Inspection of the eight nut plates on the vertical aft fin for cracks in the body or base of nut plates.

81-7-6: Inspect and replace if needed the AC fuel pump on O-200 engines.

81-15-3: Replace Brackett engine air filter.

81-16-5: Inspect the Slick magneto coil for cracks. Replace as needed.

82-13-1: Periodic inspection and/or replace the gripper bushing block and check pistons and valves on engines with S-1200 series Bendix magnetos.

82-20-1: Inspect the Bendix impulse couplers prior to 300 hours usage on the magnetos.

83-17-6: Balance the ailerons on some Robertson STOL conversions.

84-26-2: Replace paper air filter elements each 500 hours.

86-5-2: Inspect pressure sensitive altimeters.

86-15-7: If a larger engine than O-200 is installed—modify CG (center of gravity). Possible limitation to pilot only.

86-24-7: Modify engine control rod ends.

86-26-4: Inspect and/or modify the shoulder harnesses.

87-20-3: Inspect and repair the seat rails.

87-21-5: Placard against spins (150 through Model M, A150, 152 and A152).

88-15-6: Secure the battery cable to battery box cover lock pin.

Model 152

78-25-7: Replace the vertical fin brackets on some Aerobats.

79-2-6: Inspect or replace the heater muffler.

79-13-8: Replace the Airborne dry air pump, if installed after 5-15-79.

79-18-5: Replace LiS02 ELT batteries.

80-1-6: Modify the flap actuator assembly.

80-6-3: Install a new flap cable clamp.

80-6-5: Test the magnetic impulse coupling.

80-11-4: Inspection of the eight nut plates on the vertical aft fin for cracks in the body or base of nut plates.

80-25-2: Check and record valve tappet clearances on some engines (see AD for serial numbers).

80-25-7: Check the Stewart-Warner oil cooler for oil leaks. Replace if needed.

81-5-1: Check the fuel gauge markings.

81-16-5: Inspect the Slick magneto coil for cracks. Replace as needed.

81-18-4: Replace the oil pump impeller and shaft on Lycoming O-235 engines.

83-22-6: Modify or replace the aileron hinges on 152 S/N 15282032-85783 and A1520809-1022.

84-26-2: Replace paper air filter elements each 500 hours.

86-24-7: Modify engine control rod ends.

87-20-3: Inspect and repair the seat rails.

87-21-5: Placard against spins (150 through Model M, A150, 152 and A152).

88-2-4: Remove and check part number on model MA-3PA carburetor on Lycoming engine.

89-26-10: Inspect and rework the propeller hub bolt holes.

91-14-22: Inspect and rework internal parts of engine at time of overhaul or damage.

DANGEROUS SEATS

"Warning," says the 1968 *Cessna Service Manual* for 150 series airplanes, "It is extremely important that the pilot's seat stops are installed (because) acceleration and deceleration could possibly permit the seat to become disengaged from the seat rails and create a hazardous situation, especially during takeoff and landing."

This is very serious. How would you feel if you had just started your climbout and suddenly were pitched over backwards, seat and all? From this new position it would be impossible to regain control of the aircraft.

For several years, letters to editors and various articles have been appearing in general aviation magazines pointing out the seat problem found in the Cessna single-engine airplanes. Basically, the pilot's seat is mounted on two aluminum tracks (rails), sliding back and forth for adjustment. A pin holds the seat position on the track.

The following is quoted from *Airworthiness Alerts*, a monthly publication of the FAA Aviation Standards National Field Office in Oklahoma City.

> Numerous reports indicate that difficulties continue to be encountered with seat attachments, structure, locking mechanisms, tracks, and stops. When required inspections are made, it is suggested the following items be examined:
>
> 1. Check the seat assembly for structural integrity.
> 2. Inspect the roller brackets for separation and wear.
> 3. Examine the locking mechanism (actuating arm, linkage, locking pin) for wear and evidence of impending failure.
> 4. Inspect the floor-mounted seat rails for condition and security, locking pin holes for wear, and rail stops for security.
> 5. Determine that the floor structure in the vicinity of the rails is not cracked or distorted.
>
> Defective or worn parts are a potential hazard that should be given prompt attention. Accomplish repair or replacement of damaged components in accordance with the manufacturer's service publications.
>
> (A note with the article said "This . . . was previously published in *Alerts* . . .. The same type problems are still being reported.")
>
> The NTSB (National Transportation Safety Board) has identified these problems as the probable cause in several fatal accidents.

Keep this seat problem in mind at preflight time and always check the seat after locking it in place. Two excellent devices designed to prevent seat slippage are the SAF-T-STOP from Texas Aero Plastics, Northwest Regional Airport, Route 9, Box 17, Roanoke, TX 76262 (817) 491-4735, and Stay Put from B&D Safety Lock Company, 14409 141st Ave. S.E., Renton, WA 98056.

EXPENSIVE STARTERS

In later 150 models, the starter switch was incorporated as a part of the ignition switch. On the earlier models, the starter was activated by pulling a T-handle mounted on the instrument panel. The latter has never been a problem except for infrequent cable breaks; however, when this happens, the pilot can either hand-prop the engine—which is dangerous to those unschooled in this method—or open the cowl, reach in, and depress the starter switch. If you elect to do the manual depress, be sure the engine throttle is set at its lowest setting, the parking brake is set, and the wheels chocked. Better yet, have a qualified person sitting in the cockpit to monitor the airplane.

If the key-start fails, you will have to hand-prop the airplane. You can count on spending several hundred dollars in repairs to the starter clutch unit. This has been a continuing problem with all key-start Model 150 airplanes. The rate of mechanical failure of the older pull system is very low and repairs are considerably more economical.

CONTROL CABLES

Flexible cables operate the control surfaces. The cables run from the controls in the cabin throughout the fuselage and wing structures. They go around corners by passing over pulleys. As the cables pass over pulleys, the cables flex and bend. Eventually fatigue will set in and the cable will fray. An unserviced cable will break, causing loss of control to the surface involved.

Some of the control cables are difficult to inspect, due to the location within the airframe, and are rarely checked. Additionally, pulleys sometimes cease to turn or sometimes break and can cause cable binding and excessive wear. Be sure that all the control cables and pulleys are checked during annual inspections.

7

Buying a used airplane

ONCE THE DECISION HAS BEEN MADE to purchase an airplane, a game plan must be set up to make the purchase in an orderly manner—perhaps a checklist arrangement. After all, pilots are familiar with checklists. The checklist should have three parts: search, inspection, and paperwork.

THE SEARCH

Locating a good used 150 or 152 should not be difficult. The hard part is in finding it where you want it, and at a price that is agreeable. The search for a Cessna 150/152 does not usually have to be wide and exhaustive because simply by sheer numbers there are so many. This is good for the buyer because it assures an adequate selection from which to choose.

Many model years and price ranges to select from are available; therefore, the purchaser is encouraged to set a range of expectations. This could be based on features desired, options available, a particular favorite model or, most likely, the cash available for such a purchase.

Where to start

The search starts locally, usually at the home airport, because it is easier to see what is available. If you know the FBO and feel comfortable with the FBO's operation, then perhaps this is a good way to do your searching. Tell the FBO what you're looking for. It could be that the FBO is considering selling a trainer, or might know of airplanes for sale—or nearly for sale that have yet to be advertised. After all, an FBO is an insider to the business.

If there is nothing of interest at your airport, then broaden the search. Check the bulletin boards at other nearby airports. While you're checking the bulletin boards, ask around. Then walk around and look for airplanes with for sale signs in the windows.

While walking around the tiedown area, pay particular attention to airplanes that appear to be little used. Sometimes the owner of a seldom-flown airplane will suddenly sell the plane if approached by a purchaser equipped with the proper interest—and money. You could even put an airplane wanted ad on the bulletin board.

Reading the ads

Most ads for airplanes for sale will make use of various more-or-less standard abbreviations. These abbreviations describe the individual airplane, and tell how it is equipped. Also in the ad will be a telephone number, but seldom a location of where the airplane is located. The clue here is the area code. A typical ad would appear as:

65 C150, 4106TT, 265 SMOH, June ANN,
FGP, NAV/COM, ELT, NDH. $12,500 firm.
999-555-1212

Translated, this ad reads: For sale, a 1965 Cessna 150 airplane with 4106 hours total time on the airframe and an engine with 265 hours since a major overhaul. The next annual inspection is due in June. It is equipped with a full gyro instrument panel, has a navigation and communication radio, an emergency locator transmitter, and, best of all, the airplane has no damage history. The price is $12,500 and the seller says bargaining is out of the question (most sellers do bargain, however). Last is the telephone number.

As you can see, a lot of information was inside those three little lines. To assist you in reading these ads, *see* appendix A for a complete listing of the popular advertising abbreviations and *see* appendix B for a listing of area codes and locations.

Where to find ads

Local newspapers sometimes have airplanes listed in the classified ads, and these should be checked; however, in this day of specialization, several publications have become leaders in airplane advertising. *Trade-A-Plane* is the king of all aviation advertising. The "Yellow Sheet," as it's sometimes called, is published three times monthly. The paper contains commercial advertising of just about everything and anything aviation-related. (*Trade-A-Plane* is required reading for all aviation buffs, even if not actively searching for an airplane.) It is available from:

Trade-A-Plane
P.O. Box 509
Crossville, TN 38555
(615) 484-5137

If you are really serious and want to find that illusive bargain, you need to be at the front of the line. This means getting *Trade-A-Plane* before everyone else does. Subscriptions are available as first-class U.S. mail, or better yet, as Federal Express 2nd day air priority delivery.

General Aviation News and Flyer is a twice monthly newspaper carrying up-to-the-minute news and information concerning general aviation. "You read it there months before the magazines print it" is a phrase I have heard more than one pilot say about *General Aviation News and Flyer*. The classifieds—typically more than

20 pages—are printed on pink paper and carried as an insert to the newspaper. Contact them at:

General Aviation News and Flyer
P.O. Box 98786
Tacoma, WA 98498-0786
(206) 588-1743

Other recommended publications containing timely used airplane listings are:

Atlantic Flyer
Civil Air Terminal
Hanscom Field
Bedford, MA 01730
(617) 274-7208

Aviators Hot Line
1003 Central Ave.
Fort Dodge, IA 50501
(515) 955-1600

A/C Flyer
P.O. Box 609
Hightstown, NJ 08520
(609) 426-7070

In Flight
P.O. Box 620477
Woodside, CA 94062
(415) 364-8110

Although listings of used airplanes can be found in the various flight-oriented magazines (*AOPA Pilot*, *Flying*, *Plane & Pilot*, *Private Pilot*), you must remember that these ads are stale. Magazines typically have a 60- to 90-day lag time between ad placement and printing.

Use the telephone

Call the phone number listed in the ad and ask questions. The very first question to ask is: Why are you selling your airplane? Often the owner is moving up to a larger plane; however, perhaps there are other circumstances (spouse says sell or perhaps the present owner can no longer afford the plane). Ask questions and take notes on the following:

- What is the general appearance and condition of the plane?
- How many total hours on the airframe?
- How many hours on the engine since new?
- How many hours since the last overhaul?
- What type of overhaul was done?
- Who did the overhaul?
- Is there any damage history?
- What is the asking price?

Remember, this telephone inquiry is to determine if you would like to see the airplane, or eliminate it from further consideration.

Traveling around

Searching for a good used airplane can be expensive and very time-consuming. You'll read ads, make telephone calls (always long distance), and travel great distances to see the airplanes that are advertised.

Often I've seen what really looked interesting in an ad (words always look good), called the telephone number, listened to the seller's spiel about the wonderful airplane, then spent my time and my money to travel halfway across the country to look at the airplane. All too often the airplane that was represented as a 10 turned out to be a gasping 2 or 3. Perhaps in the eyes of the owner the airplane was a 10, but not in mine. I would never purchase an airplane unseen, but it is done everyday and very successfully by many people. The choice, and risk, is up to the purchaser.

Some of these sight-unseen sales are handled by merely reading the ad and conversing with the seller; other sales involve photographs and copies of the logbooks. A fax machine could speed up a logbook review and a videotape could be shipped overnight, making it possible to "see" an airplane from a long distance.

Used trainers

Most but not all 150/152 airplanes have been used as trainers at one time or another. After all, this is what they were designed for. Keep this in mind when shopping. A trainer was probably kept by an FBO, and was subject to hard use—and often lots of abuse. In later years this abuse can show up in the form of unusual flying characteristics commonly known as *out of rigging*. This can be caused by stress on the airframe or improperly corrected damage to the airframe. In almost all cases, the nosewheel will shimmy from the thousands of landings at the hands of neophytes. The doors and seats have been operated thousands of times and the controls will be sloppy. In short, everything will have extensive wear.

On the brighter side, the FBO, using such airplanes on a commercial basis, had to maintain them in a stiffer manner than the individual owner. Instead of annual inspections, the FBO's aircraft had 100-hour inspections. Being used as a trainer, the plane was subjected to more careful preflight inspections than any other type of airplane. The eagle-eyed student usually will not overlook even very minor problems that the rest of us might.

With its continuous use, the trainer's engine is probably in better shape than an engine that has only been flown 20 hours in the past year. Engines thrive on constant use and lubrication. By the same token, training is hard on engines if not conducted properly. In particular, I am referring to hard climbs that overheat an engine and the fast, low-power letdowns that supercool the cylinders. Either of these scenarios will lead to early engine failure and subsequent high maintenance expenses.

Don't let an airplane that was a trainer be eliminated from your list of possibilities. Just be careful. Anything on a 150 or 152 can be repaired just like new. But such repairs will cost money.

It is certainly a tribute to these fine little airplanes that they can take the abuse and punishment of training, yet continue many thousands of hours with little or no serious structural problems. They are tough planes.

THE INSPECTION

The object of the prepurchase inspection of a used airplane is to preclude the purchase of a dog. No one wants to buy someone else's troubles. The prepurchase inspection must be completed in an orderly manner. Take your time during this inspection; a few extra minutes spent inspecting could well save you thousands of dollars later.

The very first item of inspection is a question directed to the current owner: Why are you selling the airplane? The owner might tell you about a new plane to be purchased or reminisce about good times in the plane that is for sale. You can learn a lot about the owner by listening, gaining insight into the airplane's utilization—typically the owner's flying habits—and how the plane you are considering purchasing was treated.

If the owner indicates that the airplane has become a financial burden, raise a red flag of warning. If the seller is having financial difficulties, consider the quality of maintenance that was performed on the airplane: however, financial or family pressures can work to your advantage.

Ask the seller about any known problems or defects with the airplane. Most sellers will give you an honest answer, but certain problems might be undiscovered by them or the owner's mechanic. Remember: Buyer beware. It is your money and your safety.

Definitions

Airworthy. The airplane must conform to the original type certificate, or those supplemental type certificates (STCs) issued for this particular airplane (by serial number). In addition, the airplane must be in safe operating condition, relative to wear and deterioration.

Annual inspection. All small airplanes must be inspected annually by an FAA-certified airframe and powerplant mechanic who holds an IA (inspection authorization), by an FAA-certified repair station, or by the airplane's manufacturer. This is a complete inspection of the airframe, powerplant, and all subassemblies.

100-hour inspection. A 100-hour inspection is of the same scope as the annual and is required on all commercially operated small airplanes (rental, training, and the like), and must be accomplished after every 100 hours of operation. This inspection may be performed by an FAA-certified airframe and powerplant mechanic without an IA rating. An annual inspection will fulfill the 100-hour requirement, but the reverse is not true.

Preflight inspection. The pilot performs a thorough inspection of an aircraft prior to flight. The purpose is to spot obvious discrepancies by inspection of the exterior, interior, and engine of the airplane.

Preventive maintenance. FAR Part 43 lists a number of maintenance operations that are considered preventive in nature and may be performed by a certificated pilot on an airplane owned by the pilot, provided the airplane is not flown in commercial service. (*See* chapter 9 for details about preventive maintenance.)

Repairs and alterations. Two classes of repairs or alterations are major and minor. Major repairs and alterations must be approved for a return to service by an FAA-certified airframe and powerplant mechanic holding an IA authorization, a repair station, or by the FAA. Minor repairs and alterations may be returned to service by an FAA-certified airframe and powerplant mechanic.

Airworthiness Directives. ADs are defined in FAR Part 39 and must be complied with (*see* chapter 6). Files of ADs and their requirements are kept by mechanics and the FAA offices. A compliance check of ADs is a part of the annual inspection.

Service Difficulty Reports. SDRs are prepared by the FAA from *malfunction or defect reports* (MDRs) that are initiated by owners, pilots, and mechanics. SDRs are not the word of law that ADs are; however, they should be adhered to for your own safety.

The visual inspection

The visual inspection of a used airplane is a very thorough preflight, with a few extras included. It's divided into four simple, yet logical, steps.

1. Cabin. Open the door and look inside, notice the general condition of the interior. Does it appear clean or has it recently been scrubbed after a long period of inattention? Look in the corners, just as you would if you were buying a used car. Does the air smell musty and damp? Is the headliner in one tight piece, and the upholstery unfrayed? What is the condition of the door panels? The care given the interior of an airplane can be a good indication of what care was given to the remainder of the airplane.

Look at the instrument panel. Does it have what you want or need? Are the instruments in good condition? Are knobs missing and glass faces broken? Is the equipment all original, or have there been updates made? If updates have been made, are they neat in appearance and workable? I say workable, because updating—particularly avionics—is often done haphazardly, with results that are neither attractive nor workable. Is a placard missing anywhere? Look for screw holes or old adhesive that might indicate where a placard was.

Look out the windows. Are they clear and uncrazed with no yellowing? Side windows are not expensive to replace, and you can do it yourself. Windshields are another story, and another price. Check the operation of the doors. They should open and close and lock with little effort. Make sure the doors close snugly. No outside light should be seen around edges of the doors.

Check the seats for freedom of movement and adjustability. Check the seat tracks and the adjustment locks for damage. The seat tracks and locks have long been a recognized problem with Cessna airplanes.

2. Airframe. Do a complete walk-around of the airplane. Is the paint in good condition, or is some of it lying on the ground underneath the airplane? Paint jobs are expensive, yet necessary for the protection of the metal surfaces from corrosive elements. Paint jobs should also please the eye of the beholder. A good paint job might cost in excess of $3000.

Dents, wrinkles, or tears of the metal skin might indicate prior damage—or just careless handling. Each discrepancy must be examined very carefully by an experienced mechanic. Total consideration of all the dings and dents should tell if the airplane has had an easy or a rough life.

Corrosion or rust on skin surfaces or control systems should be cause for alarm. Corrosion is to aluminum what rust is to iron. It's destructive. Any corrosion or rust should be brought to the attention of a mechanic for judgment. Corrosion that appears as only minor skin damage might continue, unseen, into the interior structure. Damage such as this creates dangerous structural problems that can be very costly to repair. Having a little corrosion in the wing structure is similar to having a little lung cancer. The word "little" is irrelevant.

Check for fuel leaks around the wings, in particular where the wings attach to the fuselage. If leakage evidence is seen, have a mechanic check its source. The landing gear should be checked for evidence of being sprung. Check the tires for signs of unusual wear that might indicate other structural damage. Also look at the nosewheel oleo strut for signs of fluid leakage and proper extension.

Move all the control surfaces to check each for damage. Control movement should be free and smooth. When the controls are centered, the surfaces should also be centered. If the controls are not centered, a problem in the control rigging exists.

3. Engine. Open or remove the cowling to inspect the engine. If you cannot see the engine, you cannot inspect it. Search for signs of oil leakage. Do this by looking at the engine, the inside of the cowl, and on the firewall. If the leaks are bad enough, there will be oil dripping to the ground or onto the nosewheel. Naturally, the seller has probably cleaned all the old oil drips away; however, oil leaves stains. Look for these stains.

Check all the fuel and vacuum hoses/lines for signs of deterioration or chafing. Also check the connections for tightness and/or signs of leakage. Check engine control linkages and cables for obvious damage and ease of movement. Be sure none of the cables are frayed. Check the battery box and battery for corrosion or other damage.

Check the propeller for damage, such as nicks, cracks, or gouges. Even very small defects can cause stress areas on the prop (*see* chapter 5). Any visible damage to a propeller must be checked by a mechanic. Also check it for movement that would indicate propeller looseness at the hub.

Check the exhaust pipes for rigidity, then reach inside with a finger and rub along the inside wall. A light gray dusty coating indicates proper operation. If your finger comes back perfectly clean, you can be assured that someone has cleaned the inside of the pipe—possibly to remove the oily deposits that form there when an engine is burning a lot of oil. If your finger has found a black oily goo, have your mechanic determine the cause. Perhaps a carburetor needs adjustment. The goo could also be caused by a large amount of oil blowby, indicating that the engine needs an expensive overhaul.

Check for exhaust stains on the belly of the plane to the rear of the exhaust pipe. This area has probably been washed, but look anyway. If you find black oily goo, then, as above, see your mechanic.

4. Logbooks. If you are satisfied with what you've seen up to this point, then go back to the cabin, have a seat, and check that all required paperwork is with the airplane. This includes:

- Airworthiness certificate
- Aircraft registration certificate
- FCC station license

- Flight manual or operating limitations
- Logbooks (airframe, engine and propeller)
- Current equipment list
- Weight and balance chart

These items are required by the FARs to be in the plane when flown (except for the logs, which must be available).

Pull out the logbooks and start reading them. (This is an excellent time to look around the cockpit again.) Be sure you're looking at the proper logs for this particular aircraft and that they are the original logs. Sometimes logbooks get "lost" and are replaced with new ones. This can happen because of carelessness or theft. This is why many owners do not keep their logs in the plane and might only provide copies for a sales inspection. Replacement logs might be lacking very important information or could be outright frauds. Fraud is not unheard of in the used airplane business. Be on your guard if the original logs are not available.

Start with the airframe log by looking in the back for the AD compliance section (*see* chapter 6 for a basic list of ADs). Check that the list is up-to-date and that any required periodic inspections have been made. Now go back to the most recent entry, probably an annual or 100-hour inspection. The annual inspection will be a statement that reads:

> March 21, 1993 Total Time: 3126 hrs. I certify that this aircraft has been inspected in accordance with an annual inspection and was determined to be in airworthy condition.
> Signed
> IA # 0000000

From this point back to the first entry in the logbook you'll be looking for similar entries, always keeping track of the total time to ensure continuity and to indicate the regularity of usage (number of hours flown between inspections). Also, you will be looking for indications of major repairs and modifications that will be signaled by the phrase "Form 337 filed." A copy of this form should be with the logs and will tell what work was done. The work might also be described in the logbook. Form 337, Major Repair and Alteration, is filed with the FAA, and copies are a part of the official record of each airplane. Any Form 337s for an airplane are retrievable from the FAA, for a fee.

The engine log will be quite similar in nature to the airframe log, and will contain information from the annual/100-hour inspections. Total engine time will be given, and possibly an indication of time since any overhaul work, although you might have to do some math here. It's quite possible that this log—and engine—will not be the original for the aircraft. As long as the facts are well-documented in both logs, there is no cause for alarm. After all, this would be the case if the original engine was replaced with a factory rebuilt engine or a used engine from another plane.

Pay particular attention to the numbers that indicate the results of a differential compression check. These numbers are the best single indicator of the overall health of an engine. Each number is given as a fraction, with the bottom number always being 80; indicating the industry standard of 80 pounds per-square-inch air pressure that was utilized for the check. The top number is the air pressure that the combustion chamber was able to maintain while being tested. A perfect 80 is not attainable; therefore, the top number will always be less. The reason for the lower number is the air pressure loss that results from loose, worn, or broken rings; scored or cracked cylinder walls; or burned, stuck, or poorly seated valves. Mechanics use different methods to determine the cause and, of course, repair the damage.

Normal readings would be no less than 70/80, and should be uniform (within 2 or 3 lbs) for all cylinders. A discrepancy between cylinder readings might indicate the need for a top overhaul of one or more cylinders. The FAA says that a loss in excess of 25 percent is cause for further investigation. That would be a reading of 60/80. (Such a low reading as this indicates a very tired engine in need of considerable work and expenditures.)

Read the information from the last oil change. The information might contain a statement about debris found on the oil screen or in the oil filter; however, oil changes are often performed by owners and might not be recorded in the log, even though the FARs require all maintenance to be logged. If the oil changes are recorded, how regular were they? I prefer every 25 hours, but 50 is the norm. Is there a record of oil analysis available? If so, ask for it.

If the engine has been top overhauled or majored, there will be a description of the work performed, a date, and the total time on the engine when the work was accomplished.

Check to see if the ADs have been complied with and the appropriate AD entries made in the log (*see* chapter 6 for a basic list of the ADs).

The test flight

The test flight is a flight to determine if the airplane feels right to you. The flight should last at least 30 minutes, but two hours would not be too much.

For insurance purposes, either the owner or a competent flight instructor should accompany you on the test flight. This will also eliminate problems of currency, ratings, and the like, with the FAA, and it will foster better relations with the owner.

After starting the engine, pay particular attention to the gauges. Do they jump to life, or are they sluggish? Watch the oil pressure gauge in particular. Did the oil pressure rise within a few seconds after the engine started? Check the other gauges. Are they indicating as should be expected? Check them during your ground runup, then again during the takeoff and climbout. Do the numbers match those called for in the operations manual? In order to pay more attention to the gauges, it might be advisable to have the other pilot make the takeoff.

After you're airborne, check the gyro instruments for stability. Check the ventilation and heating system for proper operation. Do a few turns, stalls, and some level flight. Does the airplane perform as expected? Can it be trimmed for hands-off flight?

Check all the avionics for proper operation (NAV/COMM, MBR, ADF, LORAN, ILS). A complete check might require a short cross-country flight to an ILS-equipped airport. The short cross-country will give you time to see if you like the plane. Return to the airport and make a couple of landings. Check for proper brake operation and for nosewheel shimmy.

After returning to the parking ramp, open the engine compartment and look again for oil leaks. Also, check along the belly for indications of oil leakage and blowby. A short flight should be enough to dirty things up again, if they had been dirty to begin with.

If you decide not to purchase the airplane, it would be ethical to at least offer to pay for the fuel used during the flight test.

Mechanic's inspection

If you are still satisfied with the airplane and desire to pursue the matter further, then have it inspected by an A&P or AI. This inspection will cost you; however, the inspection could save you thousands. The average for a prepurchase inspection is three to four hours labor, at shop rates. That might be fewer than $100 at a small FBO or several hundred dollars at a large operation specializing in business type aircraft.

The mechanic will accomplish a search of ADs, a complete check of the logs, and an overall check of the plane. A compression check and a *borescope examination* must be made to determine the internal condition of the engine. A borescope examination means looking into a cylinder—with a very small light and lens at the end of a flexible rod, a borescope, that goes through a spark plug hole—and viewing the top of the piston, the valves, and the cylinder walls.

Always use your own mechanic for the prepurchase inspection. You are paying someone to watch out for your interests, not someone who might have an interest in the sale of the plane (employee of the seller).

Have the plane checked even if an annual was just done, unless you know and trust the AI who did the inspection. You might be able to make a deal with the owner over the cost of the mechanic's inspection, particularly if an annual is due.

It's not uncommon to see airplanes listed for sale with the phrase "annual at date of sale." I am always leery of this because I don't know who will do the annual, or how complete the annual will be. All annuals are not created equal. An annual at the date of sale is coming with the airplane, done by the seller, as part of the sale. Who is looking out for your interests?

If an airplane seller refuses you anything that has been mentioned in this chapter, then say thanks for the help, walk away, and look elsewhere. (In retrospect, considering a few sales pitches I've heard over the years, after refusing to fulfill your request, thanking a seller for anything is optional.) Do not let a seller control the situation. Your money, your safety, and possibly your very life are at stake. Airplanes are not hot sellers and there is rarely a line forming to make a purchase. You are the buyer; you have the final word.

THE PAPERWORK

You have decided this airplane is it and just cannot do without it. All inspections have been made and you are satisfied the airplane will suit your needs. Is the price agreeable?

Used airplane prices

Used airplane prices can fluctuate to the extreme and are dependent upon more than the physical airframe and its contents. The actual selling price is the amount mutually agreed upon by the seller and buyer. This agreed-upon sum is arrived at by bargaining.

Bargaining, or the trading of price offers and counter-offers, is the norm in aircraft trade. The concept of bargaining is to find the point where the owner's selling price equals the buyer's purchase price. The selling price is the least amount the owner will take for the airplane and the purchasing price is the most the buyer will pay.

A friend who has bought and sold airplanes for a living sums it up thus, "The selling price is that asked for the one-owner, super-clean, low-time, family pride of an airplane. The purchasing price is that offered for the same box of rocks."

To sum it up, how badly does the seller want to sell, and how badly does the buyer want to buy?

Now you're ready to sit down and complete the paperwork that will lead to ownership.

Title search

The first step when purchasing an airplane is to ensure that the craft has a clear title. A title search is accomplished by checking the aircraft's individual records at the Mike Monroney Aeronautical Center in Oklahoma City, Oklahoma. These records include title information, chain of ownership, major repair/alteration (Form 337) information, and other data pertinent to a particular airplane. The FAA files this information by N-number.

The object of a title search is to ascertain that there are no liens or other hidden encumbrances, against the ownership of the airplane. This search may be done by you, your attorney, or other representative selected by you. Because most prospective purchasers would find it inconvenient to travel to Oklahoma City to do the search themselves, it is advisable to contract with a third party specializing in this service to do the searching. For further information, contact:

King Aircraft Title, Inc.
1411 Classen Blvd. Suite 114
Oklahoma City, OK 73106
(800) 688-1832

or

Aircraft Owners and Pilots Association
Aircraft and Airmen Records Dept.
P.O. Box 19244 Southwest Station
Oklahoma City, OK 73144
(800) 654-4700

Other organizations that provide similar services may be found in *Trade-A-Plane* advertisements.

In addition to title searches, AOPA offers inexpensive title insurance, which protects the owner against unrecorded liens, FAA recording mistakes, or other clouds on the title.

Documents

The following documents must be given to you with the airplane:

- Bill of sale
- Airworthiness certificate
- Logbooks (airframe and engine/propeller)
- Equipment list (including weight and balance data)
- Flight manual

Forms to be completed

Changing official ownership of an airplane requires several FAA and FCC forms to be completed.

AC Form 8050-2, Bill of Sale, is the standard means of recording transfer of ownership (Figs. 7-1, 7-2).

UNITED STATES OF AMERICA

DEPARTMENT OF TRANSPORTATION — FEDERAL AVIATION ADMINISTRATION

AIRCRAFT BILL OF SALE INFORMATION

PREPARATION: Prepare this form in duplicate. Except for signatures, all data should be typewritten or printed. *Signatures must be in ink.* The name of the purchaser must be identical to the name of the applicant shown on the application for aircraft registration

When a trade name is shown as the purchaser or seller, the name of the individual owner or co-owners must be shown along with the trade name.

If the aircraft was not purchased from the last registered owner, conveyances must be submitted completing the chain of ownership from the last registered owner, through all intervening owners, to the applicant.

REGISTRATION AND RECORDING FEES: The fee for issuing a certificate of aircraft registration is $5.00. An additional fee of $5.00 is required when a conditional sales contract is submitted in lieu of bill of sale as evidence of ownership along with the application for aircraft registration ($5.00 for the issuance of the certificate, and $5.00 for recording the lien evidenced by the contract). The fee for recording a conveyance is $5.00 for each aircraft listed thereon. (There is no fee for issuing a certificate of aircraft registration to a governmental unit or for recording a bill of sale that accompanies an application for aircraft registration and the proper registration fee.)

MAILING INSTRUCTIONS:

If this form is used, please mail the original or copy which has been signed in ink to the FAA Aircraft Registry, P.O. Box 25504, Oklahoma City, Oklahoma 73125.

Fig. 7-1. Aircraft bill of sale information.

UNITED STATES OF AMERICA
DEPARTMENT OF TRANSPORTATION FEDERAL AVIATION ADMINISTRATION

AIRCRAFT BILL OF SALE

FOR AND IN CONSIDERATION OF $ THE
UNDERSIGNED OWNER(S) OF THE FULL LEGAL
AND BENEFICIAL TITLE OF THE AIRCRAFT DES-
CRIBED AS FOLLOWS:

UNITED STATES
REGISTRATION NUMBER **N**

AIRCRAFT MANUFACTURER & MODEL

AIRCRAFT SERIAL No.

DOES THIS   DAY OF   19

HEREBY SELL, GRANT, TRANSFER AND

DELIVER ALL RIGHTS, TITLE, AND INTERESTS

IN AND TO SUCH AIRCRAFT UNTO:

Do Not Write In This Block
FOR FAA USE ONLY

PURCHASER

NAME AND ADDRESS
(IF INDIVIDUAL(S), GIVE LAST NAME, FIRST NAME, AND MIDDLE INITIAL.)

DEALER CERTIFICATE NUMBER

AND TO   EXECUTORS, ADMINISTRATORS, AND ASSIGNS TO HAVE AND TO HOLD
SINGULARLY THE SAID AIRCRAFT FOREVER, AND WARRANTS THE TITLE THEREOF.

IN TESTIMONY WHEREOF   HAVE SET   HAND AND SEAL THIS   DAY OF   19

NAME (S) OF SELLER (TYPED OR PRINTED)	SIGNATURE (S) (IN INK) (IF EXECUTED FOR CO-OWNERSHIP, ALL MUST SIGN.)	TITLE (TYPED OR PRINTED)

SELLER

ACKNOWLEDGMENT   (NOT REQUIRED FOR PURPOSES OF FAA RECORDING: HOWEVER, MAY BE REQUIRED
BY LOCAL LAW FOR VALIDITY OF THE INSTRUMENT.)

ORIGINAL: TO FAA

AC FORM 8050-2 (8-85) (0052-00-629-0002)

Fig. 7-2. Aircraft bill of sale.

AC Form 8050-1, Aircraft Registration, is filed with the Bill of Sale, or its equivalent (Figs. 7-3, 7-4). If you are purchasing the airplane under a Contract of Conditional Sale, then that contract must accompany the registration application in lieu of the AC Form 8050-2. The pink copy of the registration is retained by you, and will remain in the airplane until the new registration is issued by the FAA.

AC 8050-41, Release of Lien, must be filed by the seller if a lien is recorded (Fig. 7-5).

AC 8050-64, Assignment of Special Registration Number, is for vanity registration numbers. All U.S. aircraft registration numbers consist of the prefix N, and are followed by

- One to five numbers or one to four numbers, and a letter suffix
- One to three numbers and a two-letter suffix

This is similar to obtaining personalized license plates for your automobile.

FCC (Federal Communications Commission) Form 404, Application for Aircraft Radio Station License, must be completed if you have any radio transmitting equipment on board (Figs. 7-6, 7-7, & 7-8). The tear-off section will remain in your airplane as temporary authorization until the new license is sent to you (Fig. 7-7).

Most forms sent to the FAA or FCC will result in the issuance of a document to you. Be patient—it all takes time.

Assistance

Although not complicated, many forms must be completed when purchasing an airplane, and you might wish to seek assistance filling them out. Check with your FBO, or call upon another party, such as AOPA, which provides closing services via telephone, then prepares and files the necessary forms to complete the transaction (for a small fee). This is particularly nice if the parties involved in the transaction are spread all over the country, for instance when purchasing an airplane sight unseen.

Aircraft Owners and Pilots Association
421 Aviation Way
Frederick, MD 21701
(301) 695-2000

Another source of assistance in completing the necessary paperwork is your bank. This is particularly true if the bank has a vested interest in your airplane (they hold the note).

Insurance

No one can afford to take risks. Insure your airplane from the moment you sign on the dotted line. You will be concerned with two types of insurance coverage: *liability* and *hull*.

UNITED STATES OF AMERICA-DEPARTMENT OF TRANSPORTATION

FEDERAL AVIATION ADMINISTRATION-MIKE MONRONEY AERONAUTICAL CENTER

AIRCRAFT REGISTRATION INFORMATION

PREPARATION: Prepare this form in triplicate. Except for signatures, all data should be typewritten or printed. Signatures must be in ink. The name of the applicant should be identical to the name of the purchaser shown on the applicant's evidence of ownership.

EVIDENCE OF OWNERSHIP: The applicant for registration of an aircraft must submit evidence of ownership that meets the requirements prescribed in Part 47 of the Federal Aviation Regulations. AC Form 8050-2, Aircraft Bill of Sale, or its equivalent may be used as evidence of ownership. If the applicant did not purchase the aircraft from the last registered owner, the applicant must submit conveyances completing the chain of ownership from the registered owner to the applicant.

The purchaser under a CONTRACT OF CONDITIONAL SALE is considered the owner for the purpose of registration and the contract of conditional sale must be submitted as evidence of ownership.

A corporation which does not meet citizenship requirements must submit a certified copy of its certificate of incorporation.

REGISTRATION AND RECORDING FEES: The fee for issuing a certificate of aircraft registration is $5; therefore, a $5 fee should accompany this application. An additional $5 recording fee is required when a conditional sales contract is submitted as evidence of ownership. There is no recording fee for a bill of sale submitted with the application.

MAILING INSTRUCTIONS: Please send the WHITE original and GREEN copy of this application to the Federal Aviation Administration Aircraft Registry, Mike Monroney Aeronautical Center, P.O. Box 25504, Oklahoma City, Oklahoma 73125. Retain the pink copy after the original application, fee, and evidence of ownership have been mailed or delivered to the Registry. When carried in the aircraft with an appropriate current airworthiness certificate or a special flight permit, this pink copy is temporary authority to operate the aircraft.

CHANGE OF ADDRESS: An aircraft owner must notify the FAA Aircraft Registry of any change in permanent address. This form may be used to submit a new address.

AC Form 8050-1 (3/90) (0052-00-628-9006) Supersedes Previous Edition

Fig. 7-3. Aircraft registration information.

UNITED STATES OF AMERICA DEPARTMENT OF TRANSPORTATION
FEDERAL AVIATION ADMINISTRATION-MIKE MONRONEY AERONAUTICAL CENTER
AIRCRAFT REGISTRATION APPLICATION

CERT. ISSUE DATE

UNITED STATES REGISTRATION NUMBER **N**
AIRCRAFT MANUFACTURER & MODEL

AIRCRAFT SERIAL No.

FOR FAA USE ONLY

TYPE OF REGISTRATION (Check one box)

☐ 1. Individual ☐ 2. Partnership ☐ 3. Corporation ☐ 4. Co-owner ☐ 5. Gov't. ☐ 8. Non-Citizen Corporation

NAME OF APPLICANT (Person(s) shown on evidence of ownership. If individual, give last name, first name, and middle initial.)

TELEPHONE NUMBER: (   )

ADDRESS (Permanent mailing address for first applicant listed.)

Number and street:

Rural Route: P.O. Box:

CITY	STATE	ZIP CODE

☐ **CHECK HERE IF YOU ARE ONLY REPORTING A CHANGE OF ADDRESS**
ATTENTION! Read the following statement before signing this application.
This portion MUST be completed.

A false or dishonest answer to any question in this application may be grounds for punishment by fine and / or imprisonment (U.S. Code, Title 18, Sec. 1001).

CERTIFICATION

I/WE CERTIFY:

(1) That the above aircraft is owned by the undersigned applicant, who is a citizen (including corporations) of the United States.

(For voting trust, give name of trustee: _____), or:

CHECK ONE AS APPROPRIATE:

a. ☐ A resident alien, with alien registration (Form 1-151 or Form 1-551) No. _____

b. ☐ A non-citizen corporation organized and doing business under the laws of (state) _____
and said aircraft is based and primarily used in the United States. Records or flight hours are available for inspection at _____

(2) That the aircraft is not registered under the laws of any foreign country; and
(3) That legal evidence of ownership is attached or has been filed with the Federal Aviation Administration.

NOTE: If executed for co-ownership all applicants must sign. Use reverse side if necessary.

TYPE OR PRINT NAME BELOW SIGNATURE

	SIGNATURE	TITLE	DATE
EACH PART OF THIS APPLICATION MUST BE SIGNED IN INK.	SIGNATURE	TITLE	DATE
	SIGNATURE	TITLE	DATE

NOTE   Pending receipt of the Certificate of Aircraft Registration, the aircraft may be operated for a period not in excess of 90 days, during which time the PINK copy of this application must be carried in the aircraft.

AC Form 8050-1 (3/90) (0052-00-628-9006) Supersedes Previous Edition

Fig. 7-4. Aircraft registration (keep the pink copy as the temporary registration).

THIS FORM SERVES TWO PURPOSES

PART I acknowledges the recording of a security conveyance covering the collateral shown.
PART II is a suggested form of release which may be used to release the collateral from the terms of the conveyance.

PART I — CONVEYANCE RECORDATION NOTICE

NAME (last name first) OF DEBTOR

NAME and ADDRESS OF SECURED PARTY/ASSIGNEE

NAME OF SECURED PARTY'S ASSIGNOR (if assigned)

Do Not Write In This Block
FOR FAA USE ONLY

FAA REGISTRA-TION NUMBER	AIRCRAFT SERIAL NUMBER	AIRCRAFT MFd. (BUILDER) and MODEL

ENGINE MFR. and MODEL	ENGINE SERIAL NUMBER(S)

PROPELLER MFR. and MODEL	PROPELLER SERIAL NUMBER(S)

THE SECURITY CONVEYANCE DATED_____COVERING THE ABOVE COLLATERAL WAS RECORDED BY THE FAA AIRCRAFT REGISTRY ON_____ AS CONVEYANCE NUMBER_____.

_____
FAA CONVEYANCE EXAMINER

PART II — RELEASE — (This suggested release form may be executed by the secured party and returned to the FAA Aircraft Registry when terms of the conveyance have been satisfied. See below for additional information.)

THE UNDERSIGNED HEREBY CERTIFIES AND ACKNOWLEDGES THAT HE IS THE TRUE AND LAWFUL HOLDER OF THE NOTE OR OTHER EVIDENCE OF INDEBTEDNESS SECURED BY THE CONVEYANCE REFERRED TO HEREIN ON THE ABOVE-DESCRIBED COLLATERAL AND THAT THE SAME COLLATERAL IS HEREBY RELEASED FROM THE TERMS OF THE CONVEYANCE. ANY TITLE RETAINED IN THE COLLATERAL BY THE CONVEYANCE IS HEREBY SOLD, GRANTED, TRANSFERRED, AND ASSIGNED TO THE PARTY WHO EXECUTED THE CONVEYANCE, OR TO THE ASSIGNEE OF SAID PARTY IF THE CONVEYANCE SHALL HAVE BEEN ASSIGNED: PROVIDED, THAT NO EXPRESS WARRANTY IS GIVEN NOR IMPLIED BY REASON OF EXECUTION OR DELIVERY OF THIS RELEASE.

This form is only intended to be a suggested form of release, which meets the recording requirements of the Federal Aviation Act of 1958, and the regulations issued thereunder. In addition to these requirements, the form used by the security holder should be drafted in accordance with the pertinent provisions of local statutes and other applicable federal statutes. This form may be reproduced. There is no fee for recording a release. Send to FAA Aircraft Registry, P. O. Box 25504, Oklahoma City, Oklahoma 73125.

ACKNOWLEDGEMENT (If Required By Applicable Local Law):

DATE OF RELEASE: ....

....
(Name of security holder)

SIGNATURE (in ink) ....

TITLE ....

(A person signing for a corporation must be a corporate officer or hold a managerial position and must show his title. A person signing for another should see Parts 47 and 49 of the Federal Aviation Regulations (14 CFR).

Fig. 7-5. Release of lien.

Liability insurance protects you, or your heirs, in instances of claims against you, or your estate, resulting from your operation of an airplane (death, bodily injury, property damage, and the like). In this the age of litigation, you can be sure you will be sued if anyone is injured or killed while riding in your airplane, or struck by it on the ground.

UNITED STATES OF AMERICA
FEDERAL COMMUNICATIONS COMMISSION

Approved by OMB
3060-0040
Expires 7/31/94
See below for public
burden estimate

APPLICATION FOR AIRCRAFT RADIO STATION LICENSE

Public reporting burden for this collection of information is estimated to average twenty minutes per response, including the time for reviewing instructions, searching existing data sources, gathering and maintaining the data needed, and completing and reviewing the collection of information. Send comments regarding this burden estimate or any other aspect of this collection of information, including suggestions for reducing the burden to Federal Communications Commission, Information Resources Branch, Room 416, Washington, DC 20554, and to the Office of Management and Budget, Office of Information and Regulatory Affairs, Paperwork Reduction Project (3060-0040), Washington, DC 20503.

GENERAL INFORMATION

RULES AND REGULATIONS

Before preparing this application, refer to FCC Rules, Part 87, "Aviation Services". Contact the U.S. Government Printing Office, Washington, DC 20402, telephone (202) 783-3238 for the correct price.

CORRECT FORM

Use FCC 404 to apply for:
● A new station license when the station aboard an aircraft is first licensed or the ownership of the aircraft is changed and the previous owner is not to continue as the licensee of the station.
● A modified station license when the licensee remains the same, but the operation is to be different from that provided in the license. If the licensee's name or mailing address changes, notify the Commission by letter, see FCC Rules, Part 87.

To renew your license use FCC 405-B which is normally sent to each licensee at the address of record approximately 60 days prior to license expiration. If you have not received FCC 405-B, you may use FCC 404.

Do not use FCC 404 when applying for transmitters or radio frequencies in radio services other than the aviation services (e.g., Amateur, Industrial) even though these facilities may be placed aboard the aircraft. FCC 404 cannot be used to file for a Ground Radio Station License or Restricted Radiotelephone Operator's Permit.

NUMBER OF APPLICATIONS

Submit a separate application form for each aircraft and for each portable radio (see COMPLETING THE APPLICATION, Item 14), unless the application is for a fleet license. See FCC Rules, Part 87 for those eligible for a fleet license.

FEES AND MAILING INSTRUCTIONS

Each application must be accompanied by a single check or money order payable to the FCC for the Total Fee Due. Mail your application and fee to: FEDERAL COMMUNICATIONS COMMISSION, AVIATION AIRCRAFT SERVICE, P. O. BOX 358280, PITTSBURGH, PA 15251-5280.

FEE EXEMPTIONS: No fee is required for governmental entities. Fee exempt applications should be mailed to:
FEDERAL COMMUNICATIONS COMMISSION, 1270 FAIRFIELD ROAD, GETTYSBURG, PA 17325-7245.

COMPLETING THE APPLICATION

ITEM 1. Enter the legal name of the person or entity applying for the license. If you are an individual doing business in your own name, enter your full individual name, (last name, first name, and middle initial).

EXAMPLE: Smith, John A.

If you are an individual doing business under a firm or trade name (sole proprietorship), enter both your name and the firm or trade name.

EXAMPLE: Doe, John H. DBA Doe Construction Co.

Do not apply in the name of more than one individual, except on behalf of a legally recognized partnership. If the applicant is a partnership, list the name of the partner whose address appears in items 2 through 6. List the other partners in item 15. If you are a member of a partnership doing business under a firm or company name, insert the full name of each partner having an interest in the business and the firm or company trade name.

EXAMPLE: Doe, John H. & Doe, Richard A. DBA

Doe Construction Company

If you are filing as a corporation, insert the exact name of the corporation as it appears in the Articles of Incorporation. If you are an unincorporated association,

insert the name of the association as it appears in the Articles of Association or By-Laws. If you are a governmental entity, insert the name of the Government entity having jurisdiction of the station.

EXAMPLE: State of California   City of Houston, TX
County of Fairfax, VA

ITEMS 2–6. Enter a permanent mailing address in the United States to which the authorization and any future correspondence related to your station is to be mailed.

ITEM 7. The FAA registration number must be entered on applications submitted for a new station license except those for which FAA registration is not required or those for a fleet or portable license. If exempt from FAA registration, provide an explanation in item 15. When a fleet or portable license is involved, a control number will be assigned by the Commission. When applying for modification or renewal of an existing aircraft radio station license, the FAA registration number or the control number appearing on the license must be entered in item 7.

GOVERNMENTAL ENTITIES ARE EXEMPT FROM FEE REQUIREMENTS AND SHOULD SKIP ITEMS 8 THROUGH 10 OF THE APPLICATION

FCC 404 INSTRUCTIONS
SEPTEMBER 1991

(CONTINUED ON REVERSE)

Fig. 7-6. Application for aircraft radio station license general information.

ITEM 8. Refer to the Private Radio Services Fee Filing Guide for the appropriate Fee Type Code to enter for this application.

ITEM 9. Enter the number of aircraft to be licensed as the Fee Multiple. Normally, the Fee Multiple will be "1", unless the application is for a fleet license, in which case you must show the number of aircraft in the fleet for a new station license, or the number to be added if application is for a modification.

ITEM 10. Refer to the Private Radio Services Fee Filing Guide to determine the fee amount associated with the Fee Type Code in item 8. Multiply the fee amount by the Fee Multiple in item 9, enter the result in item 10, Fee Due. Your check or money order should be for this amount. We will not accept multiple checks.

ITEM 11. Check only one block for the appropriate type of applicant.

ITEM 12. Check the appropriate block for the purpose of filing this application, if for a modification, briefly explain proposed modifications.

ITEM 13. Indicate if application is for a fleet license, if "YES", show the total number of aircraft for a new fleet license, or show the number of aircraft being added or deleted for a modification.

ITEM 14. Check the desired frequencies based on the following information:

PRIVATE AIRCRAFT: These frequencies include those normally available for air traffic control, aeronautical advisory, aeronautical multicom, ground traffic control, and navigation. Refer to Part 87 of the Rules for the specific frequencies available. Private aircraft frequencies are avail-able to any aircraft except those weighing more than 12,500 pounds which are used in carrying passengers or cargo for hire. Do not apply for private aircraft frequencies if the aircraft falls within the latter category.

AIR CARRIER: Refer to Part 87 of the Rules for specific frequencies available.

DO NOT CHECK BOTH PRIVATE AIRCRAFT AND AIR CARRIER IN ITEM 14A.

FLIGHT TEST HF OR VHF OR BOTH: Submit a statement showing that the applicant is a manufacturer of aircraft or major aircraft components. Any request for VHF flight test frequencies must be accompanied by AFTRCC Coordination.

PORTABLE: Submit a statement that it is necessary for the applicant to move the transmitting equipment aboard various U.S. registered aircraft. NOTE: No license is required for a portable radio used only as a back-up on an aircraft which has a station license.

OTHER: Specify any other frequencies you require that are not regularly available for use in accordance with the provisions of Part 87 of the Rules. Each request for "Other" frequencies must be accompanied by a statement showing the need for assignment, including reference to any governmental contracts which may be involved and a description of the proposed use. The emission, power, points of communication, and area of operation should also be included in the statement. In certain cases, AFTRCC Coordination is required.

Application must bear an original signature. Failure to sign the application may result in dismissal of the application and forfeiture of any fees paid.

FCC 404 INSTRUCTIONS
SEPTEMBER 1991

DETACH HERE

✂ -

UNITED STATES OF AMERICA
FEDERAL COMMUNICATIONS COMMISSION

Approved by OMB
3060-0040
Expires 7/31/94
See instructions for
public burden estimate.

TEMPORARY AIRCRAFT RADIO STATION
OPERATING AUTHORITY

Use this form if you want temporary operating authority while your regular application, FCC 404, is being processed by the FCC. This authority authorizes the use of transmitters operating on the appropriate frequencies listed in Part 87 of the Commission's Rules.

DO NOT use this form if you already have a valid aircraft station license.
DO NOT use this form when renewing your aircraft license.
DO NOT use this form if you are applying for a fleet license.
DO NOT use this form if you do not have an FAA Registration Number.

ALL APPLICANTS MUST CERTIFY:

1. I am not a representative of a foreign government.
2. I have applied for an Aircraft Radio Station License by mailing a completed FCC Form 404 to the FCC.
3. I have not been denied a license or had my license revoked by the FCC.
4. I am not the subject of any adverse legal action concerning the operation of a radio station license.
5. I ensure that the Aircraft Radio Station will be operated only by individuals properly licensed or otherwise permitted by the Commission's Rules.

WILLFUL FALSE STATEMENTS MADE ON THIS FORM ARE PUNISHABLE BY FINE AND/OR IMPRISONMENT (U.S. CODE, TITLE 18, SECTION 1001), AND/OR REVOCATION OF ANY STATION LICENSE OR CONSTRUCTION PERMIT (U.S. CODE, TITLE 47, SECTION 312(A)(1)), AND/OR FORFEITURE (U.S. CODE, TITLE 47, SECTION 503).

Name of Applicant (Print or Type)	Signature of Applicant
FAA Registration Number (Use as Temporary Call Sign)	Date FCC 404 Mailed

Your authority to operate your Aircraft Radio Station is subject to all applicable laws, treaties and regulations and is subject to the right of control of the Government of the United States. This authority is valid for 90 days from the date FCC 404 is mailed to the FCC.

YOU MUST POST THIS TEMPORARY OPERATING AUTHORITY ON BOARD YOUR AIRCRAFT

FCC 404-A
September 1991

Fig. 7-7. Application for aircraft radio station license and temporary operating authority (tear off bottom and retain until license comes in the mail).

UNITED STATES OF AMERICA
FEDERAL COMMUNICATIONS COMMISSION

FOR
FCC
USE
ONLY

APPLICATION FOR AIRCRAFT RADIO STATION LICENSE

1. APPLICANT NAME

2. MAILING ADDRESS (Line 1)

3. MAILING ADDRESS (Line 2)

4. CITY

5. STATE	6. ZIP CODE	7. FAA REGISTRATION OR FCC CONTROL NUMBER (If FAA registration is not required for your aircraft, explain in item 15) N_____

8. FEE TYPE CODE	9. FEE MULTIPLE	10. FEE DUE	FOR FCC USE ONLY
		$	

11. TYPE OF APPLICANT

☐ I−Individual   ☐ C−Corporation

☐ D−Individual with Business Name   ☐ A−Association

☐ P−Partnership   ☐ G−Governmental Entity

12. PURPOSE OF APPLICATION

☐ New Station   ☐ Renewal

☐ Modification (Specify) _____
_____

13. IS APPLICATION FOR A FLEET LICENSE?   ☐ YES   ☐ NO

A. If modifying a fleet license, give the number of aircraft to be added.
B. If applying for a new or modified fleet license, give the total number of aircraft.
_____

14. FREQUENCIES REQUESTED (Check appropriate box(es) in 14A and/or 14B, see Instructions)

A. CHECK ONLY ONE

☐ A−Private Aircraft

☐ C−Air Carrier

B. ADDITIONAL INFORMATION IS REQUIRED IF YOU CHECK HERE

☐ T−Flight Test HF   ☐ P−Portable (Showing required)

☐ V−Flight Test VHF   ☐ O−Other (Specify) _____

15. ANSWER SPACE FOR ADDITIONAL INFORMATION

CERTIFICATION

1. Applicant waives all claims for the use of any specific frequency regardless of prior use by license or otherwise.
2. Applicant will have unlimited access to the radio equipment and will control access to exclude unauthorized persons.
3. Neither applicant nor any member thereof is a foreign government or representative thereof.
4. Applicant certifies that all statements made in this application and attachments are true, complete, correct and made in good faith.
5. Applicant certifies that the signature that appears on this application is that of a person with the proper authority to act on behalf of the party represented.

WILLFUL FALSE STATEMENTS MADE ON THIS FORM ARE PUNISHABLE BY FINE AND/OR IMPRISONMENT (U.S. CODE, TITLE 18, SECTION 1001), AND/OR REVOCATION OF ANY STATION LICENSE OR CONSTRUCTION PERMIT (U.S. CODE, TITLE 47, SECTION 312(A)(1)), AND/OR FORFEITURE (U.S. CODE, TITLE 47, SECTION 503).

➪ SIGNATURE   DATE

FAILURE TO SIGN THIS APPLICATION MAY RESULT IN DISMISSAL OF THE APPLICATION AND FORFEITURE OF ANY FEES PAID.

FCC 404
September 1991

Fig. 7-8. Application for aircraft radio station license.

Hull insurance protects your investment from loss caused by the elements of nature, fire, theft, vandalism, or accident. Limited coverage policies are available that provide for losses to the airplane while on the ground, but not while in the air. You can save money here; however, discussion of coverages available is best left between you and the insurance agent you are doing business with. Your lending institution will require hull insurance for their protection.

A check of any of the various aviation publications will produce telephone numbers for several aviation underwriters. The larger insurance companies have toll-free telephone numbers. Call all of them because services, coverage, and rates do differ.

Don't buy a policy that has complicated exclusions or other specific rules involving maximum preset values for replacement parts or payment of losses. Purchase a policy that you can read and understand, one that is written in plain English.

Something else to consider is your personal health and life insurance coverage. Be sure you are covered while flying a private airplane. Some policies do not, and in the event of injury or death, there might be no payoff.

SAFEKEEPING AN AIRPLANE

You cannot make your airplane theftproof; however, it can be made less attractive to the thief. Less attractive means more difficult to steal. The thief doesn't want to spend large amounts of time stealing an airplane. The idea is get in and go; therefore, any delays might sufficiently discourage the thief. Locks of one type or another typically delay the thief:

- Store the airplane in a locked hangar
- Use cut-resistant chain and locks for the tiedowns
- Install a throttle lock or another similar control lock

Unfortunately, another type of criminal is loose in America. This type will attempt to steal your property, and if unable to do so, will retaliate by destroying the property. The reasoning is simple: If the criminal can't have the property, neither will you. This criminal element is primarily found in urban areas breaking into Mercedes, BMW, and Volvo automobiles, but this disease has spread to some close-in airports during the past several years.

How to report a stolen airplane

What would you do if you drove out to the airport and your airplane had been stolen, or the plane had been broken into and some of the avionics were missing?

Naturally, you would notify the local police or other law enforcement agency that has jurisdiction over the airport. They will come to the airport—maybe—and make a report of the theft, and possibly even process the crime scene by fingerprinting. The latter will be accomplished only if there is a chance for prints. Fingerprinting is negated if it has rained since the break-in, or if the scene has been contaminated by you or others touching the airplane.

Don't expect the local or state police to do very much about your loss. The reports will be filed and entries will be made into the NCIC (National Crime Information Center) computer including registration number, serial number, and the like. This will give a chance of recovery in the event that another police department on the other side of the country comes into contact with the stolen items.

Notify the FAA because they will issue a Nationwide Stolen Aircraft Alert. If the registration numbers are not changed, and a controller is sharp, you have a chance of recovery. Contact the Aviation Crime Prevention Institute at telephone (301) 694-5444 or FAX (301) 695-6955. Inform your insurance carrier of the loss, and be ready to supply them with copies of all police reports, purchase receipts, and other pertinent information.

8

Tender loving care

WHEN YOU OWN AN AIRPLANE, you have to take care of it. Basically, the owner needs to be concerned with four areas of care: proper handling, effective storage, cleaning, and preventive maintenance. All four areas provide the owner with methods of becoming intimately acquainted with the airplane. Additionally, by properly caring for the airplane, the personal investment will be protected, flying safety greatly increased, and a considerable amount of money saved. The first three areas of care are explained in this chapter. Preventive maintenance is explained in chapter 9 because that area is more complex and is affected by regulations.

GROUND HANDLING

Proper handling of an airplane while on the ground (moving by hand) is extremely important. If care is not taken, major structural damage can be done to the airplane that could cost thousands of dollars to repair.

Towing

A tow bar properly attached to the nose gear should be used for pulling, pushing, steering, and maneuvering the aircraft while on the ground (Figs. 8-1 and 8-2). When moving the aircraft, never turn the nosewheel more than 30 degrees either side of center or the nose gear will be damaged. If no tow bar is available, apply downward pressure at the horizontal stabilizer front spar adjacent to the fuselage to raise the nosewheel off the ground. When the nosewheel is clear of the ground, the aircraft can be maneuvered by pivoting on the main wheels. This is not the recommended procedure, but can be used in a pinch. The best method is to use a tow bar.

If more pushing or pulling power is needed when moving the aircraft with the tow bar, use only the wing struts and landing gear legs as push points. Don't push on the wing edges, control surfaces, cabin doors, and the like. Never use the propeller as a push point. The engine could fire from only a slight movement, causing severe injury or death. If you are unconcerned about that possibility, then think

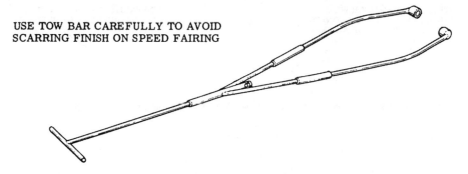

USE TOW BAR CAREFULLY TO AVOID
SCARRING FINISH ON SPEED FAIRING

Fig. 8-1. Old-style tow bar. Cessna Aircraft Company

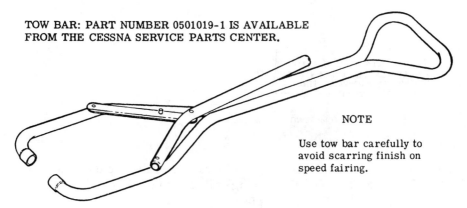

TOW BAR: PART NUMBER 0501019-1 IS AVAILABLE
FROM THE CESSNA SERVICE PARTS CENTER.

NOTE

Use tow bar carefully to
avoid scarring finish on
speed fairing.

Fig. 8-2. New-style tow bar. Cessna Aircraft Company

about propeller blade failure caused by bending. Blade failure means complete separation caused by metal fatigue developed from stress caused by bending (*see* chapter 5). Everyone has seen airplanes pushed and pulled by their propellers— but don't you do it.

Parking

Parking procedures will depend principally upon the local conditions of your airport, and the weather. Under normal conditions, most pilots will park the airplane, for short periods of time, merely by applying the parking brake and locking the controls. Further caution would call for wheel chocks. This procedure is adequate for short periods of time such as fueling, pit stops, and other short layovers when the airplane will not be out of sight. This only applies if there is no wind blowing.

If the airplane is going to be left unattended for more than a few minutes, then tie it down (Fig. 8-3). When tying down the aircraft in the open, face it into the wind if possible. Lock the control surfaces with the internal control lock, and set

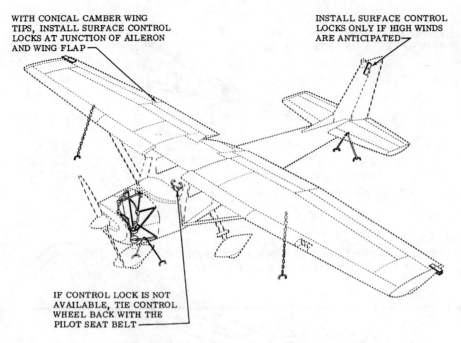

WITH CONICAL CAMBER WING TIPS, INSTALL SURFACE CONTROL LOCKS AT JUNCTION OF AILERON AND WING FLAP

INSTALL SURFACE CONTROL LOCKS ONLY IF HIGH WINDS ARE ANTICIPATED

IF CONTROL LOCK IS NOT AVAILABLE, TIE CONTROL WHEEL BACK WITH THE PILOT SEAT BELT

Fig. 8-3. Recommended tiedown. Cessna Aircraft Company

the brakes. If no standard Cessna control lock is available, tie the controls down with the seat belt. Do not set the parking brakes during cold weather or when the brakes are overheated. Then accomplish the following:

1. Attach ropes, cables, or chains to the wing tiedown fittings. These fittings are located at the upper end of each wing strut. Secure the opposite ends to ground anchors.
2. Secure a tiedown rope (not a chain or cable) to the exposed portion of the engine mount and secure the opposite end to a ground anchor.
3. Fasten the middle of a rope to the tail tiedown ring, pull each end of the rope away at a 45-degree angle, and secure to ground anchors at each side of the tail.
4. Install surface control locks between the wingtip and aileron, and over the fin and rudder.

Tie the airplane down whether the wind is blowing or not. If you neglect to secure your airplane, and leave it unattended, you could return to find that unexpected winds damaged your plane or your plane caused damage to other airplanes. Unexpected winds often visit in the form of dust devils in the summertime. A dust devil is similar to a miniature tornado and is quite capable of picking up a lightplane such as the 150 and slamming it back down.

AIRPLANE STORAGE

Storing an airplane is much more than merely hangaring or parking. Unfortunately a large number of owners pay little attention to the proper storage of the airplane during periods of nonuse. What really concerns me is the large number of uncared-for airplanes. Some airplanes are parked in October and not moved (or even visited) until May. Most people wouldn't do that with their cars, but look at all the airplanes. This unattended, uncared-for, sitting routine causes airplanes to die. Resurrection is expensive; proper care is cheap.

Three categories of storage are time-based, with the planned length of storage time determining the category:

- Flyable storage. The airplane is flown daily or at least every few days.
- Temporary storage. The storage of the airplane for up to three months.
- Indefinite storage. Mothballing for an undetermined period of time. (If serious consideration is being given to mothballing, it is time to ponder the viability of continued airplane ownership.)

Flyable storage

Flyable storage is really the daily care of the airplane. Daily usage, or nearly daily usage, is the best form of storage for an airplane. Your body stays in best shape when you exercise regularly, and so does an airplane. Regular use is of prime importance for the engine. Routine care—including exterior and interior cleaning and surface protection—is also important. At the end of each flight, service the aircraft according to Cessna's instructions. This includes refueling, tiedown, and the like, as prescribed in the owner's handbook.

If you do not fly the aircraft at least weekly:

- Pull the propeller through every seven days by hand-rotating without running the engine.
- Rotate the engine six revolutions and stop the propeller 45 to 90 degrees from the original position.

Note: If the engine has fewer than 50 hours of operating time, pull the propeller through every five days because an engine with few operating hours has not attained the varnish residue coating on the inside of the cylinders; therefore, the engine is more susceptible to oxidation than an engine with more than 50 hours.

Caution: For maximum safety, accomplish propeller rotation as follows:

1. Check that the magneto switches are in the OFF position.
2. Move the throttle to the CLOSED position.
3. Set the mixture control to IDLE CUTOFF.
4. Set the parking brake and block the aircraft's wheels.

5. Leave the aircraft tiedowns installed.

6. Open the cabin door.

7. Do not stand within the arc of the propeller blades.

Fly the airplane at least once every two weeks. This biweekly flight should last a minimum of 30 minutes, allowing the engine to reach, but not exceed, normal oil and cylinder operating temperatures. If the flight cannot be accomplished on schedule due to weather, maintenance, and the like, pull the propeller through daily and fly as soon as possible.

If the aircraft still cannot be flown, it should be placed in temporary or indefinite storage. Ground running is not an acceptable substitute for flying. For future reference, the propeller pull-through and flight time may be recorded in the engine log, or informally on a note pad.

Temporary storage

Temporary storage of the aircraft is storage for a limited period, no longer than three months, such as during the winter months. Cessna aircraft are constructed of corrosion-resistant Alclad aluminum alloy, which will last indefinitely under normal conditions; however, these alloys are subject to corrosion if not properly cared for. The first indication of corrosion on unpainted surfaces is the formation of white deposits or spots. These spots might resemble a scattering of salt crystals. On painted surfaces, the paint becomes discolored or blistered. Storage in a dry hangar is essential to good preservation and such storage should be procured, if possible.

Note: If the aircraft is not returned to flyable status at the expiration of the temporary storage, it must be placed into indefinite storage.

To prepare an airplane for temporary storage:

1. Service the aircraft as you would at the end of a flight, including filling the fuel tanks with the correct grade of fuel.

2. Clean and wax the entire aircraft, inside and out.

3. Remove any grease or oil residue from the tires and coat them with a tire preservative.

4. Cover the nosewheel to protect it from oil dripping from the engine.

5. Block up the fuselage to remove the weight from the tires. Tires will take a set, causing them to become out-of-round, if an aircraft is left unmoved for extended periods.

6. Remove the top spark plug and spray preservative oil (MIL-L-46002, Grade 1) through the upper spark plug hole of each cylinder with the piston approximately in bottom dead center position. Rotate the crankshaft after each pair of opposite cylinders is sprayed. Stop the crankshaft with no piston at top dead center. A pressure pot or pump-up type garden pressure sprayer may be used for applying the preservative oil; however, the spray head must have ports around the circumference to allow complete coverage of the cylinder walls. To thoroughly cover all surfaces of the cylinder

interior, move the nozzle or spray gun from the top to the bottom of the cylinder. After application has been made to each cylinder, respray inside each cylinder without rotating the engine. Reinstall the spark plugs, torquing as required. Apply the preservative to the engine interior by spraying approximately two ounces through the oil filler tube.

7. Seal all engine openings exposed to the atmosphere using suitable plugs, or moisture resistant tape, and attach red streamers at each point.

8. Affix a tag to the propeller in a conspicuous place with the following notation on the tag:
   DO NOT TURN PROPELLER
   ENGINE PRESERVED
   PRESERVATION DATE (DDMMYY)

Returning the aircraft to service is easily accomplished by the following procedure:

1. Remove all seals, tape, paper, and streamers from openings. Streamers identified seal locations.

2. Remove the bottom spark plugs from the cylinders, and hand-turn the propeller several revolutions. This will clear excess preservative oil from the cylinders. Reinstall the spark plugs, torquing as needed.

3. Do a complete and very thorough walkaround inspection (preflight).

4. Start the engine as you normally would.

5. A test flight is recommended.

Indefinite storage

Indefinite storage is mothballing. The aircraft is placed into a state of storage where it can remain until used again. This could be for months, or even years. In addition to preparing the airplane as you would for temporary storage:

1. Lubricate all movable airframe parts.

2. Cover all openings to the airframe to keep vermin, insects, and birds out.

3. Remove the battery and store it in a cool dry place, servicing it periodically.

4. Place covers over the windshield and rear windows.

5. Inspect the airframe at least monthly for signs of corrosion. Clean and wax as necessary.

6. Drain the engine oil and refill with MIL-C-6529 Type II.

7. The aircraft must then be flown for 30 minutes, allowing normal oil and cylinder temperatures to be attained. Allow the engine to cool to ambient temperature.

8. Using MIL-C-6529 Type II, follow the temporary storage procedures for preservative application to the cylinders of the engine. Do no reinstall the top

spark plugs. (MIL-C-6529 Type II can be formulated by thoroughly mixing one part compound MIL-C-6529 Type I Esso Rust-Ban 628, Cosmoline No. 1223 or equivalent with three parts new lubricating oil of the grade recommended for service (all at room temperature). Single-grade oil is recommended.)

9. Apply preservative to the engine interior by spraying MIL-L-46002, Grade 1 oil (approximately two ounces) through the oil filler tube.

10. Install dehydrator plugs in each of the top spark plug holes, making sure that each plug is blue in color when installed. Protect and support the spark plug leads.

11. If the carburetor is removed from the engine, place a bag of desiccant in the throat of the carburetor air adapter.

12. Seal the adapter with moisture-resistant paper and tape on a cover plate.

13. Place a bag of desiccant in the exhaust pipes and seal the openings with moisture-resistant tape.

14. Seal the cold air inlet to the heater muff with moisture-resistant tape to exclude moisture and foreign objects.

15. Seal the engine breather by inserting a dehydrator plug in the breather hose and clamping in place.

16. Attach a red streamer to each place on the engine where bags of desiccant are placed. Attach red streamers to each sealed area.

17. Attach a tag to the propeller in a conspicuous place with the following notation on the tag:
DO NOT TURN PROPELLER
ENGINE PRESERVED
PRESERVATION DATE (DDMMYY)

Aircraft in indefinite storage should be inspected every two weeks to check the dehydrator plugs for a change in color. Reapply preservative oil to the inside of any cylinder that displays a plug with changed color, and replace the dehydrator plug. If the color on more than two of the cylinders has changed, all desiccant material on the engine should be replaced.

Every six months the cylinder bores should be resprayed with corrosion preventive mixture—more frequently if a bore inspection indicates corrosion has started earlier than six months. Before spraying, make a bore inspection of at least one cylinder. If the cylinder shows the start of rust on the cylinder walls, the entire engine must be represerved. Also, remove at least one rocker box cover from the engine and inspect the valve mechanism. Replace all desiccant and dehydrator plugs.

To return the aircraft to normal service, accomplish the following:

1. Remove the aircraft from the blocks and check the tires for proper inflation.

2. Check the nose strut for proper inflation.

3. Remove all airframe covers and plugs, and inspect the interior of the airframe for debris and foreign matter.

4. Thoroughly search for vermin damage.

5. Check the battery and reinstall.

6. Remove the cylinder dehydrator plugs from each engine cylinder.

7. Remove all paper, tape, desiccant bags, and streamers used to preserve the engine.

8. Drain the corrosion preventive mixture from the crankcase and reservice with the recommended lubricating oil.

9. If the carburetor has been preserved with oil, drain it and flush with avgas, then reinstall.

10. Remove the bottom spark plugs and rotate the propeller to clear excess preservative oil from the cylinders.

11. Reinstall the spark plugs and rotate the propeller by hand through compression strokes of all the cylinders to check for possible liquid lock. **Caution:** Disconnect the ignition harness from all spark plugs during this procedure.

12. Start the engine in a normal manner, allowing normal oil pressure to be attained and any remaining cylinder preservative oil to be burned off. Then shut the engine down.

13. Clean the interior and exterior of the aircraft.

14. Give the aircraft a thorough visual inspection and cleaning.

15. Test-fly the aircraft.

CLEANING

Airplane ownership is a source of pride. To display this pride, you should own a clean airplane. But pride alone is not the sole reason for keeping the appearance of an airplane in top shape. A clean airplane retains its economic value, normally indicates the owner cares for his airplane, and forces close inspection of the aircraft during cleaning.

Exterior care

Complete washing with automotive-type cleaners will produce good results, and the materials used will be much cheaper than so-called aircraft cleaners. Automotive protective coatings, formerly called wax, will protect painted and unpainted surfaces. These new space-age silicone preparations are very easy to apply, won't whiten rubber components, and will protect your airplane's finish for many months. Just remember, there are a lot of surfaces on an airplane . . . many square feet. So, use the best products available, unless you like to make a career of airplane polishing.

For those interested in polishing a bare metal airplane, there is the Cyclo Wonder Tool, a dual orbital polishing machine. I can say from personal experience that this machine is well worth the investment if you wish to keep a shiny unpainted bird in tip-top condition. It is also useful in stripping before painting and will polish hard waxes. For further information contact:

Cyclo Manufacturing Co.
1438 S. Cherokee
Denver, CO 80223
(303) 744-8043

My personal arsenal to keep an airplane looking really sharp includes:

- Engine degreaser for cleaning the engine area and front strut. It dissolves grease and can be washed off with water. When using a degreaser inside the engine compartment, you must cover the magnetos and alternator with plastic bags to keep the cleaner and rinse water out. Degreaser is also good for cleaning the belly of the airplane if it is oil-stained. Available from discount department stores and auto supply houses.

- Rubbing compound to clean away stains caused by engine exhaust. Rubbing compounds are available in several strengths (abrasiveness); use the mildest. Avoid being overzealous in the application of rubbing compound, as you could remove paint by overdoing it. Available from discount department stores and auto supply houses.

- Micro-mesh, which is a specialized product designed to clean and polish Plexiglas. Plexiglas is a product of Rohm & Haas Company and is used for windshields and windows. Micro-mesh is available from:

UNIVAIR Aircraft Corporation
2500 Himalaya Road
Aurora, CO 80011
(303) 375-8882

- Protect All Quick and Easy Wash is used to clean exterior surfaces, applied by sponge or cloth and wiped off with a chamois or dry cloth. It is ideal for washing airplanes where no running water is available and leaves an excellent shine. Protect All does just what the name says—it protects all. Available in spray cans and by bulk, Protect All can be used to shine the entire airplane. Protect All products are available at most recreational vehicle centers or from:

Protect All, Inc.
1910 East Via Burton St.
Anaheim, CA 92806
(800) 322-4491
(714) 635-4491

Interior care

The interior of the airplane is seen by all, including the pilot and his passengers. It is probably the most judged area of the airplane, yet can be a major problem to keep clean. I recommend cleaning with standard automobile cleaning methods, using automobile cleaning products.

Protect All may be used on the instrument panel, hard and soft plastic surfaces, and metals. It is easy to apply, has a UV blocker, and is very durable.

Household products are also worthwhile for aircraft upkeep:

- 409 is an excellent cleaner for the hard-to-remove stuff. Keep it away from the windshield, instruments, and painted surfaces.
- Windex is an excellent product for small cleanup jobs; however, never use it on the windshield or other windows. Windex contains ammonia, and its use on such surfaces will cause a characteristic clouding—spoiling the clear qualities. In time, you will have to replace the window.
- Scotch Guard is a spray-on product for seats, carpets, and other cloth areas. It will allow quick mop-up of small spills, and it prevents most liquids from soaking into upholstery.
- WD-40 is a spray lubricant used to stop squeaks and reduce friction between any moving parts. It's good on cables, controls, seat runners, door hinges, and latches. Keep it off the windows.

Heat and sunlight protection

The interior temperature of a parked aircraft can reach as much as 185°F. This heat buildup will not only damage avionics, but will cause problems with instrument panels, upholstery, and many plastic things. A quick look around at the local airport will show four methods of heat protection:

- None
- A chart or towel on the panel
- An interior reflective cover
- An exterior protective cover

The first method is seen most often on older, already sad-looking airplanes. There is certainly no ownership pride here, and the situation will only get worse. Some owners of older planes recognize the need for protection from the sun's rays, so they lay a towel or chart over the top of the instrument panel. This is merely an exercise in futility, and prevents no heat buildup at all. The only use for such a measure would be when parking for a short period of time, such as refueling.

Inside covers—heat shields—have a reflective surface that protects the interior of an aircraft by reflecting the sun's rays. The shield attaches to the interior of the aircraft with Velcro fasteners. Interior reflective heat shields are available from many sources and are advertised in all the aviation periodicals.

Exterior airplane covers provide similar protection for the interior of the aircraft, yet give additional exterior protection by covering the windshield, refueling caps, and fresh air vents. Exterior covers are also advertised in aviation periodicals.

9

Preventive maintenance

AN OWNER CAN DO EVEN MORE than cleaning and polishing an airplane. Federal Aviation Regulations (FARs) specify that preventive maintenance may be performed by owners of airplanes that are not utilized in commercial service. Preventive maintenance is simple or minor preservation procedures and the replacement of small standard parts not involving complex assembly operations. Preventive maintenance is not a replacement for a licensed mechanic because complex and sensitive components in an aircraft require the mechanical expertise of a licensed A&P mechanic.

The reader is advised that when a question comes up about maintenance, consult a competent licensed mechanic. The instructions and advice you receive might help you avoid making costly mistakes. You might have to pay the mechanic for the time, but it will be money well-spent. After all, the mechanic's time is money.

FAA COMMENT

In case your FBO is concerned about your attempts at saving money and tries to stop your efforts, be aware that the FAA is on your side. Here's a partial reprint of Advisory Circular 150/5190-2A (April 4, 1972):

> Restrictions on Self-Service. Any unreasonable restriction imposed on the owners and operators of aircraft regarding the servicing of their own aircraft and equipment may be considered as a violation of agency policy. The owner of an aircraft should be permitted to fuel, wash, repair, paint, and otherwise take care of his own aircraft, provided there is no attempt to perform such services for others. Restrictions which have the effect of diverting activity of this type to a commercial enterprise amount to an exclusive right contrary to law.

With these words the FAA has allowed the owner of an aircraft to save their hard-earned dollars—and to become very familiar with the airplane—consequently contributing to safety. Additionally, properly performed preventive maintenance gives the owner a tremendous feeling of accomplishment.

LOGBOOK REQUIREMENTS

Entries must be made in the appropriate logbook whenever preventive maintenance is performed. A logbook entry must include:

- Description of work done
- Date work is completed
- Name of the person doing the work
- Approval for return to service (signature and certificate number) by the pilot approving the work

The FARs require that all preventive maintenance work must be done in such a manner, and by use of materials of such quality, that the airframe, engine, propeller, or assembly worked on will be at least equal to its original condition.

TOOLS YOU SHOULD HAVE

Get your own tools; don't borrow from your friend the mechanic, or the friendship won't last much longer. A small quantity of quality tools should allow the owner to perform maintenance on an airplane. A carrying bag or box will be very handy to keep the tools in order and protected.

An ideal basic tool kit would be:

- Multipurpose knife (Swiss Army knife)
- ⅜-inch ratchet drive (flex head optional)
- 2-, 4-, and 6-inch ⅜ inch extensions
- Sockets from ⅜ inch to ¾ inch in 1/16-inch increments
- 6-inch crescent wrench
- 10-inch monkey wrench
- 6- or 12-point closed (box) wrenches from ⅜ inch to ¾ inch
- Set of open-end wrenches from ⅜ inch to ¾ inch
- Pair of channel-lock pliers (medium size)
- Phillips screwdriver set
- Blade screwdriver set
- Plastic electrical tape
- Container of aircraft-grade assorted nuts and bolts
- Spare set of spark plugs
- 10× magnifying glass
- Inspection mirror

PREVENTIVE MAINTENANCE ITEMS

FAR Part 43 lists 28 preventive maintenance items—only those procedures listed in the FAR are considered preventive maintenance. Procedures applicable to the

Model 150/152 airplanes are presented. Specific procedural instructions for Cessna airplanes follow the list.

1. Removal, installation, and repair of landing gear tires.
2. (Does not apply to 150/152 aircraft.)
3. Servicing landing gear struts by adding oil, air, or both.
4. Servicing landing gear wheel bearings, such as cleaning and greasing.
5. Replacing defective safety wiring or cotter pins.
6. Lubrication not requiring disassembly other than removal of nonstructural items such as cover plates, cowlings, and fairings.
7. (Does not apply to 150/152 aircraft.)
8. Replenishing hydraulic fluid in the hydraulic reservoir.
9. Refinishing decorative coatings of the fuselage, wing, and tail-group surfaces (excluding balanced control surfaces), fairings, cowlings, landing gear, cabin, or cockpit interior when removal or disassembly of any primary structure or operating system is not required.
10. Applying preservative or protective material to components when no disassembly of any primary structure or operating system is involved and when such coating is not prohibited or is not contrary to good practices.
11. Repairing upholstery and decorative furnishings of the cabin or cockpit when it does not require disassembly of any primary structure or operating system or affect the primary structure of the aircraft.
12. Making small, simple repairs to fairings, nonstructural cover plates, cowlings and small patches, and reinforcements not changing the contour so as to interfere with the proper airflow.
13. Replacing side windows where that work does not interfere with the structure or any operating system, such as controls and electrical equipment.
14. Replacing safety belts.
15. Replacing seats or seat parts with replacement parts approved for the aircraft, not involving disassembly of any primary structure or operating system.
16. Troubleshooting and repairing broken landing light wiring circuits.
17. Replacing bulbs, reflectors, and lenses of position and landing lights.
18. Replacing wheels and skis where no weight and balance computation is required.
19. Replacing any cowling not requiring removal of the propeller or disconnection of flight controls.
20. Replacing or cleaning spark plugs and setting of spark plug gap clearance.
21. Replacing any hose connection except hydraulic connections.
22. Replacing prefabricated fuel lines.
23. Cleaning fuel and oil strainers.

24. Replacing batteries and checking fluid level and specific gravity.

25. (Does not apply to 150/152 aircraft.)

26. (Does not apply to 150/152 aircraft.)

27. Replacement or adjustment of nonstructural standard fasteners incidental to operations.

28. (Does not apply to 150/152 aircraft.)

PROCEDURAL INSTRUCTIONS

The following instructions and notes will assist you in performing preventive maintenance and understanding other maintenance. You should have a service manual available. If you do not have a manual and wish to purchase one, contact:

ESSCO
1615 S. Arlington St.
Akron, OH 44306
(216) 724-1249

Tires

Maintain the tire pressure as specified in your aircraft owner's manual. When checking tire pressure, examine the tires for wear, cuts, bruises, and slipping. Damage to tires is very common when operating from unpaved runways. Remove oil and grease from the tires with soap and water. Petroleum products can rot rubber tires, rendering them unsafe. **Note:** Recommended tire pressures should be maintained, especially in cold weather because any drop in the temperature of air inside a tire causes a corresponding drop in air pressure.

Main wheel removal

1. Jack up one main wheel of the aircraft at a time. Place the jack at the universal jack point; do not use the brake casting as a jacking point. When using the universal jack point, flexibility of the gear strut will cause the main wheel to slide inboard as the wheel is raised, tilting the jack. The jack must be lowered for a second operation. Jacking both main wheels simultaneously with universal jack points is not recommended (Fig. 9-1).

2. Remove the speed fairing (if installed) (Fig. 9-2).

3. Remove the hub cap, cotter pin, and axle nut.

4. Remove the bolts and washers attaching back plate to brake cylinder and remove back plate.

5. Pull the wheel from the axle (Figs. 9-3, 9-4).

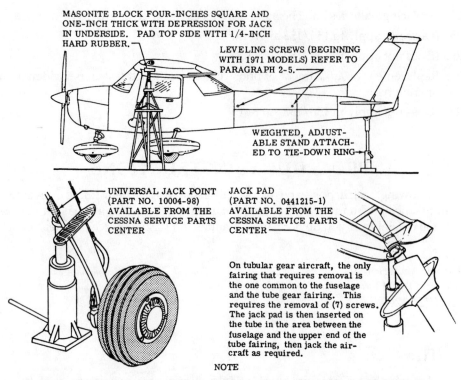

MASONITE BLOCK FOUR-INCHES SQUARE AND ONE-INCH THICK WITH DEPRESSION FOR JACK IN UNDERSIDE. PAD TOP SIDE WITH 1/4-INCH HARD RUBBER.

LEVELING SCREWS (BEGINNING WITH 1971 MODELS) REFER TO PARAGRAPH 2-5.

WEIGHTED, ADJUST-ABLE STAND ATTACH-ED TO TIE-DOWN RING.

UNIVERSAL JACK POINT (PART NO. 10004-98) AVAILABLE FROM THE CESSNA SERVICE PARTS CENTER

JACK PAD (PART NO. 0441215-1) AVAILABLE FROM THE CESSNA SERVICE PARTS CENTER

On tubular gear aircraft, the only fairing that requires removal is the one common to the fuselage and the tube gear fairing. This requires the removal of (7) screws. The jack pad is then inserted on the tube in the area between the fuselage and the upper end of the tube fairing, then jack the air-craft as required.

NOTE

Wing jacks available from the Cessna Service Parts Center are REGENT Model 4939-30 for use with the SE-576 wing stands. Combination jacks are the REGENT Model 4939-70 for use without wing stands. The 4939-70 jack (70-inch) may be converted to the 4939-30 jack (30-inch) by remov-ing the leg extensions and replacing lower braces with shorter ones. The base of the adjustable tail stand (SE-767) is to be filled with concrete for additional weight as a safety factor. The SE-576 wing stand will also accommodate the SANCOR Model 00226-150 jack. Other equivalent jacks, tail stands, and adapter stands may be used.

1. Lower aircraft tail so that wing jack can be placed under front wing spar just outboard of wing strut.

2. Raise aircraft tail and attach tail stand to tie-down ring. BE SURE the tail stand weighs enough to keep the tail down under all conditions and is strong enough to support aircraft weight.

3. Raise jacks evenly until desired height is reached.

4. The universal jack point may be used to raise only one main wheel. Do not use brake casting as a jack point.

CAUTION

When using the universal jack point, flexibility of the gear strut will cause the main wheel to slide inboard as the wheel is raised, tilting the jack. The jack must be lowered for a second operation. Jacking both main wheels simultaneously with universal jack points is not recom-mended.

Fig. 9-1. Proper jacking instructions. Cessna Aircraft Company

Wheel disassembly

1. Remove the valve core and deflate the tire. Break the tire beads loose from the wheel rims. **Warning:** Injury can result from attempting to separate

wheel halves with the tire inflated. Avoid damaging wheel flanges when breaking tire beads loose.

2. Remove the through-bolts and separate the wheel halves, removing the tire, tube, and brake disc (Figs. 9-5 and 9-6).

3. Remove the grease seal rings, felts, and bearing cones from the wheel halves.

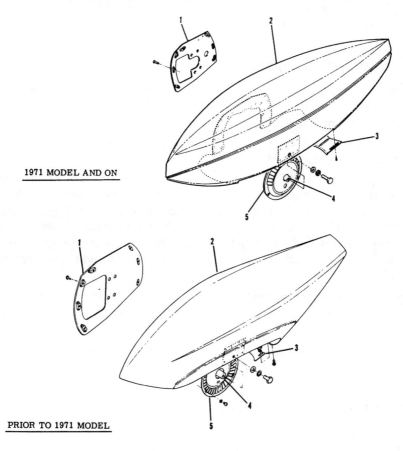

1971 MODEL AND ON

PRIOR TO 1971 MODEL

1. Attach Plate
2. Speed Fairing
3. Scraper
4. Axle Nut
5. Hub Cap

Fig. 9-2. Main wheel speed fairings. Cessna Aircraft Company

Wheel inspection and repair

1. Clean all metal parts and the grease seal felts in solvent and dry thoroughly.

2. Inspect the wheel halves for cracks. Cracked wheel halves shall be discarded and new parts used. Sand out nicks, gouges, and corroded areas.

Where the protective coating has been removed, the area should be cleaned thoroughly, primed with zinc chromate, and repainted with aluminum lacquer.

3. If excessively warped or scored, the brake disc should be replaced with a new part. Sand smooth small nicks and scratches.

4. Carefully inspect the bearing cones and cups for damage and discoloration. After cleaning, pack the cones with clean aircraft wheel bearing grease before installing them in the wheel half.

Main wheel assembly

1. Insert the through-bolts through the brake disc and position (the disc) in the inner wheel half, using the bolts to guide the disc. Ascertain that the disc is bottomed in the wheel half.

2. Position the tire and tube with the tube inflation valve through the hole in the outboard wheel half.

3. Place the inner wheel half in position on the outboard wheel half. Apply a light force to bring the wheel halves together. While maintaining the light force, assemble a washer and nut on one through-bolt and tighten snugly. Assemble the remaining washers and nuts on the through-bolts and torque to the value marked on the wheel. **Caution:** Uneven or improper torque of the through-bolt nuts can cause failure of the bolts, with resultant wheel failure.

4. Clean and pack the bearing cones with new aircraft wheel bearing grease.

5. Assemble the bearing cones, grease seal felts, and rings into the wheel halves.

6. Inflate the tire to seat the tire beads, then adjust inflation to the correct pressure according to the owner's manual.

Main wheel installation

1. Place the wheel assembly on the axle.

2. Install the axle nut and tighten until a slight bearing drag is obvious when the wheel is rotated. Back off the axle nut to the nearest castellation and install a cotter pin.

3. Place the brake back plate in position and secure it with bolts and washers.

4. Install the hub cap. **Caution:** If the landing gear has speed fairings, be sure to check the scraper clearance before aircraft operation.

Nosewheel removal

1. Weight or tie down the tail of the aircraft to raise the nosewheel off the ground.

2. Remove the nosewheel axle bolt (Figs. 9-7 through 9-9).

3. Pull the nosewheel assembly from the fork and remove the spacers and axle tube from the nosewheel. Loosen the scraper if necessary. Wheel disassembly, inspection and repair, and reassembly of the nosewheel follow similar procedures to those of the main wheels.

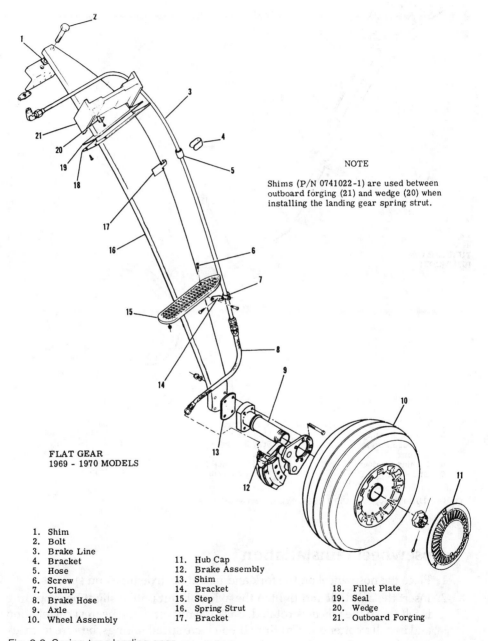

NOTE

Shims (P/N 0741022-1) are used between outboard forging (21) and wedge (20) when installing the landing gear spring strut.

FLAT GEAR
1969 - 1970 MODELS

1. Shim
2. Bolt
3. Brake Line
4. Bracket
5. Hose
6. Screw
7. Clamp
8. Brake Hose
9. Axle
10. Wheel Assembly
11. Hub Cap
12. Brake Assembly
13. Shim
14. Bracket
15. Step
16. Spring Strut
17. Bracket
18. Fillet Plate
19. Seal
20. Wedge
21. Outboard Forging

Fig. 9-3. Spring-type landing gear. Cessna Aircraft Company

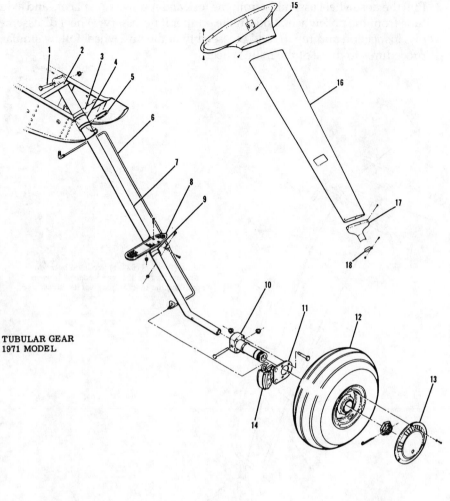

TUBULAR GEAR
1971 MODEL

1. Bolt	7. Spring-Strut	13. Hub Cap
2. Inboard Forging	8. Step	14. Brake Assembly
3. Outboard Forging	9. Step Bracket	15. Fuselage Fairing
4. Bushing	10. Axle	16. Spring-Strut Fairing
5. Bushing Retainer	11. Brake Torque Plate	17. Fairing Cap
6. Brake line	12. Wheel Assembly	18. Clamp

Fig. 9-4. Tubular-type landing gear. Cessna Aircraft Company

Nosewheel reinstallation

1. Place the nosewheel on the fork and install the axle tube and spacers.
2. Insert the axle bolt and tighten the axle bolt nut until a slight bearing drag is felt when the wheel is rotated. Back the nut off to the nearest castellation and install a cotter pin. **Caution:** If you have speed fairings, be sure to check the scraper clearance before aircraft operation.

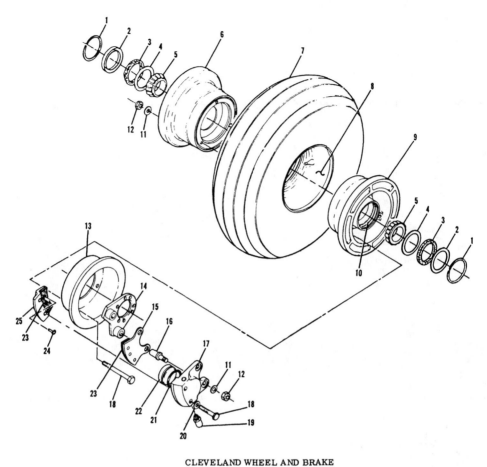

CLEVELAND WHEEL AND BRAKE

1. Snap Ring	9. Inboard Wheel Half	18. Bolt
2. Grease Seal Ring	10. Bearing Cup	19. Bleeder Valve
3. Grease Seal Felt	11. Washer	20. Washer
4. Grease Seal Ring	12. Nut	21. O-Ring
5. Bearing Cone	13. Brake Disc	22. Brake Piston
6. Outboard Wheel Half	14. Torque Plate	23. Brake Lining
7. Tire	15. Pressure Plate	24. Rivet
8. Tube	16. Anchor Bolt	25. Back Plate
	17. Brake Cylinder	

Fig. 9-5. Cleveland main wheel and brake. Cessna Aircraft Company

Nose gear shock strut

The nose gear shock strut requires periodic checking to ensure that the strut is filled with hydraulic fluid and is inflated to the correct air pressure (Fig. 9-10). Al-

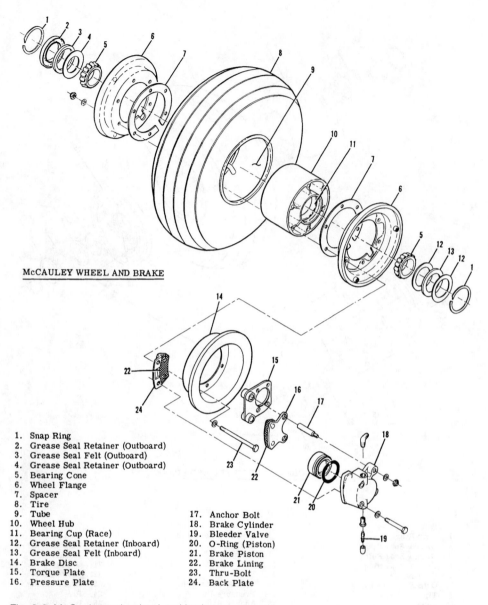

McCAULEY WHEEL AND BRAKE

1. Snap Ring
2. Grease Seal Retainer (Outboard)
3. Grease Seal Felt (Outboard)
4. Grease Seal Retainer (Outboard)
5. Bearing Cone
6. Wheel Flange
7. Spacer
8. Tire
9. Tube
10. Wheel Hub
11. Bearing Cup (Race)
12. Grease Seal Retainer (Inboard)
13. Grease Seal Felt (Inboard)
14. Brake Disc
15. Torque Plate
16. Pressure Plate
17. Anchor Bolt
18. Brake Cylinder
19. Bleeder Valve
20. O-Ring (Piston)
21. Brake Piston
22. Brake Lining
23. Thru-Bolt
24. Back Plate

Fig. 9-6. McCauley main wheel and brake. Cessna Aircraft Company

lowing the strut to collapse can result in propeller contact with the ground. To service the nose gear strut, proceed as follows:

1. Remove the valve cap and release the air pressure (Fig. 9-11).
2. Remove the valve housing.
3. Compress the nose gear to its shortest length and fill the strut with hydraulic fluid to the bottom of the filler hole.

4. Raise the nose of the aircraft, extend and compress the strut several times to expel any entrapped air, then lower the nose of the aircraft and repeat step 3.

5. With the strut compressed, install the valve housing assembly.

6. With the nosewheel off the ground, inflate the strut according to the owner's manual for exact pressure. **Note:** Keep the nose gear shock strut clean of dust and grit that might harm the seals in the strut barrel.

Nose gear shimmy dampener

The shimmy dampener should be serviced at least every 100 hours. The shimmy dampener must be filled completely with fluid, free of entrapped air, to serve its purpose. To service the shimmy dampener, proceed as follows:

1. Remove the shimmy dampener from the aircraft (Fig. 9-12).

2. While holding the dampener in a vertical position with the fitting end pointed downward, pull the fitting end of the dampener shaft to its limit of travel.

3. While holding the dampener in this position, fill the dampener through the open end of the cylinder.

4. Push the shaft upward slowly to seal off the filler hole.

5. Clean the dampener with solvent. Be sure to keep the shaft protruding through the filler hole until the dampener is installed on the aircraft.

6. Install the dampener on the aircraft. **Note:** Keep the shimmy dampener clean—especially the exposed portions of the dampener piston shaft—to prevent the collection of dust and grit that could cut the seals in the dampener barrel. Keep the machined surfaces wiped free of dirt and dust, using a clean, lint-free cloth saturated with hydraulic fluid or kerosene. All surfaces should be wiped free of excess hydraulic fluid.

Airframe lubrication

Lubrication requirements are noted in Figs. 9-13 through 9-15. Before adding grease to grease fittings, wipe all dirt from the fitting. Lubricate until grease appears around the parts being lubricated, then wipe excess grease away.

Wheel bearings should be cleaned and repacked at 500-hour intervals, unless heavy use or dirt strip operations occur. If the latter is the case, then service every 100 hours.

Lubricate the nose gear torque links every 50 hours of operation (more often when flying in dusty conditions).

Engine lubrication

Proper lubrication of the inside of the engine is essential (Figs. 9-16 through 9-18). No lubrication, no engine. Engine lubrication will be determined by check-

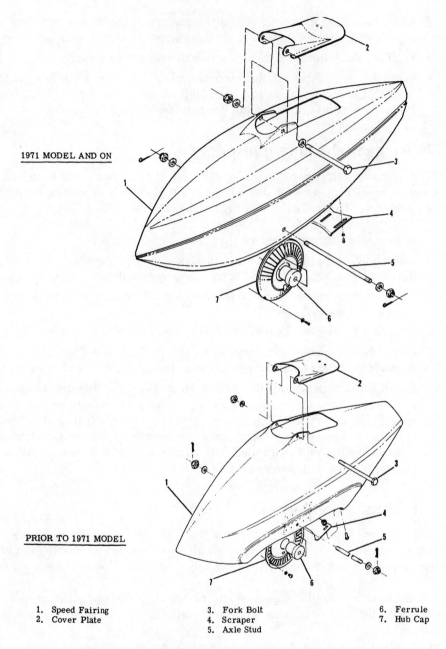

1971 MODEL AND ON

PRIOR TO 1971 MODEL

1. Speed Fairing	3. Fork Bolt	6. Ferrule
2. Cover Plate	4. Scraper	7. Hub Cap
	5. Axle Stud	

Fig. 9-7. Nosewheel speed fairings. Cessna Aircraft Company

ing the aircraft owner's manual; however, as a rule of thumb, never exceed 50 hours between oil changes. Oil is comparatively cheap, and I never heard of an engine that failed due to clean oil.

Oil changing for the airplane owner is no more complicated than for the fam-

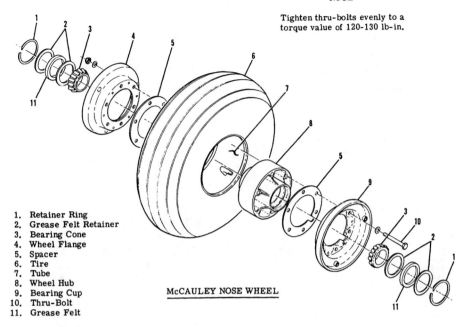

NOTE

Tighten thru-bolts evenly to a
torque value of 120-130 lb-in.

1. Retainer Ring
2. Grease Felt Retainer
3. Bearing Cone
4. Wheel Flange
5. Spacer
6. Tire
7. Tube
8. Wheel Hub
9. Bearing Cup
10. Thru-Bolt
11. Grease Felt

McCAULEY NOSE WHEEL

Fig. 9-8. McCauley nosewheel. Cessna Aircraft Company

ily automobile; however, there is something you should do with the oil that is not normally done with auto oil. This is to obtain an engine oil analysis at each oil change. Engine oil analysis will give indications of what is wearing—and, over a period of time, how quickly it is wearing. Engine oil analysis services are available from several companies, many of which advertise in *Trade-A-Plane* and other aviation journals.

At oil change time, you might decide to put an oil additive in the crankcase, along with the regular engine oil. The object of an additive is to reduce engine wear, resulting in longer engine life. One such additive is Microlon, a Teflon product, approved by the FAA under FAR 33. Microlon is added to the oil only once in the life of the engine. After initial introduction to the crankcase oil, the product is claimed to bond itself to all surfaces within the engine, providing extremely good lubricating properties. Note that Lycoming and Continental state that the use of oil additives will void an engine warranty. Microlon is available from:

Microlon, Inc.
1305 Fraser Street Suite D-5
Bellingham, WA 98226
(800) 962-4152
(206) 647-1350

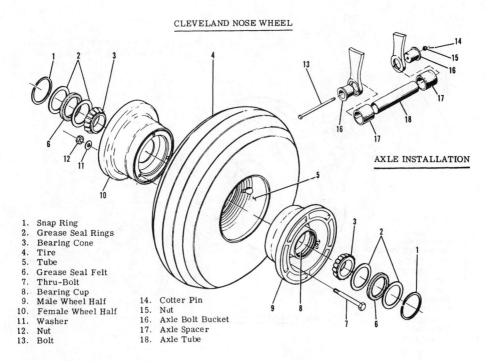

CLEVELAND NOSE WHEEL

AXLE INSTALLATION

1. Snap Ring
2. Grease Seal Rings
3. Bearing Cone
4. Tire
5. Tube
6. Grease Seal Felt
7. Thru-Bolt
8. Bearing Cup
9. Male Wheel Half
10. Female Wheel Half
11. Washer
12. Nut
13. Bolt
14. Cotter Pin
15. Nut
16. Axle Bolt Bucket
17. Axle Spacer
18. Axle Tube

Fig. 9-9. Cleveland nosewheel. Cessna Aircraft Company

Spark plugs

Spark plugs require constant attention for proper engine operation. If they fail to operate properly, the engine will fail to produce its rated power, run rough, or fail completely.

Before you attempt spark plug maintenance, see your mechanic. You will need the mechanic's advice and instruction on the proper method of plug removal, cleaning, gapping, and installation (including proper torquing using a torque wrench) (Fig. 9-19).

Spark plugs can be examined for damage, color of residue, and the like, that indicate what is happening inside your engine's combustion chambers. For a color chart depicting these important clues, write to any of the spark plug manufacturers and request a spark plug information kit.

Hydraulic brake systems

Check brake master cylinders and refill with hydraulic fluid every 100 hours. Bleed the brake system of entrapped air whenever there is a spongy response to the brake pedals.

Fiberglass and metal repair

The wheel fairings, wingtips, and cowlings on the 150/152 are all subject to cracking. Repairs to these fiberglass or metal surfaces are easy and effective.

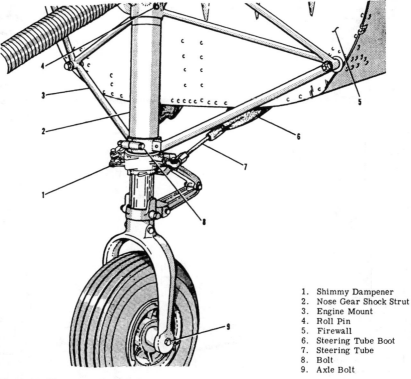

Fig. 9-10. Nose gear installation. Cessna Aircraft Company

1. Shimmy Dampener
2. Nose Gear Shock Strut
3. Engine Mount
4. Roll Pin
5. Firewall
6. Steering Tube Boot
7. Steering Tube
8. Bolt
9. Axle Bolt

For fiberglass:

1. Remove the fairing and drill a hole at the end of the crack to stop the crack from getting larger.
2. Dust the inside of the surface to be repaired with baking soda, then position a small piece of fiberglass cloth over the crack and saturate the entire area with cyanoacrylate (Super Glue). Repeat step 2.
3. From the outside, fill the crack with baking soda and harden with cyanoacrylate.
4. Sand smooth and repaint.

A commercially available product for repairing most plastic materials is Poly-fix, available from:

Redam Corp.
321 Ross Ave.
Hamilton, OH 45013
(800) 234-4583
(513) 863-9393

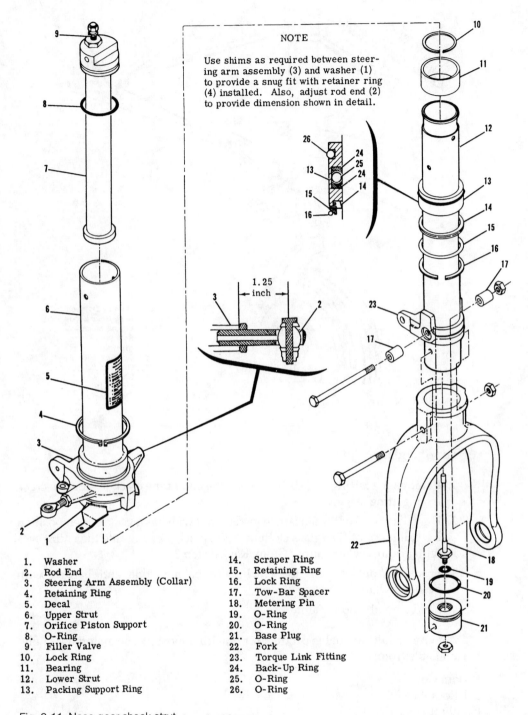

NOTE

Use shims as required between steering arm assembly (3) and washer (1) to provide a snug fit with retainer ring (4) installed. Also, adjust rod end (2) to provide dimension shown in detail.

1.25 inch

1.	Washer	14. Scraper Ring
2.	Rod End	15. Retaining Ring
3.	Steering Arm Assembly (Collar)	16. Lock Ring
4.	Retaining Ring	17. Tow-Bar Spacer
5.	Decal	18. Metering Pin
6.	Upper Strut	19. O-Ring
7.	Orifice Piston Support	20. O-Ring
8.	O-Ring	21. Base Plug
9.	Filler Valve	22. Fork
10.	Lock Ring	23. Torque Link Fitting
11.	Bearing	24. Back-Up Ring
12.	Lower Strut	25. O-Ring
13.	Packing Support Ring	26. O-Ring

Fig. 9-11. Nose gear shock strut. Cessna Aircraft Company

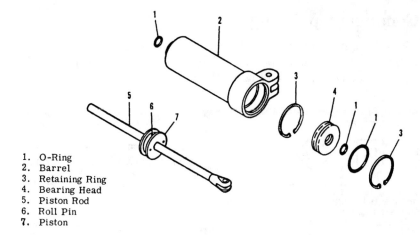

1. O-Ring
2. Barrel
3. Retaining Ring
4. Bearing Head
5. Piston Rod
6. Roll Pin
7. Piston

Fig. 9-12. Nose gear shimmy damper. Cessna Aircraft Company

For metal:

1. Remove the fairing and drill a stop hole at the end of the crack to keep it from continuing farther.
2. Cut a small piece of metal of the same type as the fairing being repaired. This should extend about one inch out from the crack in all directions.
3. Drill holes through the patch and fairing, then rivet together.
4. Touch up with paint as needed.

Paint touch-up

Touching-up a small area on the wings or fuselage of an airplane is very easy, and really makes a marked improvement in the plane's appearance. Many colors of touch-up paint are available in small spray cans from automobile parts houses. It is usually possible to select a close match in color to your airplane from among these products.

Touch-up is easy if you follow the following steps:

1. Thoroughly wash the area to be touched up. All preservatives such as wax and silicone products must be removed.
2. If there is any loose or flaking paint, it must be removed. Carefully use very fine sandpaper for this purpose. Do not sand the bare metal.
3. If bare metal is exposed, it must be primed with an aircraft-type zinc chromate primer.
4. Using sweeping spray strokes, apply at least two coats of touch-up paint.

Complete repainting

Although most owners would never attempt to paint their airplane, they should know what makes a good paint job. This information is general in nature, but applies to all current repainting methods.

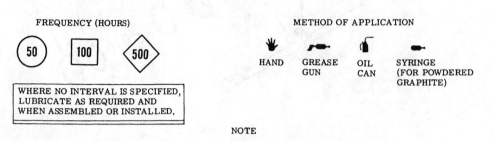

FREQUENCY (HOURS)

50   100   500

WHERE NO INTERVAL IS SPECIFIED, LUBRICATE AS REQUIRED AND WHEN ASSEMBLED OR INSTALLED.

METHOD OF APPLICATION

HAND   GREASE GUN   OIL CAN   SYRINGE (FOR POWDERED GRAPHITE)

NOTE

The military specifications listed are not mandatory, but are intended as guides in choosing satisfactory materials. Products of most reputable manufacturers meet or exceed these specifications.

LUBRICANTS

PG —— MIL-G-6711   POWDERED GRAPHITE
GG —— MIL-G-7711   GENERAL PURPOSE GREASE
GA —— MIL-G-25760   AIRCRAFT WHEEL BEARING GREASE
GH —— MIL-G-23827   AIRCRAFT AND INSTRUMENT GREASE
GL —— MIL-G-21164   HIGH AND LOW TEMPERATURE GREASE
OG —— MIL-L-7870   GENERAL PURPOSE OIL
PL —— VV-P-236   PETROLATUM
GS ——   SIL-GLYDE (OR EQUIVALENT)

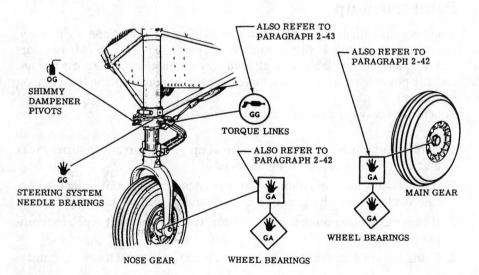

Fig. 9-13. Lubrication chart A. Cessna Aircraft Company

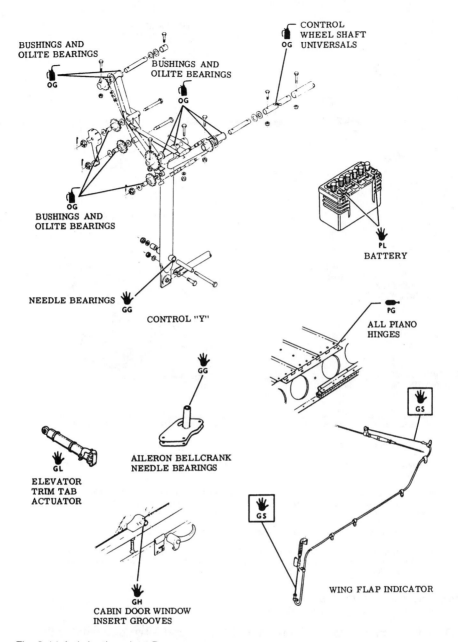

BUSHINGS AND
OILITE BEARINGS

OG

BUSHINGS AND
OILITE BEARINGS

OG

CONTROL
WHEEL SHAFT
OG UNIVERSALS

BUSHINGS AND
OILITE BEARINGS

OG

BUSHINGS AND
OILITE BEARINGS

OG

PL
BATTERY

NEEDLE BEARINGS
GG

CONTROL "Y"

PG
ALL PIANO
HINGES

GG

GS

GL
ELEVATOR
TRIM TAB
ACTUATOR

AILERON BELLCRANK
NEEDLE BEARINGS

GS

WING FLAP INDICATOR

GH
CABIN DOOR WINDOW
INSERT GROOVES

Fig. 9-14. Lubrication chart B. Cessna Aircraft Company

Stripping the aircraft. Aircraft paint removers are fast-acting water-washable products designed for use on aircraft aluminum surfaces. While using remover, always wear rubber gloves and protect your eyes from splashes. If remover gets on your skin, flush with plenty of water. If any comes in contact with your eyes, flood repeatedly with water and call a physician. Have adequate ventilation.

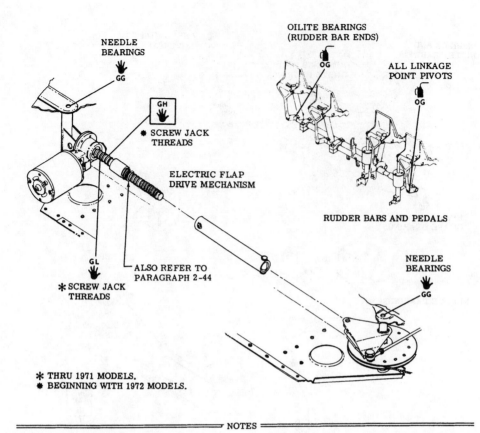

NEEDLE
BEARINGS
GG

GH
❋ SCREW JACK
THREADS

OILITE BEARINGS
(RUDDER BAR ENDS)
OG

ALL LINKAGE
POINT PIVOTS
OG

ELECTRIC FLAP
DRIVE MECHANISM

RUDDER BARS AND PEDALS

GL
✳ SCREW JACK
THREADS

ALSO REFER TO
PARAGRAPH 2-44

NEEDLE
BEARINGS
GG

✳ THRU 1971 MODELS.
❋ BEGINNING WITH 1972 MODELS.

═══════ NOTES ═══════

Sealed bearings require no lubrication.

Do not lubricate roller chains or cables except under seacoast conditions. Wipe with a clean, dry cloth.

Lubricate unsealed pulley bearings, rod ends, Oilite bearings, pivot and hinge points, and any other friction point obviously needing lubrication, with general purpose oil every 1000 hours or oftener if required.

Paraffin wax rubbed on seat rails will ease sliding the seats fore and aft.

Lubricate door latching mechanism with MIL-F-7711 general purpose grease, applied sparingly to friction points, every 1000 hours or oftener if binding occurs. No lubrication is recommended on the rotary clutch.

Fig. 9-15. Lubrication chart C. Cessna Aircraft Company

Do not let remover come in contact with any fiberglass components of the aircraft such as wingtips, fairings, and the like. Make sure that these parts are well-masked or removed from aircraft while stripping is in progress.

Apply the remover liberally by brush to the metal surface. When brushing, be sure to brush in only one direction. Keep surface wet with remover. If an area dries before the paint film softens or wrinkles, apply more remover. It is sometimes advisable to lay an inexpensive polyethylene drop cloth over the applied remover in order to hold the solvents longer, giving more time for penetration of the film. Af-

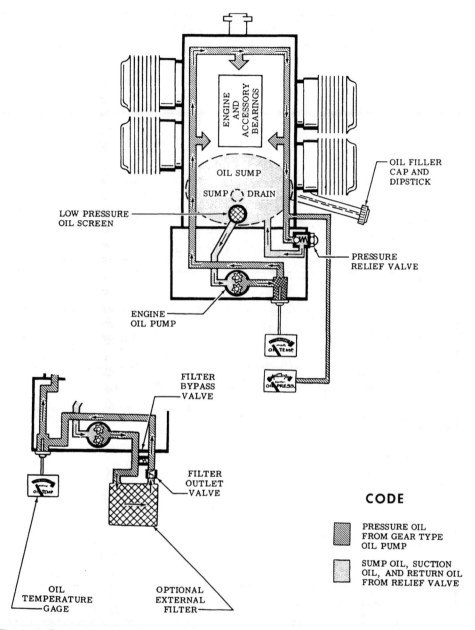

Fig. 9-16. Engine oil schematic. Cessna Aircraft Company

ter the paint softens and wrinkles, use a pressure water hose to thoroughly flush off all residue. In the case of an acrylic lacquer finish, the remover will only soften and will not wrinkle the film. A rubber squeegee or stiff bristle brush can be used to help remove this type of finish.

After all paint has been removed, flush the entire aircraft off with a pressure

PROBABLE CAUSE	ISOLATION PROCEDURE	REMEDY
NO OIL PRESSURE.		
No oil in sump.	Check with dipstick.	Fill sump with proper grade and quantity of oil.
Oil pressure line broken, dis-connected, or pinched.	Inspect oil pressure line.	Replace or connect.
Oil pump defective.	Remove and inspect.	Examine engine. Metal particles from damaged pump may have entered engine oil passage.
Defective oil pressure gage.	Check with another gage. If second reading is normal, air-craft gage is defective.	Replace gage.
Oil congealed in gage line.	Disconnect line at engine and gage; flush with kerosene.	Pre-fill line with kerosene and install.
Pressure relief valve defective.	Remove and check for dirty or defective parts.	Clean and reinstall; replace defective parts.
LOW OIL PRESSURE.		
Low oil supply.	Check with dipstick.	Fill sump with proper grade and quantity of oil.
Low oil viscosity.		Drain sump. Refill with correct grade.
Plugged oil screen.	Inspect screen.	Remove and clean.
Dirt on oil pressure relief valve seat.	Remove and inspect.	Clean plunger and seat.
Oil pressure relief valve plunger sticking.	Remove and inspect.	Clean plunger.
Oil pump suction tube screen plugged.		Engine overhaul.
Oil pressure gage defective.	Test gage.	Replace or repair gage.
Internal oil leak.		Engine overhaul.
HIGH OIL PRESSURE.		
High oil viscosity.		Drain oil and refill sump with correct grade and quantity of oil.
Defective oil pressure gage.	Test gage.	Replace or repair gage.
HIGH OIL TEMPERATURE.		
Low oil supply.	Check with dipstick.	Fill sump with correct grade and quantity of oil.

Cessna Aircraft Company

Fig. 9-17. Oil pressure troubleshooting chart A.

water hose. Let dry. Using clean cotton rags, wipe all surfaces thoroughly with methyl ethyl ketone (MEK).

Corrosion removal. After paint stripping, any traces of corrosion on the aluminum surface must be removed with aluminum wool or a Scotch Brite pad.

PROBABLE CAUSE	ISOLATION PROCEDURE	REMEDY
HIGH OIL TEMPERATURE (Cont).		
Dirty or diluted oil.	Check with dipstick.	Drain sump, and fill with fresh oil of proper grade.
Winter baffles installed.	Check for baffles installed.	Remove winter baffles.
Prolonged ground operation at high engine speed.		Avoid prolonged running on the ground.
Excessive rate of climb.		Avoid low airspeed.
Lean fuel-air mixture.		Avoid excessive lean mixture operation.
Defective oil temperature gage.	Test gage.	Replace or repair gage.
Defective oil temperature bulb.	Check for correct oil pressure, oil level, and cylinder head temperature. If they are correct, check oil temperature gage for being defective; if a similar reading is observed, bulb is defective.	Replace temperature bulb.

Fig. 9-18. Oil pressure troubleshooting chart B.

Fig. 9-19. A one-piece 152 cowling 152 makes engine inspection and maintenance easier.

Never use steel wool or a steel brush, as bits of steel will embed in the aluminum, causing additional corrosion.

Metal pretreatment. In the case of an aircraft that has been stripped of its previous coating, make sure that all traces of paint or paint remover residue have been removed. Give special attention to areas such as seams and around rivet heads. Aircraft should be flushed with plenty of clean water to ensure removal of all contaminants. Let dry. Using clean cotton rags, wipe all surfaces thoroughly with MEK.

Apply a metal pretreatment liberally to all the aluminum surfaces of the aircraft. While keeping these surfaces thoroughly wet with the pretreatment, scrub briskly with a Scotch Brite pad. Wear rubber gloves and protect your eyes from splash during this procedure.

The pretreatment may be applied with clean rags or a brush. After the entire aircraft has been treated with this procedure, flush very thoroughly with plenty of clean water. Let dry.

The next step is to thoroughly wipe down the entire aluminum surface with MEK using clean cotton rags. This will ensure all contaminants are removed prior to application of primer. Let dry and tack-rag all surfaces.

Priming the cleaned areas. The best aircraft primers available today are the two-part epoxy primers. They are specifically designed for aircraft and afford the best in corrosion protection. Epoxy primers give the best adhesion possible to the substrata aluminum surface and to the finish top coat.

Mix the components of the epoxy primer per the manufacturer's instructions, then let stand for 15 to 20 minutes prior to starting application. Pot life after mixture is limited and will vary from manufacturer to manufacturer.

Care must be taken that only enough primer be used to prime the surface evenly to about 0.0005 in. (a half-mil film thickness). This means that the aluminum substrate should show through, with a light yellow coating of the primer coloring the metal. Drying time of the primer will vary slightly due to differences in temperature and relative humidity at the time of application. As a general rule, primer should be ready for application of the finish coat within four to six hours.

After the primer is thoroughly dry, wipe the entire surface with clean, soft, cotton rags using a little pressure, as in polishing. Next, tack-rag the entire surface. You are now ready for application of the top coat finishing system you have selected.

Conditions for painting. For optimum results, temperature should be more than 70°F and relative humidity should be 20–60 percent. Departure from these limits could result in various application or finish problems. Drying time of the finish coating will vary with temperature, humidity, amount of thinner used, and thickness of paint film.

Painting safety tips.

- Ground the surface you are painting or sanding
- Do not use an electric drill to mix dope or paint
- Wear leather-soled shoes in the painting area
- Wear cotton clothes while painting
- Keep solvent-soaked rags in a fireproof safety container

- Keep spray area and floor clean and free of dust buildup. (Rinse with hose or wet-sweep the floor.)
- Have adequate ventilation
- Do not allow mist or fumes to build up in a confined area
- Do not smoke or have any type of open flame in the area

Application of the top coat. Several types of top coat systems are discussed, complete with application instructions.

Polyurethane enamel. Polyurethane enamels are the finest aircraft finishes available today. They offer such important characteristics as superior gloss, excellent color retention, resistance to abrasion, chemical damage, fuel staining, hydraulic fluid spills, and thermal shock. These characteristics remain with little or no maintenance over many years of active flying.

Mix the several parts of the polyurethane enamel per the manufacturer's instructions. Pot life after mixing is approximately six hours, but will vary with temperature and humidity.

Spray a relatively light tack coat on the first application. Let dry for at least 15 minutes. The second coat is applied as a full, wet cross-coat. Care should be taken to ensure that not too much paint is applied, resulting in runs or sags. Polyurethane enamel is a high-solid material giving excellent hiding characteristics without excessive paint buildup.

An overnight dry is preferable before taping for trim color application unless forced drying is used. Forced drying for one or two hours at 140°F is sufficient.

After masking, and before applying the trim color, lightly scuff the trim color surface using #400 wet-or-dry sandpaper. Tack-rag and apply the trim color. Remove masking tapes as soon as paint has started to set.

Acrylic lacquer. Acrylic lacquers have been used by some of the largest aircraft and automobile manufacturers for many years. These are proven paints, with outstanding durability, good color, and excellent gloss retention characteristics.

Mix the paint and associated other elements per the manufacturer's instructions. Adjustments to this mixture might be necessary due to the spray equipment used or operator technique.

Spray a relatively light tack coat on the first application. Let dry for approximately 30 minutes. Follow this first coat with at least three full, wet cross-coats, letting each dry for approximately 30 minutes between coats. If the material is too heavy, orange peel or pinhole imperfections are likely to appear.

An overnight dry is preferable before taping for trim color application. Remove the masking tape as soon as the trim paint has started to set.

Enamel. Enamels have been in use for many years and can provide good service. Mix the enamel as instructed by the manufacturer. Spray on a light tack coat. Allow to dry for 15 to 20 minutes, then apply a full, wet cross-coat. Allow to dry at least 48 hours before taping for trim colors.

After masking and before applying trim color, lightly scuff the trim color surface using #400 wet-or-dry sandpaper. Tack-rag and apply trim color. Remove masking tape as soon as the paint has started to set.

Refinishing fiberglass components

When refinishing any fiberglass component of the aircraft, such as wingtips, antenna, fairings, and the like, it is extremely important that they are protected from paint remover or solvents. The only safe method of removing paint from these components is to sand it off. After the paint is removed by sanding, tack-rag the surface and apply a light coat of primer (automotive primer is acceptable).

When the primer is dry, briskly wipe the entire surface clean with soft, cotton rags. Next, tack-rag the surface and finish with the paint you are using on the airframe.

Headliner removal and installation

Probably the worst hair-tearing job for the do-it-yourself airplane fixer-upper is the removal and installation of a headliner. Follow these simple instructions taken from the *Cessna Service Manual*, and you can't miss (Fig. 9-20):

Removal.

1. Remove the sun visors, all inside-finish strips and plates, doorpost upper shields, front-spar trim shield, dome light panel, and any other visible retainers securing the headliner.

2. Work the edges of the headliner free from the metal tabs that hold the fabric.

3. Starting at the front of the headliner, work the headliner down, removing the screws through the metal tabs that hold the wire bows to the cabin top. Pry loose the outer ends of the bows from the retainers above the doors. Detach each wire bow in succession. **Note:** Always work from front to rear when removing the headliner; it is impossible to detach the wire bows when working from rear to front.

4. Remove the headliner assembly and bows from the airplane. **Note:** Due to the difference in length and contour of the wire bows, each bow should be tagged to assure proper relocation in the headliner.

5. Remove the spunglass soundproofing panels (these are held in place by glue).

Installation.

1. Before installing the headliner, check all items concealed by the headliner to see that they are mounted securely. Use wide cloth tape to secure loose wires to the fuselage, and to seal any openings in the wing roots. Straighten any tabs bent during the removal of the old headliner.

2. Apply cement to the skin areas where the soundproofing panels are not supported by wire bows, and press the panels into place.

3. Insert wire bows into the headliner seams, and secure the rearmost edges of the headliner after positioning the two bows at the rear of the headliner. Stretch the material along the edges to make sure it is properly centered, but do not stretch it tight enough to destroy the ceiling contours or distort the wire bows. Secure the edges of the headliner with sharp tabs, or, where necessary, rubber cement.

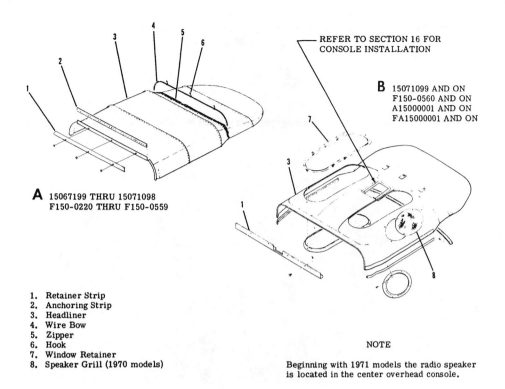

REFER TO SECTION 16 FOR
CONSOLE INSTALLATION

B 15071099 AND ON
F150-0560 AND ON
A15000001 AND ON
FA15000001 AND ON

A 15067199 THRU 15071098
F150-0220 THRU F150-0559

1. Retainer Strip
2. Anchoring Strip
3. Headliner
4. Wire Bow
5. Zipper
6. Hook
7. Window Retainer
8. Speaker Grill (1970 models)

NOTE

Beginning with 1971 models the radio speaker
is located in the center overhead console.

Fig. 9-20. Cabin headliner diagram. Cessna Aircraft Company

4. Work the headliner forward, installing each wire bow in place with the tabs.
Wedge the ends of the wire bows into the retainer strips. Stretch the headliner just taut enough to avoid wrinkles and maintain a smooth contour.

5. When all bows are in place and fabric edges are secured, trim off any excess
fabric and reinstall all items removed.

Seats and seat re-covering

Re-covering the seats is generally easier (less hair pulled out) than installing a
headliner. My only advice in seat re-covery is to work in a well-ventilated area, or
the glue you'll be working with will have you flying without the airplane.

Due to the wide selection of materials and styles of seat covers available, I recommend you either contract the job with a professional aviation interior shop, or
contact a supplier of complete interiors or slip covers (Fig. 9-21). The latter method
is recommended if you are the hands-on type, and also want to save a dollar. Suppliers of seat covers are:

Cooper Aviation Supply Co.
2149 E. Pratt Blvd.
Elk Grove Village, IL 60007
(708) 364-2600

Fig. 9-21. Seat covers you can install yourself.

Garrett Leather Corp.
P.O. Box 29
359 Niagara Street
Buffalo, NY 14201
(800) 342-7738
(716) 852-7720

Also check *Trade-A-Plane* for listings of other suppliers. Another alternative source of seats and carpets is the aircraft wrecking yards, which are also advertised in *Trade-A-Plane*.

Individual seats are equipped with manually operated reclining seat backs. Rollers permit the seats to slide forward and backward on seat rails. Pins, which engage various holes in the seat rails, lock the seats in selected positions. Stops limit ultimate travel.

Removal of a seat is accomplished by removing the stops and moving the seats forward and backward on the rails to disengage them from the rails. Installation is in reverse order (Figs. 9-22 and 9-23). **Warning:** It is extremely important that the pilot's seat stops be installed because acceleration and deceleration could possibly permit the seat to become disengaged from the seat rails and create a hazardous situation, especially during takeoff and landing.

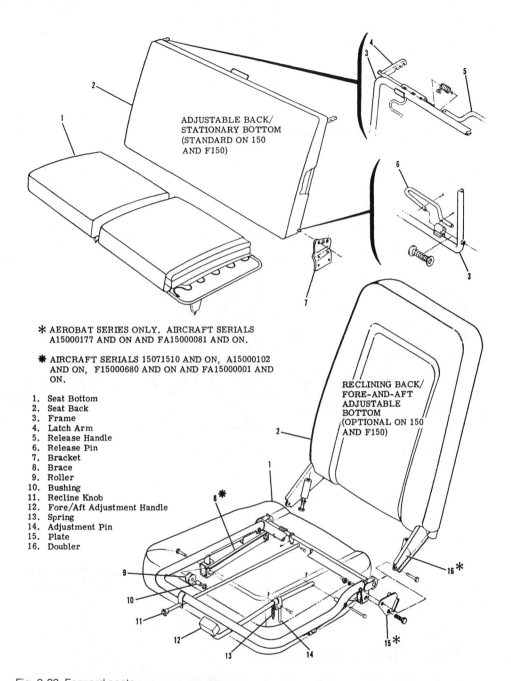

ADJUSTABLE BACK/
STATIONARY BOTTOM
(STANDARD ON 150
AND F150)

RECLINING BACK/
FORE-AND-AFT
ADJUSTABLE
BOTTOM
(OPTIONAL ON 150
AND F150)

✱ AEROBAT SERIES ONLY. AIRCRAFT SERIALS
A15000177 AND ON AND FA15000081 AND ON.

✸ AIRCRAFT SERIALS 15071510 AND ON, A15000102
AND ON, F15000680 AND ON AND FA15000001 AND
ON.

1. Seat Bottom
2. Seat Back
3. Frame
4. Latch Arm
5. Release Handle
6. Release Pin
7. Bracket
8. Brace
9. Roller
10. Bushing
11. Recline Knob
12. Fore/Aft Adjustment Handle
13. Spring
14. Adjustment Pin
15. Plate
16. Doubler

Fig. 9-22. Forward seats. Cessna Aircraft Company

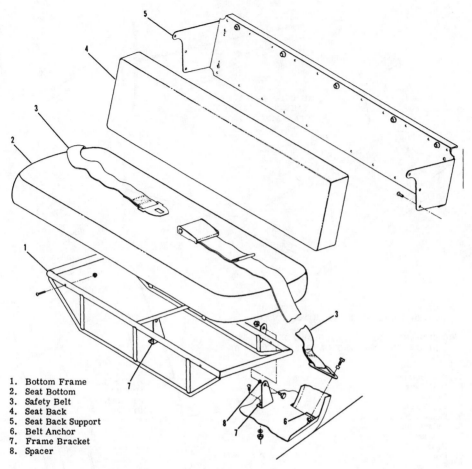

1. Bottom Frame
2. Seat Bottom
3. Safety Belt
4. Seat Back
5. Seat Back Support
6. Belt Anchor
7. Frame Bracket
8. Spacer

Fig. 9-23. Auxiliary seat. Cessna Aircraft Company

Safety belts

Safety belts must be replaced when they are frayed, cut, or the latches become defective. Attaching hardware should be replaced if faulty. Use only approved safety belts.

Side window replacement

A movable window, hinged at the top, is installed in doors. The window assembly may be replaced by pulling the hinge pins and disconnecting the window stop. To remove the frame from the plastic, it is necessary to drill out the blind rivets where the frame is spliced. When replacing a window in a frame, make sure that the sealing strip and an adequate coating of a sealing compound are used all around the edges of the plastic panel (Fig. 9-24).

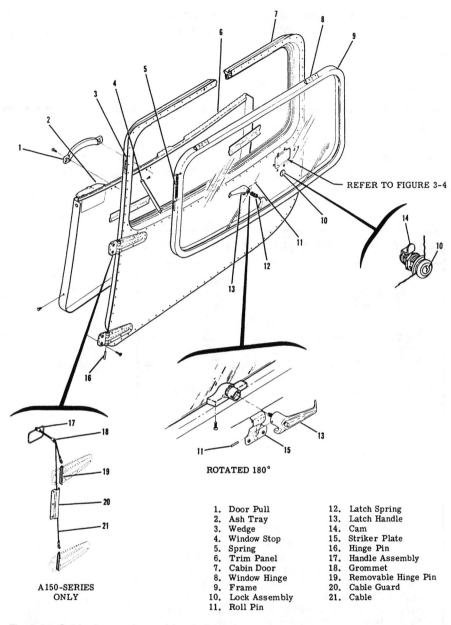

REFER TO FIGURE 3-4

ROTATED 180°

A150-SERIES
ONLY

1.	Door Pull	12.	Latch Spring
2.	Ash Tray	13.	Latch Handle
3.	Wedge	14.	Cam
4.	Window Stop	15.	Striker Plate
5.	Spring	16.	Hinge Pin
6.	Trim Panel	17.	Handle Assembly
7.	Cabin Door	18.	Grommet
8.	Window Hinge	19.	Removable Hinge Pin
9.	Frame	20.	Cable Guard
10.	Lock Assembly	21.	Cable
11.	Roll Pin		

Fig. 9-24. Cabin door and movable window. Cessna Aircraft Company

Battery

Battery servicing involves adding distilled water to maintain the electrolyte level with the horizontal baffle plate at the bottom of the filler holes. Be sure to flush the area with plenty of clean water after refilling to wash away any spilled battery acid.

The use of a hydrometer is required for checking the charge condition of the battery (Fig. 9-25). Charging and starting problems can be solved by referring to Fig. 9-26.

Electrical lighting system

For troubleshooting the lighting system, a complete set of *Cessna Service Manual* diagrams and aids is shown (Figs. 9-27 through 9-30). Most troubleshooting can be accomplished with a multimeter. Landing, navigation, strobe, and beacon lights will unfortunately require replacement on an all-too-often basis. Aircraft lights don't have the long life of auto headlights and accessory bulbs (Figs. 9-31 through 9-34).

BATTERY HYDROMETER READINGS

READINGS	BATTERY CONDITION
1.280 Specific Gravity	100% Charged
1.250 Specific Gravity	75% Charged
1.220 Specific Gravity	50% Charged
1.190 Specific Gravity	25% Charged
1.160 Specific Gravity	Practically Dead

NOTE

All readings shown are for an electrolyte temperature of 80° Fahrenheit. For higher temperatures the readings will be slightly lower. For cooler temperatures the readings will be slightly higher. Some hydrometers will have a built-in temperature compensation chart and a thermometer. If this type tester is used, disregard this chart.

Cessna Aircraft Company

Fig. 9-25. Battery Hydrometer readings.

Fuel system

Understanding the *Cessna Service Manual* diagram of the fuel system will help you see where most problems will occur in the fuel system, and why you must be careful about water and debris in the system (Fig. 9-35).

PROBABLE CAUSE	ISOLATION PROCEDURE	REMEDY
BATTERY WILL NOT SUPPLY POWER TO BUS OR IS INCAPABLE OF CRANKING ENGINE.		
Battery discharged.	1. Measure voltage at "BAT" terminal of battery contactor with master switch and a suitable load such as a taxi light turned on. Normal battery will indicate 11.5 volts or more.	If voltage is low, proceed to step 2. If voltage is normal, proceed to step 3.
Battery faulty.	2. Check fluid level in cells and charge battery at 20 amps for approximately 30 minutes or until the battery voltage rises to 15 volts. Check battery with a load type tester.	If tester indicates a good battery, the malfunction may be assumed to be a discharged battery. If the tester indicates a faulty battery, replace the battery.
Faulty contactor or wiring between contactor or master switch.	3. Measure voltage at master switch terminal (smallest) on contactor with master switch closed. Normal indication is zero volts.	If voltage reads zero, proceed to step 4. If a voltage reading is obtained, check wiring between contactor and master switch. Also check master switch.
Open coil on contactor.	4. Check continuity between "BAT" terminal and master switch terminal of contactor. Normal indication is 16 to 24 ohms (Master switch open).	If ohmmeter indicates an open coil, replace contactor. If ohmmeter indicates a good coil, proceed to step 5.
Faulty contactor contacts.	5. Check voltage on "BUS" side of contactor with master switch closed. Meter normally indicates battery voltage.	If voltage is zero or intermittant, replace contactor. If voltage is normal, proceed to step 6.
Faulty wiring between contactor and bus.	6. Inspect wiring between contactor and bus.	Repair or replace wiring.

Cessna Aircraft Company

Fig. 9-26. Troubleshooting the battery charging system.

Stainless steel screw kits

Have you noticed all those rusted screws on an airplane? It's easy to replace them with nonrusting stainless steel screws. Kits containing screws in the proper number and of the proper size are the recommended way to purchase supplies for this job. The use of stainless steel screws on airplanes makes sense because as they don't rust and stain the surrounding area as do stock screws. Be very careful that you don't strip out the screw holes when removing and installing screws.

Trimcraft Aviation has packaged kits of stainless steel screws (Fig. 9-36). Each kit contains everything you will need. Their kits are available from various suppliers that advertise in the airplane magazines and *Trade-A-Plane*. Direct supply is available from:

Trimcraft Aviation
P.O. Box 488
Genoa City, WI 53128
(414) 279-6896

PROBABLE CAUSE	ISOLATION PROCEDURE	REMEDY
LANDING AND TAXI LIGHTS OUT.		
Short circuit in wiring.	1. Inspect fuse.	If fuse is open, proceed to step 2. If fuse is OK, proceed to step 3.
Defective wiring.	2. Test each circuit separately until short is located.	Repair or replace wiring.
Defective switch.	3. Check voltage at lights with master and landing and taxi light switches ON. Should read battery voltage.	Replace switch.
LANDING OR TAXI LIGHT OUT.		
Lamp burned out.	1. Test lamp with ohmmeter or new lamp.	Replace lamp.
Open circuit in wiring.	2. Test wiring for continuity.	Repair or replace wiring.
FLASHING BEACON DOES NOT LIGHT.		
Short circuit in wiring.	1. Inspect fuse.	If fuse is open, proceed to step 2. If fuse is OK, proceed to step 3.
Defective wiring.	2. Test circuit until short is located.	Repair or replace wiring.
Lamp burned out.	3. Test lamp with ohmmeter or a new lamp.	Replace lamp. If lamp is good, proceed to step 4.
Open circuit in wiring.	4. Test circuit from lamp to flasher for continuity.	If no continuity is present, repair or replace wiring. If continuity is present, proceed to step 5.
Defective switch.	5. Check voltage at flasher with master and beacon switch on. Should read battery voltage.	Replace switch. If voltage is present, proceed to step 6.
Defective flasher.	6. Install new flasher.	
FLASHING BEACON CONSTANTLY LIT.		
Defective flasher.	1. Install new flasher.	
ALL NAV LIGHTS OUT.		
Short circuit in wiring.	1. Inspect fuse.	If fuse is open, proceed to step 2. If fuse is OK, proceed to step 3.
Defective wiring.	2. Isolate and test each nav light circuit until short is located.	Repair or replace wiring.

Cessna Aircraft Company

Fig. 9-27. Troubleshooting the aircraft lighting system chart A.

D&D Aircraft Supply
Div. of Hunter Industries
4 Stickney Terrace
P.O. Box 1200
Hampton, NH 03842
(800) 469-8000
(603) 926-8881

Plastic parts

Interior molded plastic parts, such as door panels, post covers, access covers, headliners, seat trim backs, and the like, are available from:

AirFlite Industries, Inc.
P.O. Box 8
Grand Ledge, MI 48837
(800) 345-7753
(517) 627-9322

Kinzie Industries, Inc.
P.O. Box 847
Alva, OK 73717
(405) 327-1565

Texas Aero Plastics
Northwest Regional Airport
Route 9 Box 17
Roanoke, TX 76262
(817) 491-4735

PROBABLE CAUSE	ISOLATION PROCEDURE	REMEDY

INSTRUMENT LIGHTS WILL NOT LIGHT (Cont).

PROBABLE CAUSE	ISOLATION PROCEDURE	REMEDY
Defective wiring.	2. Test circuit until short is located.	Repair or replace wiring.
	3. Test for open circuit.	Repair or replace wiring. If no short or open circuit is found, proceed to step 4.
Defective rheostat.	4. Check voltage at instrument light with master switch on. Should read battery voltage with rheostat turned full clockwise and voltage should decrease as rheostat is turned counterclockwise.	If no voltage is present or voltage has a sudden drop before rheostat has been turned full counterclockwise, replace rheostat.
Lamp burned out.	5. Test lamp with ohmmeter or new lamp.	Replace lamp.

CONTROL WHEEL MAP LIGHT WILL NOT LIGHT THRU 1970 AIRCRAFT ONLY.

PROBABLE CAUSE	ISOLATION PROCEDURE	REMEDY
Nav light switch turned off.	1. Nav light switch has to be ON before map light will light.	
Short circuit in wiring.	2. Check lamp fuse on terminal board located on back of stationary panel with ohmmeter.	If fuse is open, proceed to step 3. If fuse is OK, proceed to step 4.
Defective wiring.	3. Test circuit until short is located.	Repair or replace wiring.
	4. Test for open circuit.	Repair or replace wiring. If a short or open circuit is not found, proceed to step 5.
Defective map light assembly.	5. Check voltage at map light assembly with master and nav switches on.	If battery voltage is present, replace map light assembly.

⟨CAUTION⟩

Failure to observe polarity shown on wiring diagram (page 20-19), will result in immediate failure of the transistor on the map light circuit board assembly.

CONTROL WHEEL MAP LIGHT WILL NOT LIGHT 1971 AIRCRAFT & ON.

PROBABLE CAUSE	ISOLATION PROCEDURE	REMEDY
Nav light switch turned off.	1. Nav light switch has to be ON before map light will light.	
Short circuit in wiring.	2. Check lamp fuse on terminal board located on back of stationary panel with ohmmeter.	If fuse is open, proceed to step 3. If fuse is OK, proceed to step 4.
Defective wiring.	3. Test circuit until short is located.	Repair or replace wiring.

Cessna Aircraft Company

Fig. 9-28. Troubleshooting the aircraft lighting system chart B.

PROBABLE CAUSE	ISOLATION PROCEDURE	REMEDY
ALL NAV LIGHTS OUT (Cont).		
Defective switch.	3. Check voltage at nav light with master and nav light switches on. Should read battery voltage.	Replace switch.
ONE NAV LIGHT OUT.		
Lamp burned out.	1. Inspect lamp.	Replace lamp.
Open circuit in wiring.	2. Test wiring for continuity.	Repair or replace wiring.
ONE ANTI-COLLISION STROBE LIGHT DOES NOT LIGHT.		
Flash tube burned out.	Test with new flash tube.	Replace flash tube.
Faulty wiring.	Test for continuity.	Repair or replace.
Faulty trigger head.	Test with new trigger head.	Replace trigger head.
BOTH ANTI-COLLISION STROBE LIGHTS WILL NOT LIGHT.		
Circuit breaker open.	Inspect.	Reset.
Faulty power supply.	Listen for whine in power supply to determine if power is operating.	
Faulty switch.	Test for continuity.	Repair or replace.
Faulty wiring.	Test for continuity.	Repair or replace.
DOME LIGHT TROUBLE.		
Short circuit in wiring.	1. Inspect fuse.	If fuse is open, proceed to step 2. If fuse is OK, proceed to step 3.
Defective wiring.	2. Test circuit until short is located.	Repair or replace wiring.
	3. Test for open circuit.	Repair or replace wiring. If no short or open circuit is found, proceed to step 4.
Lamp burned out.	4. Test lamp with ohmmeter or new lamp.	Replace lamp.
Defective switch.	5. Check for voltage at dome light with master and dome light switch on. Should read battery voltage.	Replace switch.
INSTRUMENT LIGHTS WILL NOT LIGHT.		
Short circuit in wiring.	1. Inspect fuse.	If fuse is open, proceed to step 2. If fuse is OK, proceed to step 3.

Fig. 9-29. Troubleshooting the aircraft lighting system chart C.

PROBABLE CAUSE	ISOLATION PROCEDURE	REMEDY
CONTROL WHEEL MAP LIGHT WILL NOT LIGHT 1971 AIRCRAFT & ON (Cont).		
	4. Test for open circuit.	Repair or replace wiring. If a short or open circuit is not found, proceed to step 5.
Defective map light assembly.	5. Check voltage at map light assembly with master and nav switches on.	If battery voltage is present, replace map light assembly.

Fig. 9-30. Troubleshooting the aircraft lighting system chart D.

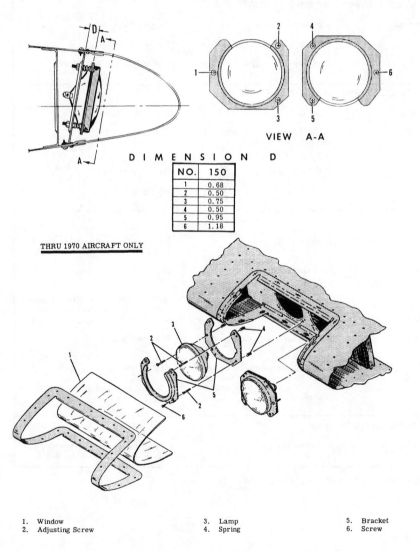

VIEW A-A

D I M E N S I O N   D

NO.	150
1	0.68
2	0.50
3	0.75
4	0.50
5	0.95
6	1.18

THRU 1970 AIRCRAFT ONLY

1.	Window	3.	Lamp	5.	Bracket
2.	Adjusting Screw	4.	Spring	6.	Screw

Fig. 9-31. Landing and taxi light installation, 1959 through 1970.

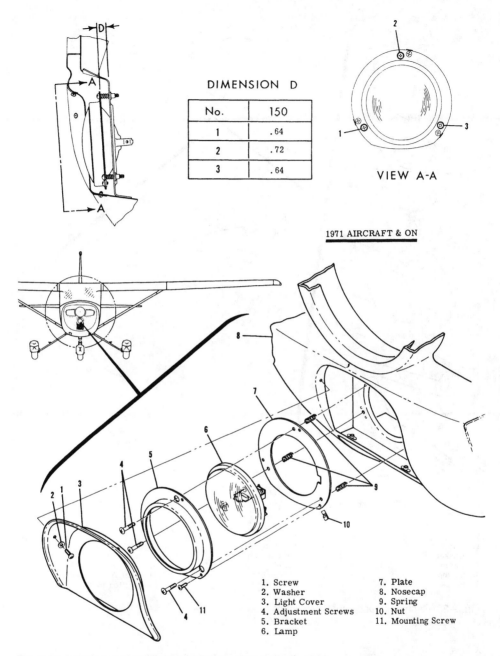

DIMENSION D

No.	150
1	.64
2	.72
3	.64

VIEW A-A

1971 AIRCRAFT & ON

1. Screw
2. Washer
3. Light Cover
4. Adjustment Screws
5. Bracket
6. Lamp
7. Plate
8. Nosecap
9. Spring
10. Nut
11. Mounting Screw

Fig. 9-32. Landing and taxi light installation, 1971 through 1983. Cessna Aircraft Company

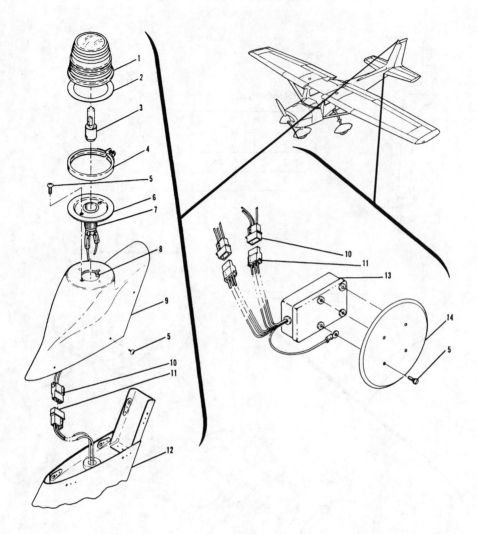

1. Dome
2. Gasket
3. Lamp
4. Clamp Assembly
5. Screw

6. Plate - Mounting
7. Socket Assembly
8. Nutplate
9. Tip Assembly - Fin

10. Housing - Plug
11. Housing - Cap
12. Fin Assembly
13. Flasher Assembly
14. Inspection Plate

Fig. 9-33. Flashing beacon light installation. Cessna Aircraft Company

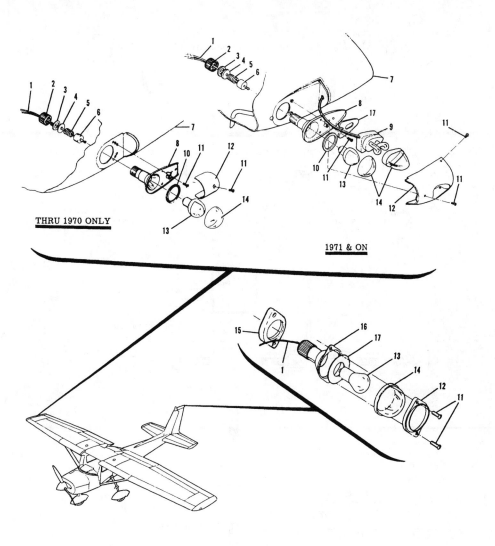

THRU 1970 ONLY

1971 & ON

1. Electrical leads	7. Wing Tip	13. Bulb
2. Cap	8. Wing Navigation Light	14. Lens
3. Washer	9. Flash Tube Assembly	15. Mount
4. Insulated Washer	10. Seal	16. Tail Navigation Light
5. Spring	11. Screw	17. Gasket
6. Insulator	12. Lens Retainer	

Fig. 9-34. Navigation and anticollision strobe light installation. Cessna Aircraft Company

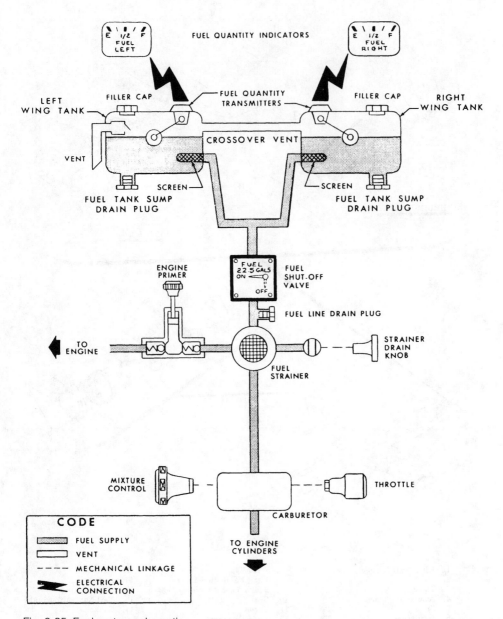

Fig. 9-35. Fuel system schematic. Cessna Aircraft Company

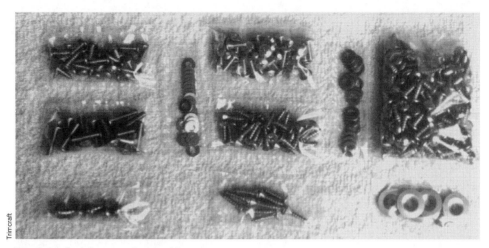

Trinrcraft

Fig. 9-36. Stainless steel screw kit.

10

Modifications and STCs

THE *SUPPLEMENTAL TYPE CERTIFICATE* (STC) is required when a change or modification is made to an airplane and that change or modification will be applied to more than a single airplane. These STC changes can be as minor as approving a certain type of brake modification, or as complex as recontouring the flying surfaces of the airplane.

POPULAR MODIFICATIONS

Because so many 150/152 airplanes are flying, numerous modifications are available to improve the airplanes' performance, appearance, and more.

STOL

STOL conversions are perhaps king of all the modifications available to the 150/152 owner. STOL is the military designation for *short takeoff and landing* aircraft. STOL has extended into general aviation markets, resulting in some rather spectacular aircraft performance figures. The typical STOL modification involves changes to the overall shape of the wing (usually in the form of a leading-edge cuff), the addition of stall fences to stop the stall from proceeding outward along the wing span (Fig. 10-1), gap seals, modified wingtips (Fig. 10-2), vortex generators to aid in directional control at low speed, and an increase in power (larger engine).

Sometimes an owner will make STOL modifications one part at a time, often with STCs from several sources. Before proceeding with this piecemeal change, check with your local FAA office about the various STCs you are considering because some are not compatible with others.

A typical STOL conversion consisting of a modified leading edge, stall fences, gap seals, and wingtips will cost fewer than $1000 for materials and take a competent mechanic about 25 hours for the installation.

Fig. 10-1. Stall fence installed as part of an STOL package.

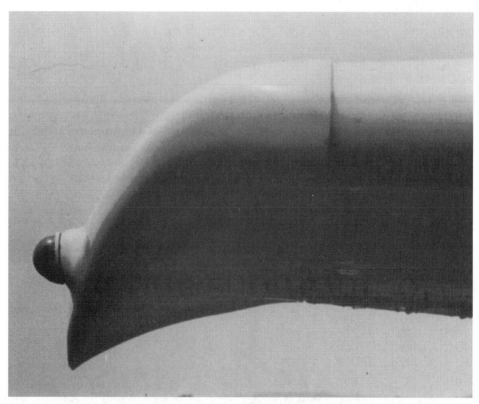

Fig. 10-2. Wingtips sometimes used in STOL conversions, generally called *droop tips*.

The specifications, as listed by Horton STOLcraft for a converted Cessna 150 (Compare these to the factory specifications in chapter 3.):

Gross weight: 1500 lbs
Takeoff Speed: 33 mph
Takeoff over 50-ft obs: 770 ft
Cruise Speed: 120 mph
Approach Speed: 36 mph
Landing over 50-ft obs: 540 ft
(These figures represent maximum performance)

For further information about STOL modifications contact:

Horton STOLcraft
Wellington Municipal Airport
Wellington, KS 67152
(800) 835-2051
(316) 326-2241

Bush Conversions
P.O. Box 431
Udall, KS 67146
(800) 752-0748

Power

Power increases are another popular modification made to the 150/152s, and are often done in conjunction with a STOL modification. These mods consist of engine replacement to increase the useful load and improve flight performance figures of the aircraft. The usual engine will be in the 150-horsepower range, although there are some 180-horsepower 150s around. The modifications can be extensive—and costly, although most are not much above the level of a good engine rebuild charge. Generally, a power conversion will cost $2000 to $3000 for the materials and use better than 50 hours labor. Of course, the cost of the replacement engine is added to this, making a power mod's total cost in excess of $15,000.

Aircraft Conversion Technologies (ACT) claims the following performance figures for its 150- and 180-hp conversions:

Speed
    Cruising (10,000 ft): 154 TAS
    Stall: 47 mph
Takeoff distance 250 ft
Rate of climb: 1590 fpm
Service ceiling: 21,500 ft
Gross weight: 1760 lbs

Compare these figures to those found in chapter 3 and you will quickly see why the big iron power-up conversions are popular. For further information about these engine modifications, contact:

Aircraft Conversion Technologies
1410 Flightline Dr.
Hangar A
Lincoln Airport
Lincoln, CA 95648
(916) 645-3264

Wingtips

Wingtips are often changed to increase performance. Dr. Sighard Hoerner, Ph.D, designed a high-performance wingtip for the U.S. Navy that provided information that led to the development of improved wingtips for small planes. A properly designed wingtip can provide an increase of 3–5 mph in cruise speed and a small increase in climb performance, but most important are the improved low-speed handling characteristics: 10–20 percent reduction in takeoff roll, 4–5 mph slower stall speed, and improved slow-flight handling. Installation time can be as low as 2–3 hours. Improved wingtips are one of the most popular modifications for 150/152s (Fig. 10-3).

Met-Co-Aire

Fig. 10-3. Hoerner wingtips.

Wingtips will not break the bank, typically costing fewer than $300 and taking only a few hours to install. For more information, contact:

Met-Co-Aire
P.O. Box 2216
Fullerton, CA 92633
(714) 870-4610

An alternate type of wingtip is the drooptip (Fig. 10-2), which is supposed to increase speed by 7–10 percent, increase the rate of climb by 20 percent, reduce stall speed 20 percent, reduce the takeoff roll, and improve stability. Drooptips are available from:

Madras Air Service
1914 NW Deemers Dr.
Madras, OR 97741
(503) 475-2360

Taildraggers

Taildragger conversion has become another popular modification among the owners of 150/152s. Basically, the nosewheel is removed, the main gear moved forward, and a tailwheel installed (Fig. 10-4). Performance benefits of 8–10 mph increase in cruise, shorter takeoff distances, and better rough-field handling are claimed. The cost for this conversion will be nearly $2500 for materials and take an estimated 50 hours labor.

Fig. 10-4. Taildragger conversion.

If an owner must have a rough-field airplane, a proper STOL and power modification should also be made in addition to the taildragger conversion. This will cost more money, but the results will be a very stable, safe, dependable, go-anywhere airplane.

Before you run out and have your tricycle-geared airplane modified, consider the difficulties you might encounter with your piloting skills. Taildraggers require more precision when landing, and are far less forgiving of error than nosewheel airplanes.

A particularly nice taildragger conversion is the Texas Taildragger available from ACT. This is a well-planned kit that will take 50–60 hours labor. It even allows return to tricycle configuration at a later date with only a few hours labor. The tailwheel is hard rubber; however, a Scott or Maule tailwheel can be purchased as part of the STC. ACT claims the following benefits from converting to a taildragger configuration:

- Speed increase of 9 mph
- 465 fpm rate of climb increase
- Better fuel economy
- Increase of 10 lbs in useful load
- More propeller-to-ground clearance
- No nosewheel shimmy
- More versatile aircraft

For further information about taildragger conversions contact:

Aircraft Conversion Technologies
1410 Flightline Dr.
Hangar A, Lincoln Airport
Lincoln, CA 95648
(916) 645-3264

AVCON Conversions
P.O. Box 654
Udall, KS 67146
(800) 872-0988

Gap Seals

Gap seals are extensions of the lower wing surface from the rear spar to the leading edge of the flap or aileron. The seals cover approximately six square feet of open space, allowing a smoother flow of air. In addition to the reduction of parasitic drag, the aircraft will cruise from 1–3 mph faster, and stall from 5–8 mph slower. The seals are often part of a STOL installation. Gap seals are available from:

Flap Seals
P.O. Box 431
Udall, KS 67146
(316) 782-3851

Fuel Systems

Larger or additional fuel tanks increase operational range. Additionally, they are required if you have a large engine installed in the aircraft. Typically, for a 150/152, long-range fuel tanks will cost $1500 (or more) and utilize 45 hours of labor. Such modifications are available from:

Aircraft Conversion Technologies
1410 Flightline Dr.
Hangar A, Lincoln Airport
Lincoln, CA 95648
(916) 645-3264

Flint Aero
1935 N. Marshall Ave.
El Cajon, CA 92020
(619) 448-1551
FAX (619) 448-1571

Noise

Noise reduction has been a problem for all small airplane owners; however, one manufacturer produces an inner window. To reduce cabin noise, the inner windows—essentially storm windows—are installed in the doors. By increasing the window thickness, and including dead airspace, interior noise is reduced (Fig. 10-5). For further information, contact:

Las Vegas Aero Specialties, Incorporated
2772 North Rancho Dr.
Las Vegas, NV 89130
(702) 647-6121

Fig. 10-5. Sound-reducing windows.

Doors

Door catches on older 150s are usually rusted and no longer function to hold the doors open. The installation of a Sky Catch will eliminate this problem. For further information, contact:

R.W. Traves Associates
829 Oak Street
Medina, OH 44256
(216) 723-2778

Drain Valve

Production 150/152 airplanes have no method of properly draining water from the lowest point of the fuel system, the very place where water will gather. The installation of a belly drain at this lowest point will facilitate proper contamination removal. The drain unit costs only a few dollars and can be installed in about 10 minutes. For further information, contact:

C-MODs
P.O. Box 15388
Durham, NC 27704

Oil Filters

Many early aircraft engines were built without spin-on oil filters. In the case of Cessna 150s, a kit is available that fits the O-200 and O-200A engines (Fig. 10-6). For further information contact:

El Reno Aviation, Inc.
P.O. Box 760
El Reno, OK 73036-0760
(405) 262-2387

Fig. 10-6. Oil filter kit that fits the Cessna 150 O-200 engine.

LISTING OF CURRENT STCs

The following STC listing is complete at the time of writing. The STC number is first, followed by a brief description of the modification, then the name and address of the STC holder.

SA69NW: Installation of Matney's engine charge air-air filter assembly (150-150K); Matney's Aircraft Service, 24115 116th S.E., Kent, WA 98031.

SA71GL: Replace existing engine air filter frame assembly with Brackett Aircraft frame assembly (all 150); Brackett Aircraft Specialties, 9600 West 52nd Street, Kenosha, WI 53140.

SA308AE: Installation of A.R.P. industries Inc. carburetor ice detection system 105AP in aircraft powered with Continental, Franklin, and Lycoming engines equipped with Marvel-Schebler MA-2, MA-3, MA-3SPA, MA-4, MA-5, MA-6 and HA-6 series carburetors (all 150); Alfred Puccinelli, DER 1-145, 36 Bay Drive East, Huntington, LI, NY 11743.

SA489EA: Installation of A.R.P. industries Inc. carburetor ice detection system 107AP-12 in aircraft powered with Continental, Franklin, and Lycoming engines equipped with Marvel-Schebler MA-2, MA-3, MA-3SPA, MA-4, MA-5, MA-6 and HA-6 series carburetors (all 150); Alfred Puccinelli, DER 1-145, 36 Bay Drive East, Huntington, LI, NY 11743.

SA666NW: Installation of Teflon control yoke bushings (all 150); George Johnson, 10015 South Meridian, Puyallup, WA 98371.

SA798EA: Installation of Montair exhaust gas combustion monitor kit (all 150); Rosemount Engineering Co., 12001 West 78th Street, Eaden Prairie, MN 55343.

SA800EA: Installation of Whelen anti-collision strobe lights (150 through M, A150K-M, 152, A152); Whelen Engineering Company, Inc., Winter Avenue, Deep River, CT 06417.

SA1177WE: WECO carburetor temperature monitor (all 150); Richard Winnen, 21318 Grace Ave., Torrance, CA 90510.

SA1143CE: Installation of Aero Fabricators muffler assemblies (150, 150A-K and A150K); Aero Fabricators Inc., 1216 North Road, Lyons, WI 53148.

SA1315WE: Installation of Tri-Star Corp. mixture monitor (open exhaust gas temperature probe, gauge, and selector) (150,150A-E); Universal Corp., 730 Independent Ave., Grand Junction, CO 81505.

SA1455NM: Installation of a flame proof auxiliary heater-dryer model 12-1600 (all 150); D.C. Thermol, 311 South 16th Street, La Porte, TX 77571.

SA1626NM: Installation of Electronics International E.G.T./C.H.T. instrument and accessories (all 150/152); Electronics Internations, Inc., 5289 North East Elam Young Pkwy #G200, Hillsboro, OR 97124.

SA2350NM: Installation of Electronics International digital carburetor/outside air temperature gauges (all 150/152); Electronics Internations, Inc., 5289 North East Elam Young Pkwy #G200, Hillsboro, OR 97124.

SA2687NM: Installation of Turboplus/Electronics International digital temperature gauges and switches to reflect new Turboplus face plates to redesignate selected functions or switch positions (all 150/152); Turboplus, Inc., Tacoma Narrows Airport, 1520 26th Ave., NW, Gig Harbor, WA 98335.

SA2693NM: Installation of Electronics Int'l digital volt/amp gauges and accessories (all 150/152); Electronics Internations, Inc., 5289 North East Elam Young Pkwy #G200, Hillsboro, OR 97124.

SA3862NM: Installation of Electronics Int'l digital TIT/EGT/CHT instruments, and accessories (all 150/152); Electronics Internations, Inc., 5289 North East Elam Young Pkwy #G200, Hillsboro, OR 97124.

SA4005NM: Installation of Precise Pulselite control unit in the landing/taxi system (all 150); Precise Flight Inc., 63120 Powell Butte Rd., Bend, OR 97701.

SA1-479: Aero control AP and heading lock GD (all 150); Herbert Baer, 90 Federal Street, Boston, MA 02109.

SA1-630: Dry vacuum pump and instrument vacuum system 113A5 (all 150); Airborne Mechanisms Division, Randolph Manufacturing Company, 13229 Shaw Avenue, East Cleveland, OH 44112.

SA4-965: Autopilot (all 150); Brittain Industries, Inc., P.O. Box 51370, Tulsa, OK 74151.

SA4-1342: Full flow lube oil filter 30409A with element 1A0235 (all 150); Winslow Aerofilter Corporation, 4069 Hollis Street, Oakland, CA 94608.

SA4-1373: Brake locks AB-6531 and AB-6532 (all 150); Johns-Manville Corporation, 22 E. 40 Street, New York, NY 10001.

SA17WE: Conversion of aircraft for parachute jumping and aerial photography operations (all 150); Peterson Aviation, 3100 Airport Avenue, Santa Monica, CA 90406.

SA164WE: Fuel filter PFF-100 (all 150); Pioneer Aero Services, P.O. Box 227, Burbank, CA 91500.

SA534CE: Installation of Canairco 1214 WS supplementary light (all 150); Canairco Limited, 400 1st Avenue North, Minneapolis, MN 55401.

SA1433WE: Installation of Brittain Model CSA-1 Stability Augmentation Systems (all 150); Brittain Industries, P.O. Box 51370, Tulsa, OK 74151.

SA5733SW: Installation of long-range wing fuel tanks (all 150); Custom Aircraft Conversions, 222 West Turbo Drive, San Antonio, TX 78216.

SA1-124: Lube oil filter BP55-1 (all 150); Fram Corporation, 105 Pawtucket Avenue, Providence, RI 02916.

SA4-925: Magnetic flight director 2000 (all 150); Clarkson Company, Paul Spur, AZ.

SA220SO: Tow bar, release mechanism, and safety tow link (all 150); Gasser Banners, Inc., P.O. Box 3502, Metropolitan Airport, Nashville, TN 37217.

SA270SO: Water and ice detector in fuel gascolator and carburetor (all 150); Charles B. Shivers, Jr., 8928 Valleybrook Road, Birmingham, AL 35206.

SA316SO: Carburetor ice detector (all 150); Charles B. Shivers, Jr., 8928 Valleybrook Road, Birmingham, AL 35206.

SA971WE: Installation of Jasco 76540 (35A) alternator kit or Jasco 6555 (50A) alternator kit (all 150); Skytronics, Inc., 227 Oregon Street, El Segundo, CA 90245.

SA150NW: Installation of flap gap seals (150 through M, A150 K-M); B&M Aviation, P.O. Box 1563, Bellingham, WA 98225.

SA172NW: Installation of drooped-type wingtips (150 through M, A150M); Robert C. Cansdale, 29511 9th Place S., Federal Way, WA 98002.

SA175GL: Installation of conventional landing gear (150 through M, A150K-M, 152, A152); Robert L. or Barbara Williams, Box 608, Udall, KS 67146.

SA221GL: Installation of wheel replacement type skis, Fluidyne all-metal (TSO approved) model A2000A main skis, Fluidyne Model AT2000A tail ski (150 through M, A150K-M, 152); Robert L. or Barbara Williams, Box 608, Udall, KS 67146.

SA223GL: Installation of the stall strips (150 through M, A150K-M, 152, A152); MacKenzie Aviation Company, 3847 Bassett Road, Rootstown, OH 44272.

SA268GL: Installation of wheel and ski adapters on Models 150F, G, H, J, K, L, M, 152 aircraft modified per STC SA175GL (150 through M, A150K-M, 152, A152); Robert L. or Barbara Williams, Box 608, Udall, KS 67146.

SA318GL: Installation of Bolen wheel extenders on Cessna models modified per STC SA175GL and/or SA268GL (150 through E); Robert L. or Barbara Williams, Box 608, Udall, KS 67146.

SA324GL: Installation of fuel tank caps (150 through M, A150K-M); John J. Francissen, 426 Pleasant Drive, Roseville, IL 60172.

SA326EA: Wet-to-dry vacuum pump conversion kit 300-3 (150 through H); Airborne Manufacturing Company, 711 Taylor Street, Elyria, OH 44035.

SA1398SO: Remove drain plug AN-806-6 from fuel line drain in belly of aircraft (150 through E); Middle Tennessee Acft. Components, P.O. Box 472, Smithville, TN 37166.

SA1422SO: Installation of Model CC-1 checkpoint computer (150 through M, A150M, 152, A152); Perception Systems, 4500 N. Dixie Hwy., #C-24, West Palm Beach, FL 33407.

SA1235SO: Replacement of the lower fuselage fuel drain cap (P/N AN929-6) with an adapter-type coupling, (belly drain P/N MT-101) and an exposed quick drain valve P/N CAV-160D (all 150/152); Larry L. Lofgren, P.O. Box 472, Smithville, TN 37166.

SA403CE: Install Fluidyne A2000A main skis and NA800 nose ski (150 through C); Fluidyne Engineering Corporation, 5900 Olson Memorial Highway, Minneapolis, MN 55422.

SA527CE: Installation of Hoskins Twilighter Mark I high-intensity light system (150 through G); Symbolic displays, Inc., 1762 McGaw Avenue, Irvine, CA 92705.

SA572CE: Installation of Lycoming 150 or 160-hp Model O-320 (150 through M, A150L-M normal category landplanes, 150G-K seaplanes); Barbara or Bob Williams, Box 431, 213 North Clark, Udall, KS 67146.

SA589WE: Installation of full-flow lube oil filters on aircraft for the benefit of the engine (all 150); Worldwide Aircraft Filter Corp., 1685 Abram Court, P.O. Box 175B, San Leandro, CA 94577.

SA630WE: Installation of oil filter assemblies; Nelson Filter, Division of Nelson Industries, Inc., P.O. Box 280, Stoughton, WI 53589.

SA633GL: Modify airplane to fly on unleaded automotive gasoline, 87 minimum antiknock index, per ATSM Spec. D-439, STC SE634GL; Approved unleaded automotive gasoline, 87 min. antiknock index (all 150); Experimental Aircraft Association, Wittman Airfield, Oshkosh, WI 54901.

SA672GL: Install Aero Ski Mfrg ski model M1500, M1800, or M2000 (150 through M, A150K, 152, A152); Aero Ski Manufacturing Co., Inc., P.O. Box 346, Park Rapids, MN 56470.

SA695CE: Install Frantz oil filter (150 through L, A150K); Schmidt Aero Service, Municipal Airport, Worthington, MN 56187.

SA750CE: Installation of Lycoming 150 and 160-hp Model O-320 engine and McCauley propeller 1C172/TM (150 through M, A150K-M) L; Robert L. and Barbara V. Williams, 117 East First, Udall, KS 67146.

SA844CE: Installation of electropneumatic stall warning system (most 150); Kaeton Engineering Company, 1000 West 55th Street South, Wichita, KS 67217.

SA890SW: Medairco Automatic Fuel Alert F-2 (all 150); Medairco, 3601 East Admiral Place, Tulsa, OK 74150.

SA909CE-W: Install STOL kit (wing leading edge cuffs, drooped tips, stall fences, and aileron gap seals) (150 through M, 152 landplanes and 150G-K seaplanes); Horton Stol-Craft, Wellington Municipal Airport, Wellington, KS 67152.

SA944CE: STOL kit installation (150 through L): Bob or Barbara Williams, Box 608, Udall, KS 67146.

SA917EA: Installation of Grimes Manufacturing Co. aviation white anti-collision strobe light systems, two-light or three-light series 555 for wingtips and tail,

P/N 30-0555 (150 through M, A150K-M); Grimes Manufacturing Company, 515 North Russell Street, Urbana, OH 43078.

SA1148NW: Installation of flap gap seals (150 through M, A150K-L, 152, A152); Tacoma Airways, Route 2, Box 2644, Spanway, WA 98287.

SA1261WE: Installation of control position indicator (CPI) system (150 through G); Sunstrand Data Control, Inc., Subsidiary Sunstrand Corporation, Overlake Industrial Park, Redmond, WA 98052.

SA1346CE: Chromeplate brake disc installation (150 through K, A150K); Engineering Plating & Processing, Inc., 641 Southwest Blvd., Kansas City, KS 66103.

SA1418SO: Replacement of rotor vanes in Airborne 211CC and 212CW vacuum pumps (150 and 152); U.S. Air Source, Ltd., 3640 Atlanta Highway, Athens, GA 30604.

SA1455WE: Installation of Brittain Model CSA-1 Stability Augmentation System (all 150); Brittain Industries, P.O. Box 51370, Tulsa, OK 74151.

SA1473WE: Installation of Brittain Model B2C Flight Control System (all 150); Brittain Industries, P.O. Box 51370, Tulsa, OK 74151.

SA1512WE: Installation of exhaust gas temperature monitoring systems Model EGT-1 (all 150); K S Avionics, 18145 Judy Street, Castro Valley, CA 94546.

SA1663CE: Installation of strut/wing and strut/fuselage fairings, lightning hole covers, and aerodynamic putty (150 through M, 152, A152); Aircraft Development Company, 1326 North Westlink Boulevard, Wichita, KS 67212.

SA1944WE: Installation of Madras wingtips (150 through J); Madras Air Service, Route 2, Madras, OR 97741.

SA1977WE: Installation of recontoured wing and leading edge, stall fences, wingtips and positive aileron seals (150 through L); Sierra Industries, Inc., P.O. Box 5184, Uvalde, TX 78802

SA2053WE: An adjustable lateral trim capability through spring bungee control of aileron per Strato Engineering Company (150 through E); Consulting Aerospace Engineers, 1845 Empire, Burbank, CA 91504.

SA2850SW: Installation of leading edge cuffs, stall fences, aileron seals, wingtips (150 through M, A150K-M); Bob Williams C/B/A/ Bush Conversions, P.O. Box 431, Udall, KS 67146.

SA157NE: Installation of graphic engine monitor system, Model GEM-602 S/N 403 and subsequent (all 150); Insight Instrument Corporation, Box 194, Ellicott Station, Buffalo, NY 14205.

SA2105WE: Installation of Model EGT-3 exhaust gas temperature monitor (with rising temperature alarm) (all 150); K S Avionics, 18145 Judy Street, Castro Valley, CA 94546.

SA2119WE: Installation of recontoured wing and leading edge, stall fences, wingtips and positive aileron seals (150 through L); Sierra Industries, Inc., P.O. Box 5184, Uvalde, TX 78802.

SA2219WE: Installation of Filtrator Company engine crankcase breather and vacuum pump air-oil separator (150 through L, A150L); Beryl D'Shannon Aviation Specialties, Inc., Route 1, Box 172D, Leesburg, FL 32748.

SA2790WE: Installation of angle of attack indicator (150 through L); Thompson Aircraft Company, 8219 Billy Mitchell Drive, Santee, CA 92071.

SA3112WE: Installation of flap slot closures (150 through M, A150L-M, 152, A152); Thermal Aircraft Company, 56 - 850 Thermal Street, Thermal, CA 92274.

SA3345WE: Recognition light installation on horizontal stabilizer (150 through M, A150K-M, 152, A152); Devore Aviation Corporation, Suite B, 6104 Kircher Street, N.E., Albuquerque, NM 87109.

SA4065SW: Metal chip detector in engine oil (150 through M, A150L, M, 152, A152); Aero Logistics International, P.O. Box 34395, Dallas, TX 75234.

SA4302WE: Installation of leading edge cuff on each wing (150 through M, A150M, 152, A152); Marshall E. Quackenbush, P.O. Box 2421, California City, CA 93505.

SA3037SW-D: Automatic flight system AK457 consisting of Century I autopilot with optional omni tracker (150 through M); Century Fit Systems, Inc., F.M. 1195, P.O. Box 610, Mineral Wells, TX 76067.

SA2687WE: Installation of protective device on fuel tank vent line (150C-L); S. Harry Robertson, Research Engineers, 8002 E. Cypress Street, Scottsdale, AZ 85257.

SA607SW: Installation of Mitchell automatic stabilizer model AK193 (150D-G): Century Fit Systems, Inc., F.M. 1195, P.O. Box 610, Mineral Wells, TX 76067.

SA808SW: Installation of Mitchell Model AK246 omni-tracker; Century Fit Systems, Inc., F.M. 1195, P.O. Box 610, Mineral Wells, TX 76067.

SA1809WE: Installation of one 12-gallon auxiliary fuel tank in each outboard wing panel (150D-M, A150K-M, 152, A152); Flint Aero, Inc., Division of Ironco, Inc., P.O. Box 1458, Spring Valley, CA 92077.

SA2191WE: Installation of recontoured wing and leading edge, stall fences, wingtips and positive aileron seals (150 through L); Sierra Industries, Inc., P.O. Box 5184, Uvalde, TX 78802.

SA2192WE: Installation of recontoured wing and leading edge, stall fences, wingtips and positive aileron seals (150 through L); Sierra Industries, Inc., P.O. Box 5184, Uvalde, TX 78802.

SA3733WE: Installation of a special door (right-hand side only) to facilitate aerial photography (150D-L in utility category); Robert M. Craig, 131 Burwell Road, Highland, TX 77562.

SA1431WE: Installation of rudder trim system (150E-G); Robertson Aircraft Corporation, 839 W. Perimeter Road, Renton, WA 98055.

SA287GL: Installation of Lycoming O-320-D2M engine and McCauley Model 1C172/TM propeller using the existing installation hardware on an aircraft previously modified in accordance with STC SA572CE (150F); Max L. Shankin, 1769 Rooker Road, Mooresville, IN 46158.

SA1567SO: Installation of Appalachian Accessories brake rotor P/N 75-27 (150F-K, A150K); Appalachian Accessories, P.O. Box 1077, Tri-City Airport Station, Blountville, TN 37617.

SA2035WE: Installation of Aerial photographic camera kit serial No. 101 (150F-K); Federal Water Pollution Control Administration, Pacific Northwest Water Laboratory, 200 S.W. 35th Street, Corvallis, OR 97330.

SA2846SW: Conversion from tri-gear to conventional gear configuration and reconversion to tri-gear (150F-K); Aircraft Conversion Technologies, Inc., 1410 Flightline Drive, Hangar A, Lincoln Airport, Lincoln, CA 95648.

SA4278WE: Installation of quick-drain valve at low point of aircraft fuel system (150F-M, A150K-M, 152); Aircraft Metal Products Corp., 4206 Glencoe Avenue, Venice, CA 90291.

SA1615CE: Quick drain in fuel line at tee fitting forward of fuel selector valve (150F and subsequent, A150 and subsequent, 152, A152); Wells Aircraft, Inc., Municipal Airport, P.O. Box 858, Hutchinson, KS 67501.

SA1814NM: Installation of Lompoc Aero inner Plexiglas pane in swing-out window frames presently employing a single window (150G-M, A150K-M, 152, A152); Lompoc Aero Specialties, 2772 North Rancho Drive, Las Vagas, NV 89130.

SA1395SW: Revise fuel and oil system for inverted flight (A150K-L); M.H. Spinks, Sr., P.O. Box 11099, Fort Worth, TX 76110.

SA217RM: Installation of Lycoming O-360-A1A engine (180 hp), McCauley 1A170 propeller, revised engine mount and fuel system, dorsal fin, wing leading edge cuffs, wing fences, aileron gap closures and other changes (150L normal category); Nolan E. Stallcup, 2089 Florence, Aurora, CO 80010.

SA550GL: Installation of Mitchell automatic flight system Model AK457 consisting of Century I autopilot with optional omni tracker (152); William McCormick, 55280 Ester, Utica, MI 48087.

SA1000NW: Installation of Lycoming O-235-L2C (modified) (SE792NW) engine, McCauley 1A103/TCM 6958 propeller (152); Kennis G. Blackman, Building C-52-1, Plaine Field, WA 98204.

SA1219EA: Installation of a Sensenich Model 72CKS6-0-56 or -54 metal propeller and a S72CK spinner assembly (152); Sensenich Propeller Corp., Div. of Philadelphia Bourse Inc., East Airport Road, P.O. Box 5100, Lancaster, PA 17601-0100.

SA2290NM: Installation of Elano P/N ELO99001-060 (or later FAA approved revision) muffler in lieu of original Cessna muffler (152); Del-Air, 2121 South Wildcat Way, Porterville, CA 93257.

SA789GL: Installation of Lycoming O-235-L2C engine modified with STC SE70GL in combination with propellers, Sensenich 72CK-S6-0-54 or McCauley 1A103/TCM6958. This allows airplane to fly on unleaded automotive gasoline, 87 minimum antiknock index; EAA Avn Foundation, Inc., Wittman Field, Oshkosh, WI 54903-3065.

SA1008NM: Installation of a Sensenich S72CKS6-0-52, -54 or -56 Propeller/spinner assembly on Lycoming O-235-L2C or O-235-L2C(M) engine (152, A152); Kennis G. Blackman, Building C-52-1, Paine Field, Everett, WA 98205.

SA4057WE: Installation of a muffler and exhaust heat exchanger (152, A152): Flight Research, Inc., Hangar 61, Mojave, CA 93501.

SA1384CE: Install Lycoming O-320-E2D engine and McCauley 1C172TM7458 Propeller (A152); Avcon Industries, 1006 W. 53rd Street N., Wichita, KS 67204.

SA582NW: Fabrication of wire ropes; University Swagging Corp., 800 Northwest 46th Street, Seattle, WA 98108.

SA86NW: Installation of automatic carburetor alternate air control unit; Aero-Deicers, Inc., 5407 S.E. 62nd Avenue, Portland, OR 97206.

SA121CE: Nose and main gear wheel fairing (Jetstreams) using standard unaltered Cessna landing gear and nose gear fork for model and year using 500 x 5 nose and 600 x 6 main gear tires; Creative Designs, 1338 Orkia Drive, Minneapolis, MN 55427.

SA147CE: Moni-Meters on aircraft equipped with King KY-90, KY-95, Narco Mark 4 or Mark 12 transceivers; Mobile Engineering, 220 Southdale Center, Minneapolis, MN 55435.

SA1143SW: Redesigned muffler assemblies; Comisky Engr. Co., Inc., P.O. Box 268, Mena, AR 71953.

SA2190NM: Installation of Electronics Int'l digital volt/amp gauges and accessories; Electronics Int'l, Inc., 5289 N.E. Elam Young Parkway G200, Hillsboro, OR 97124.

SA4302NM: Installation of Electronics Int'l Model SR-8 or Model US-8 digital automatic engine analyzer; Electronics Int'l, Inc., 5289 N.E. Elam Young Parkway G200, Hillsboro, OR 97124.

SA4721NM: Installation of SynCon, Inc. alarm system, model 100C, on nonpressurized metal structure aircraft; SynCon, Inc., P.O. Box 188, Loon Lake, WA 99148.

SA995SW: Increase wing leading edge radius wingtip fairings, and landing light lens; Bob or Barbara Williams, Box 608, Udall, KS 67146.

SA1371SW: Wing leading edge cuff, wingtips and upper surface flow fences; Barbara or Bob Williams, Box 431, 213 North Clark, Udall, KS 67146.

SA1474SW: Installation of MASA 1223000-7 and -8 wingtip; Barbara or Bob Williams, Box 431, 213 North Clark, Udall, KS 67146.

SA1-479: Aero control AP heading Lock GD; Herbert Baer, 80 Federal Street, Boston, MA 02109.

SA1-630: Dry vacuum pump and instrument vacuum system 113A5; Airborne Mechanisms Div. Randolph Manufacturing Co., 13229 Shaw Avenue, East Cleveland, OH 44112.

SA4-965: Autopilot; Brittain Industries, Inc., P.O. Box 51370, Tulsa, OK 74151.

SA4-1342: Full flow lube oil filter 30409A with element 1A0235; Winslow Aerofilter Corp., 4069 Hollis Street, Oakland, CA 94608.

SA4-1373: Brake blocks AB-6531 and AB-6532; Johns-Mansville Corp., 22 E. 40 Street, New York, NY 10001. SA17WE: Conversion of aircraft for parachute jumping and aerial photography operations; Peterson Aviation, 3100 Airport Avenue, Santa Monica, CA 90406.

SA164WE: Fuel filter PFF-100; Pioneer Aero Service, P.O. Box 227, Burbank, CA 91500.

SA12WE: Fiberglass wingtips; Met-Co-Aire, P.O. Box 2216, Fullerton, CA 92633.

SA124EA: Shur-Vent fuel tank filler cap; Alfred R. Puccinelli, DER 1-145, 36 Bay Drive East, Huntington, L.I., NY 11743.

SA596EA: Installation of electronic voltage alarm Drawing No. 80104; McKinley Engineering Corp., P.O. Box 275, Palisades Park, NJ 07650.

SA4319NM: Installation of an oil filter, filter base and mounting plate on the firewalls of airplanes listed on AML No. SA4318NM that are equipped with an FAA-approved Continental Model O-200-A engine installation that has been modified by the installation of an external mounted full flow oil adapter and spin-on oil filter; Aviation Products Development Co., 14337 Keil Road NE, Aurora, OR 97002.

SA1410GL: Install Aero Fabricators shoulder harness and seat belt assembly per Aero Fabricators; Aero Fabricators, Inc., Box 181, 1216 North Rd., Lyons, WI 53148.

SA2433CE: Installation of aileron and/or flap gap seals; Horton STOL-Craft, Wellington Mun. Airport, Wellington, KS 67152.

SA2776NM: Installation of exhaust gas analyzer system; OAE Concepts, Inc., P.O. Box 11196, Boulder, CO 80301.

SA3851: Installation of BAS tail pull handle in the aft fuselage; BAS, Inc., P.O. Box 190, Eatonville, WA 98328.

SA4906NM: Conversion of tricycle landing gear to conventional tailwheel landing gear; William Hilstrum, 13114 Wallace Road SE, Otalla, WA 98559.

SA2381SO: Installation of Appalachian Accessories P/N 75-92 brake rotors; Appalachian Accessories, Tri-City Airport Station, Blountville, TN 37617.

SA615EA: Installation of Whelen anti-collision strobe light system, models H through D, HR or HS (–14 (14 V) or –28 (28 V)), as replacement for originally installed anti-collision lights; Whelen Engineering Co., Inc., Winter Avenue, Deep River, CT 06417.

SA2137SO: Fabrication and installation of nose wheel fairings; Windy's Aircraft Parts, Div. of Southern Avn. of Laurel, Inc., P.O. Box 6408, Laurel, MS 39441.

SA4704NM: Installation of an Anti-Skid pressure accumulator module for the hydraulic brake system: Long's Aircraft Service, 6331 South C Street, Tacoma, WA 98408.

SA2382SO: Installation of Appalachian Accessories P/N 75-93 brake rotors; Appalachian Accessories, Tri-City Airport Station, Blountville, TN 37617.

SA2582CE: Installation of auxiliary seat per Aviation Fabricators; Aviation Fabricators, 805 N. Fourth Street, Clinton, MO 64735.

SA1761SO: Installation of Appalachian Accessories stainless steel brake rotors P/N 75-27; Appalachian Accessories, Tri-City Airport Station, Blountville, TN 37617.

SA4166NM: Installation of Fairchild voltage regulator No. UA78 GUIC to replace the original voltage regulator in Cessna turn coordinator P/N 06610060506; Paul Malkasian, 1036 Euclid Avenue, Edmonds, WA 98020.

SA2335SO: Installation of Appalachian Accessories P/N 75-5 brake discs; Appalachian Accessories, Tri-City Airport Station, Blountville, TN 37617.

SA119NE: Replace original brake discs with discs modified in accordance with Roland Langarzo procedure; Orel Aviation, Inc., 218 Hollywood Avenue, Valley Stream, NY 11581.

SA2-1533: Installation of windshield wiper; Curtiss-Wright/Marquette, Inc., 400 South Main Street, Fountain Inn, SC 29644.

SA2515CE: Installation of replacement wingtips; Horton STOL-Craft, Wellington Municipal Apt., Wellington, KS 67152.

SA1221SO: Fabrication and installation of wheel fairings; Windy's Aircraft Parts, Div. of Southern Avn. of Laurel, Inc., P.O. Box 6408, Laurel, MS 39441.

SA2356SO: Replacement of Clevland brake discs P/N 164-40 or 164-140 with Appalachian Accessories stainless steel brake rotors P/N 75-40; Appalachian Accessories, Tri-City Airport Station, Blountville, TN 37617.

SA2557NM: Installation of KS Avionics EGT/CHT-2 combined exhaust gas and cylinder head temperature monitoring system; KS Avionics, Inc., 25216 Cypress Avenue, Hayward, CA 94544.

SA2960NM: Install Stay-Put (seat locking device); B&D Safety Lock Company, 14409 141st Ave. S.C., Renton, WA 98056.

SA3659SW: Installation of Jetton Alert II alarm system; Jetton Aircraft, P.O. Box 187, Addison, TX 75001.

SA2535SO: Installation of a water fuel detection system; Jack L. Taylor, Co., 308 La Prade Road, Griffin, GA 30223.

SA2586NM: Installation of J.P. Instruments exhaust gas and/or cylinder head temperature monitoring system; J.P. Instruments, P.O. Box 7033, Huntington Beach, CA 92615.

SA6037SW-D: Installation of S-TEC System 40/50 single and two axis automatic flight guidance system, Model ST-298-40/50; S-TEC Corporation, Rt. 4, Bldg. 946, Wolters Ind. Complex, Mineral Wells, TX 76067.

SA1052SW: Installation of Lycoming O-320-E2D engine according to STC SA1034SW on floatplane version; Air Mod Engineering Co., 6611 South Meridian, Oklahoma City, OK 73159.

SA616NE: Installation of a Sensenich Model 69CKS12 or M69CKS12 fixed-pitch metal propeller; Sensenich Propeller Co., Div. of Philadelphia Bourse Inc., East Airport Road, P.O. Box 5100. Lancaster, PA 17601-0100.

SA2360NM: Installation of a Motorola alternator and regulator; Crosswinds STOL, 8134 Lake Otis Parkway, Anchorage, AK 99507.

SA2342CE: Installation of Sensenich 69CD-S12-0-52 propeller; Robert F. Schneberger, 1252 Office Park Road, Apt. 9, W. Des Moines, IA 50265.

SA4711NM: Installation of Sunrise Aviation Sunliter landing light modification; PMDB, Inc., dba Sunrise Aviation, 1314 26th Ave. N.W., Gig Harbor, WA 98335.

SA1978SO: Installation of Appalachian Accessories stainless steel brake discs P/N 75-40; Appalachian Accessories, Tri-City Airport Station, Blountville, TN 37617.

SA432NE: Installation of modified Avco Lycoming O-235-L2C engine with a McCauley propeller Model 1A103/TCM 6958; A.R. Custom Aero Engines, Ltd., 11905-99 Avenue, Surrey, BC V3V 2M6.

SA544NE: Installation of a Textron Lycoming O-290-D2 engine and a Sensenich model 76AM-2-54 propeller; Morse Aero, Inc., P.O. Box 164, Riverside Airport, Marcy, NY 13403.

SA2278NM: Installation of Lycoming O-235-L2C(M) engine and McCauley 1A135/KCM7054 propeller; Altam Corporation, 6269 Solano Drive, San Jose, CA 95119.

SA2604NM: Installation of Lycoming O-235-L2C-M engine; Snohomish Flying Svc., Inc., 9807 Airport Way, Snohomish, WA 98290.

SA867GL: Modify airplane to fly on unleaded automotive gasoline, 87 minimum antiknock index; EAA Avn. Foundation, Inc., Wittman Field, Oshkosh, WI 54903-3065.

SA3438SW-D: Installation of Century automatic flight system Model AK943; Century Flt Systems, Inc., F.M. 1195, P.O. Box 610, Mineral Wells, TX 76067.

SA3439SW-D: Installation of Century automatic flight system Model AK944; Century Flt Systems, Inc., F.M. 1195, P.O. Box 610, Mineral Wells, TX 76067.

SA1760SO: Installation of Appalachian Accessories stainless steel brake rotors P/N 75-15C; Appalachian Accessories, Tri-City Airport Station, Blountville, TN 37617.

SA534CE: Installation of Canairco 1214 WS supplementary light; Canairco Limited, 400 1st Avenue North, Minneapolis, MN 55401.

SA1433WE: Installation of Brittain Model CSA-1 stability augmentation system; Brittain Industries, P.O. Box 51370, Tulsa, OK 74151.

SA2383SO: Installation of Appalachian Accessories brake rotors P/N 75-94; Appalachian Accessories, Tri-City Airport Station, Blountville, TN 37617.

SA4795SW: Installation of Avco Lycoming O-360 or O-320 engine and increase takeoff weight to 1760 pounds; J&S Engineering, Inc., 222 W. Turbo Drive, San Antonio, TX 78216.

SA5733SW: Installation of long-range wing fuel tanks; Aircraft Conversion Technologies, Inc., 1410 Flightline Drive, Hangar A Lincoln Artp., Lincoln, CA 05648.

SA157NE: Installation of Graphic Engine Monitor (G.E.M.) System model GEM-602 S/N 403 and subsequent; Insight Instrument Corp., Box 194, Ellicott Station, Buffalo, NY 14205-0194.

SA1-124: Lube oil filter BP55-1; Fram Corporation, 105 Pawtucket Avenue, Providence, RI 02916.

SA220SO: Tow bar, release mechanism, and safety tow link; Gasser Banners, Inc., P.O. Box 3502, Metropolitan Airport, Nashville, TN 37217.

SA270SO: Water and ice detector in fuel gascolator and carburetor; Charles B. Shivers, Jr., 8928 Valleybrook Road, Birmingham, AL 35206.

SA316SO: Carburetor ice detector: Charles B. Shivers, Jr., 8928 Valleybrook Road, Birmingham, AL 35206.

SA971WE: Installation of Jasco 76540 (35A) alternator kit of Jasco 76555 (50A) alternator kit; Skytronics, Inc., 227 Oregon Street, El Segundo, CA 90245.

SA150NW: Installation of flap gap seals; Robert L. or Barbara V. Williams, Box 431, Udall, KS 67146.

SA172NW: Installation of drooped type wingtips; Robert C. Cansdale, 29511 9th Place S., Federal Way, WA 98002.

11

Modern avionics

CESSNA 150/152 AIRPLANES CAN TRACE their heritage back to 1946. The same basic method of construction is still used, but inside, on the instrument panel, there is no similarity. Modern airplanes have instrument panels that resemble those of spaceships rather than what is needed for simple flying; however, what appears complex is really straightforward in operation and is designed to make flying and navigation easier.

The small-size avionics of today are full of capabilities, such as digital displays and computerized functions. Avionics are about as similar to past equipment as a hand calculator is to a pad and pencil. Price-wise, the new equipment represents bargains as never before seen (Fig. 11-1).

Fig. 11-1. The COM 760 TSO is possibly the most communications radio for the dollar currently on the market.

Twenty years ago a good NAV/COMM cost about $1800 for 200 NAV channels and 360 COMM channels. The radio was panel-mounted, and the VOR display, CDI, was mounted separately. Considering that as a rule of thumb most consumer purchases—rent, houses, automobiles, and the like—today cost four times what they did 20 years ago, that NAV/COMM would cost $7200 today.

Electronics have changed in the past years. Today the radio for $1800 (and, in many cases, a good deal less) will be a NAV/COMM that has the same 200 NAV channels, a necessary increase to 760 COMM channels, digital display, user-programmable memory channels, plus a built-in CDI—all this in a smaller combined package than the radio alone of 20 years ago.

Don't let the price fool you. The market has been moving toward the under-$1000 complete NAV/COMM. Modern avionics really are bargains.

Avionics definitions

Seemingly everything about aviation is identified by abbreviations or buzz-words. Avionics is no different:

A-Panel or Audio Panel. Allows centralized control of all radio equipment.

ADF. Automatic direction finder.

CDI. Course deviation indicator, a panel-mounted, or built into the radio, unit giving a visual output of the navigation receiver.

COMM or COM. VHF transceiver for voice radio communications with FAA facilities, FBOs (unicom), and other airplanes.

DME. Distance measuring equipment.

ELT. Emergency locator transmitter (required by FARs for all but local flying).

HT. Handheld transceiver.

LOC/GS. Localizer/glideslope, a visual output, via CDI, of the glidepath.

Loran-C. A very accurate receiver/computer-based navigation system completely separate from the VOR system. (Loran has become one of the best bargains for navigation equipment. *See* the Loran subheading in this chapter.)

MBR. Marker beacon receiver.

NAV. VHF navigation receiver for making use of VORs.

NAV/COMM or NAVCOM. Combination of a navigation receiver and a communications transceiver in one unit.

XPNDR. Transponder (might not have altitude encoding).

YOUR AVIONICS NEEDS

Most older Cessna two-seaters are poorly equipped with avionics, partly due to the age of installed equipment and partly because those used as primary trainers had only minimal equipment in the first place; therefore, the new owner is faced with making decisions about installing updated avionics. Between the current FAA requirements and aviation industry standards, minimums of avionics equipment have been set. As to what minimums will apply, examine your current and planned flying practices.

VFR flying

In order to equip a plane for VFR flying, you must determine where the flying will be done. Are you planning to fly only from large airports, or only from small, uncontrolled fields? The equipment you install can limit you, particularly with the Class B and Class C airspace requirements.

At the barest minimum, VFR operation requires a NAV/COMM, transponder, and ELT. You could do with only the ELT, but there is just no sense to it if you plan to go anywhere except around the patch.

Although it wasn't too many years ago that most cross-country flying was done by pilotage (reading charts and looking out the windows for checkpoints), today's aviator has become accustomed to the advantages of modern navigation systems.

To properly take advantage of the modern navigation system and the safety it can provide, a VFR installation should include a NAV/COMM (760-channel), transponder, ELT, and Loran-C. With this installation you can comfortably fly pretty much wherever you want.

IFR flying

Flying IFR requires considerably more equipment—naturally, at a much higher cash investment. For operational IFR, minimum equipment would include a dual NAV/COMM (760-channel), MBR, LOC/GS, Mode C transponder, ELT, and clock. To make IFR flying more tolerable, a few items of additional equipment would include RNAV, ADF, Loran-C, audio panel, and DME.

UPDATING YOUR AIRPLANE

Several alternatives are available to fill those vacant spots on the instrument panel or replace aging original equipment (Fig. 11-2). Some alternatives are more expensive than others; some are more practical than others; generally, inexpensive and practical is the recommended path to follow.

Cessna Aircraft Company

Fig. 11-2. Example of a well-filled 1977 Cessna 150 panel with a full center stack consisting of NAV/COMM, transponder, and ADF. The marker beacon indicators and audio panel are on top of the panel. Because this is an Aerobat, an accelerometer is immediately left of the transponder.

New equipment

New equipment is state of the art, offering the newest innovations, best reliability, and—best of all—a warranty. An additional benefit of new equipment is size and efficiency; new solid-state electronic units are physically smaller and draw considerably less electrical power than the tube-type predecessors. This is extremely important for the person wanting a full panel in a small plane, such as a 150/152.

New avionics may be purchased from your local avionics dealer or from a discount house via mail order or a toll-free telephone call.

You can visit your local dealer, purchase all the equipment you want, and have it installed by the dealer. Of course, this will be the most expensive route you can take when upgrading avionics; however, in the long run, it is probably the most practical. You'll have new equipment, expert installation, and service backup. You will also have a nearby dealer you can discuss problems with, should they arise.

Discount-house prices will be considerably cheaper for the initial purchase; however, you might be left out in the cold if there is ever a need for warranty service. Some manufacturers will not honor warranty service requests unless the equipment was purchased from and installed by an authorized dealer. Check first before purchasing. Perhaps this sounds unfair to you, but the policy keeps the authorized dealers in business. If they stay in business, you can find them to repair the equipment.

Used equipment

Used avionics may be purchased from dealers or individuals. Used equipment can be a wise investment, but it can also be very risky. Unless you happen to be an avionics technician, or have access to one, I recommend against the purchase of used avionics. The sole exception to this would be if you are very familiar with the source. Even then I would not recommend the purchase of used equipment for primary IFR service.

If you do want to purchase used radios, *Trade-A-Plane* is a good source. A few words of caution about used avionics might improve the chances for reliable service:

- Don't purchase anything with tubes
- Pass it up if the radio is more than six years old
- Don't buy it if the manufacturer has gone out of business because parts availability could be a real problem
- Let the radio stay "where it is" if being sold "as is" or if the radio was "working when removed"

Reconditioned equipment

Several companies advertise reconditioned avionics at bargain—or at least low—prices. This equipment has been removed from service and completely checked out by an avionics shop. Any components that have failed or are likely to fail have been replaced; however, you are still getting what you pay for. Reconditioned is not new, not even remanufactured. It is used. Everything in the unit has been used, but not everything will be replaced during reconditioning. You will have some new parts and some old parts.

Reconditioned equipment purchases make sense for the budget-minded owner. Reconditioned radios do offer a fair-priced buy and are usually warrantied by the seller. Few pieces of reconditioned equipment will be more than six or seven years old.

Loran

Many makes of Loran-C units are on the market. Prices vary according to the capabilities of the respective units (Fig. 11-3). For instance, an inexpensive unit might have a limited memory that must be input by the pilot; an expensive unit might have navigational coordinates of every U.S. VOR and airport already in permanent memory.

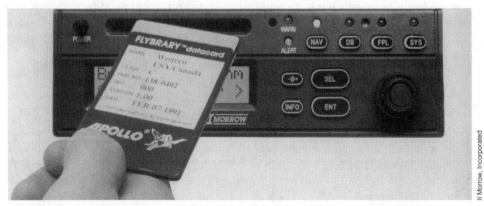

Fig. 11-3. Apollo Loran receiver by II Morrow is easily updated by inserting a card-sized database into the slot above the digital display.

Long range navigation (Loran), is based upon low-frequency radio signals, rather than the very high frequency (VHF) signals normally associated with FAA nav-aids. Loran is operated by the U.S. Coast Guard, not the FAA, and was not really intended for general aviation usage; however, with the advent of computer-based Loran-C, Loran has become the hot and affordable new equipment on the avionics market.

The first general aviation Loran units on the market were reworked marine versions, but as market demand mushroomed, receivers dedicated to aviation emerged. Most receivers are not certified for IFR operations, but this does not mean the receivers are incapable or inaccurate. This only means the manufacturer was unwilling to spend the many dollars necessary for IFR certification, which is reflected in price differences. IFR-certificated models are available for more than $8000. Uncertificated versions are generally available for fewer than $2000.

Without going into extensive theory about operation, the Loran-C unit can—by receiving several Loran signals at one time and comparing them with preprogrammed known factors—determine its exact location with accuracy of a few hundred feet. This will be displayed on the instrument's readout as latitude and longitude.

Then, by use of waypoints, the pilot can navigate. The waypoints are geographical locations entered into the Loran unit by the pilot via the keyboard. Waypoints can be geographical coordinates or—if the receiver is properly programmed—standard three-letter designators for airports or VORs (DCA, Washington National; SJT, San Angelo, Texas; BRK, Brooke VOR). The unit will then compare the known signals to the geographical inputs and give constant trip progress information concerning course direction, time elapsed, estimated time enroute, distance traveled, distance to destination, and the like—all in one box.

Loran-C offers distinct advantages over normal VHF navaids such as VORs. Due to the propagation properties of radio waves at the frequencies utilized by Loran, there is no line-of-sight range limit. This means that, unlike VORs, Loran is usable many hundreds of miles from the actual transmitting stations.

This can be very practical for typical lightplane operations conducted below 2000 ft. AGL and in remote areas, which are limiting factors for navigating by use of standard VORs. Low altitude means that the VOR might be of little or no use because the VOR's VHF signals are line-of-sight. This is where Loran shines. Loran-C is usable right down to the ground.

Other modern panel devices

High-technology consumers have become hung up on digital readouts seen every day on the clock at the bank, on wristwatches, on TVs, and the like. Airplanes are no different, and several small instruments are available with digital readouts. Among the more common are the digital outside air temperature gauge, the digital volt meter, and the digital chronometer. For engine monitoring, digital EGT and CHT gauges are available (*see* chapter 5).

Avionics advice

To some pilots, the instrument panel is a functional device; to others, it is a statement made by the owner. In either case, care must be taken when filling up the panel. Don't install instrumentation merely for the sake of filling holes. Plan it well, making it functional and easy to use. Above all else, do it economically.

Don't trade in equipment that is working properly. You cannot replace it for what a dealer will give you. Keep it as your second system.

My strongest recommendation for purchasing avionics is to save your money until you can buy new equipment. New equipment offers more features, smaller sizes, reduced electrical appetite, and better reliability. Additionally, due to inflation, new avionics prices represent a better bargain than prices of 15–20 years ago.

HEARING LOSS

After sitting for many hours in a 150 on a long trip, my ears hurt. Then, after landing, my ears will buzz for several hours. This is an all too common effect of flying in a small airplane and can lead to permanent hearing loss after repeated assaults of loud noise. Unfortunately, very little can be done to a 150/152 cabin to make it quiet.

The FAA issued Advisory Circular AC 91-35 regarding noise, hearing damage, and fatigue. The AC is partially reprinted:

> **Purpose.** This circular will acquaint pilots with the hazards of regular exposure to cockpit noise. Especially pertinent are piston-engine, fixed-wing, and rotary-wing aircraft.
>
> **Background.** Modern general aviation aircraft provide comfort, convenience, and excellent performance. At the same time that the manufacturers have developed more powerful engines, they have given the occupants better noise protection and control, so that today's aircraft are more powerful, yet quieter than ever. Still, the levels of sound associated with powered flight are high enough for general aviation pilots to be concerned about participating in continuous operations without some sort of personal hearing protection.
>
> Most long-time pilots have a mild loss of hearing. Many pilots report unusual amounts of fatigue after flights in particularly noisy aircraft. Many pilots have temporary losses of hearing sensitivity after flights. And many pilots have difficulty understanding transmissions from the ground, especially during critical periods under full power, such as takeoff.
>
> **Discussion.** Like carbon monoxide, noise exposure has harmful effects that are cumulative—they add together to produce a greater effect on the listener as sound intensity is increased and as the length of time listening is increased. A noise that could cause a mild hearing loss to a person who heard it once a week for a few minutes might make that person quite deaf if the exposure to the noise lasted eight hours.

Noise-reducing headphones

As with particularly every problem, there is a fix. In the case of a noise problem in small airplanes, the recommended fix is use of noise-reducing headphones. The headphones provide a means to use the radio, yet seal out other sounds. Headphone quality controls the amount of hearing protection afforded. For proper protection, you must use full earcover headphones, not the lightweight stereo types so popular with the high school set. Headphone manufacturers advertise in pilot magazines and *Trade-A-Plane*.

Don't make a headphone selection based solely on an advertisement. Talk to other pilots, then go to an aviation supply store and try a few on. Pay particular attention to the weight because the weight will become a fatigue factor during long periods of flying. Also, watch out for headphones that seem to grip too tightly because the headphones will feel like a vise after only a few minutes. After you find the headphones you like, purchase and use them regularly.

Intercom systems

All intercoms are designed to provide a means of communications between the pilot and passengers. Intercom systems come in all types and with varied capabilities. Some are an extension of the audio panel, primarily for the use of the pilot. A stand-alone intercom is not hooked to anything in the airplane, typically completely portable. No matter what type you select, ear protection will be provided for everyone by the headphones and the actual voice communications within the airplane are carried on via the intercom.

A few pilots supply their passengers headsets without microphones. I don't advocate this. Flying is a fun thing, and no one should be shut out, but it is an interesting point.

12

Learn to fly in your airplane

SOME YEARS AGO, Cessna Aircraft Company embarked on a campaign to encourage student pilots to purchase a new airplane and learn to fly in it. Although the price of any new airplane that is still in production has gone straight through the roof, this is not to say that a carefully selected used 150 might not be a wise first-time airplane investment for the student pilot.

In this chapter, ownership is limited to those individuals who wish to proceed with flying as a career and need to amass lots of practice time for a commercial certificate. This is probably the only time that student ownership of an airplane can be financially justified. That "financial justification"equates to saving money.

OWNERSHIP

Ownership of an airplane is a source of great pride, to say nothing of the convenience of going at any time and returning at any time, with no restrictions—disregarding restrictions of the pilot certificate and weather. The owner will never be tied to an FBO's schedule.

My research has revealed that the typical purchaser of a 150/152 pursuing a career in aviation has paid cash; therefore, expense worksheet scenarios in this chapter do not reflect that cash outlay. (If an owner has taken out a loan, the monthly payment must be multiplied by 12 and that result added to the total annual fixed cost.)

Consideration of the real costs of ownership—not included in the purchase price—requires more terminology to review:

Fixed costs. The cost of ownership, before any flying is done, that typically does not vary from month to month. Included in fixed costs are hangar or tie-down fees, state or local property tax on the aircraft, insurance premiums, and the cost—a variable figure—of the annual inspection. (Additionally, any loan payments are a fixed cost.)

Operating cost. The cost of fuel per hour (gas and oil), an engine reserve account (for the day when TBO arrives), and a general maintenance fund (to repair those usually small items that need a mechanic's or technician's attention), oil changes, periodic AD inspections, minor mechanical defects, avionics problems, and the like.

Use cost per hour. The total of the fixed costs and operating costs, divided by the number hours of operation. It is the use cost that is the all-important number that will show if ownership is practical.

Here is a worksheet to help you figure out all the costs involved with ownership. I use the term "all" very loosely because nothing regarding airplane ownership is "fixed," except that ownership will cost you money. Fill in the blanks, and follow the instructions for computations.

Fixed cost

    12 months of storage $_____

    Annual state/local tax $_____

    Insurance premium (12 months) $_____

    Annual inspection (estimated) $_____

    Annual loan payment (optional) $_____

    Total fixed cost $_____

Operating cost

    Fuel cost/gallon × GPH = $_____

    Engine reserve per hour $_____

    General maintenance per hour $_____

    Instructor fee per hour (as applicable) $_____

    Total operating cost per hour $_____

For flights without an instructor, these computations will give solo cost only. Check your local FBO's posted rates for instruction in owner-flown airplanes. The rates might be higher than in the FBO's own airplanes. Be sure to consider this when figuring your projected hourly costs.

Examples

Let's examine a hypothetical case of outright ownership without instructor charges. A check with the local FBO for rates fills in the blanks for computation.

Fixed Cost

    12 months of storage $480.00

    Annual state/local tax $120.00

    Insurance premium (12 months) $870.00

    Annual inspection (estimated) $500.00

    Total fixed cost $1970.00

Operating Cost

    Fuel at $2.25/gallon × 5 GPH = $11.25

    Engine reserve per hour $3.50

    General maintenance per hour $4.00

    Total operating cost $18.75 per hour

The example is based upon $40 per month for outside tiedown, which is very modest. A one percent local tax is applied to the $12,000 value of our hypothetical airplane. The insurance cost is an estimate based on the value of the airplane and the pilot's lack of experience. The annual inspection is a gray area because who knows what expenses lurk within an airplane waiting to be discovered at inspection time? I do feel that for a typical 150 that has had good care, the estimate given will be adequate. The 5 GPH is an estimate of 150 fuel usage. An engine reserve of $3.50 per hour should be adequate to properly maintain an engine and assure its overhaul at TBO. The general maintenance rate of $4 per flying hour will allow a reserve to build up for unforeseen mechanical difficulties (brakes, nosewheel, shimmy dampener, flap actuator jack problems, radio failure, and the like) to be repaired. At the end of our computations, we have a fixed cost of $1970 per year and an operating cost of $18.75 per hour.

Now let's take this further into our projected costs based upon the amount of planned flying. Use the following formula to determine the projected hourly costs of aircraft operation:

Annual hours flown × operating cost = $_____
+
Annual fixed costs $_____
Total $_____
Total ÷ number of hours flown = $_____ per hour

Let's apply the hypothetical costs to this formula. The first example will be for one flying hour per year.

1 hour to be flown × $18.75 = $18.75
+
Annual fixed costs $1970.00
Total $1988.75
Total ÷ number of hours flown = $1988.75 per hour

That example was a worst-case scenario, only one flying hour for the year, which serves to show that the more hours flown, the cheaper the hourly costs will be.

Now let's do the same problem for 50 hours of flying, which is often all that an airplane flies:

50 hours to be flown × $18.75 = $937.50
+
Annual fixed costs $1970.00
Total $2907.50
Total ÷ number of hours flown = $58.15 per hour

And again for 100 hours:

100 hours to be flown × $18.75 = $1875.00
+
Annual fixed costs $1970.00
Total $3845
Total ÷ number of hours flown = $38.45 per hour

And a last time for 200 hours of operation:

200 hours to be flown × $18.75 = $3750.00
+
Annual fixed costs $1970.00
Total $5720.00
Total ÷ number of hours flown = $28.60 per hour

More examples

This was a very economical example. Here is the same group of computations for what is more likely to be the cost in a metropolitan area.

Fixed Cost
    12 months of storage $1200.00
    Annual state/local tax $576.00
    Insurance premium (12 months) $940.00
    Annual inspection (estimated) $700.00
    Total fixed cost $3416.00

Operating Cost
    Fuel at $2.40/gallon × 5 GPH = $12.00
    Engine reserve per hour $3.50
    General maintenance per hour $5.00
    Total operating cost $20.50 per hour

The above example is based upon $100 per month for a tiedown, which is typical on a large airport. A 4.8 percent local property tax is applied to the $12,000 value of the hypothetical airplane. The insurance cost is an estimate based on the value of the airplane and the pilot's lack of experience and the location of the aircraft. The annual inspection remains a gray area; however, the inspection will no doubt be more expensive at a larger airport. The cost of fuel per gallon was quoted by the FBO at Dulles International Airport, and the 5 GPH is an estimate of 150 fuel usage. The engine reserve is the same as for the first series of examples, but the general maintenance reserve increases due to increased shop rates at larger facilities. At the end of the computations, is a fixed cost of $3416.00 per year, and an operating cost of $20.50 per hour.

Now let's apply this to the formulas again for a comparison to the first example.

50 hours to be flown × $20.50 = $1025.00
+
Annual fixed costs $3416.00
Total $4441.00
Total ÷ number of hours flown = $88.82 per hour

100 hours:

100 hours to be flown × $20.50 = $2050.00
+
Annual fixed costs $3416.00
Total $5466.00
Total ÷ number of hours flown = $54.66 per hour

200 hours:

200 hours to be flown × $20.50 = $4100.00
+
Annual fixed costs $3416.00
Total $7516.00
Total ÷ number of hours flown = $37.58 per hour

Compare these figures with straight rental of a similar airplane at your local FBO. Keep in mind that you can sometimes purchase blocks of time from an FBO for a reduced rate, often reduced by as much as 10 percent. Just out of interest, my local FBO charges $43.50 per hour (solo) for a 152 (summer of 1992).

AGAINST OWNERSHIP

At the first part of this chapter I mentioned the pride of ownership, and the convenience of being free of the FBO's control. This is all very true, but there is a price to be extracted for ownership.

All maintenance will be your responsibility; you won't have a squawk book to report complaints and have the FBO repair them before you fly again. You will have to either fix them yourself or pay to have them fixed out of your own pocket.

Do you like the clean airplane the FBO rents you? If you own it, you will have to keep it clean. Know how big the airplane is? Just the top surfaces of the wings are better than 150 square feet, and that's a lot when you are washing and polishing—just think of the total surface to be cleaned and polished. I have not mentioned the windshield, windows, upholstery, carpets, oil-stained belly, and the like.

If the real incentive for ownership is to log hours cheaply, you might find ownership a financial advantage—providing you purchase a good airplane that can be later sold at a similar price to that of purchase.

If you desire an airplane to learn in, then keep for personal use, you will not view the various maintenance and cleaning tasks as loading yourself down with work. That will all be found under pride of ownership.

Advice

Seek out a reputable flight training center and get their advice. A science has been made of pilot training, including video tapes, simulators, and computers. Training centers have good answers to just about any question you could possibly ask. Compare the costs of certificates and ratings with the cost of ownership before buying a plane to save money.

A LITTLE STORY

This talk about pilot training brings to mind a story related to me by a friend at the Cessna factory. It seems that Cessna ran an advertisement in Popular Mechanics magazine publicizing the company's guaranteed-price pilot training program that read:

"Cessna will make you a pilot for $2990. Guaranteed."

A short time after this ad first appeared, Cessna received a letter from a small group of women. The letter read:

> Dear Cessna,
>   In response to your ad in the latest *Popular Mechanics* magazine, we would like to order a pilot. The following particulars should be built into your design: Male—quick learner, height six feet two inches to six feet five inches, weight 190 pounds, chest 46 inches, waist 34 inches, shoe size 11—optional: hairy chest, muscular build, dark blue eyes, and wavy brown hair.
>   We see by your ad that this pilot is guaranteed, but we would prefer to take him on approval. We have several other people also interested in your pilot program. Could we get a discount on case lots?

13

Hangar flying
the Little Wonders

GO TO ANY AIRPORT, SIT AROUND, AND TALK AND LISTEN. This is hangar flying. Pilot's probably log more hangar flying than any other type of flying. Although you sometimes have to filter out the rumors, tall tales, and the like, you can learn a lot from hangar flying just by listening. This chapter is comprised of hangar flying anecdotes to help you attain a better understanding of the 150/152 airplanes. The hangar flying includes bits and pieces about clubs, comments from owners, pilots, mechanics, and line service. Charts at the end of the chapter compare the relative safety of the 150/152 to other lightplanes.

CLUBS

The single most useful productive action an owner can do is join a club that supports the airplane of interest. The Cessna 150/152 Club is the sole organization that supports only these airplanes. This unique club offers a monthly newsletter, the *Cessna 150-152 News*, which includes maintenance and modification ideas; the exchange of technical information and manufacturers' service letters; service difficulty reports, airworthiness directives, and airworthiness alerts; want ads; and help is as close as a telephone. Contact:

Cessna 150-152 Club
P.O. Box 15388
Durham, NC 27704
(919) 471-9492

The Cessna Owner Organization publishes a monthly full-color magazine, the *Cessna Owner Magazine*, for its members. The magazine includes news, safety articles, ADs, service difficulty reports, classified ads, and product reviews. Want ads are included in each issue. The organization supports all models of Cessna airplanes including 150/152s. Contact:

Cessna Owner Organizations
P.O. Box 337
Iola, WI 54945
(800) 331-0038

WHAT THEY SAY

Because so many 150/152s are flying and because so many pilots learned to fly in these planes, comments about the little two-seaters abound. The following is a synopsis of what everyone from pilots to insurance carriers have said about the Cessna 150/152s.

Pilots

The 150's not the greatest on takeoff in the summer, but it gets there, even with two big guys aboard.

The nosewheel shimmies.

I jazzed mine up with a new interior and a set of sheepskin seat covers.

I have the large wheels and heavy nose gear on mine, and will land anywhere that a taildragger will. I've been doing it for years, and have never bent anything. Just keep the weight off the nosewheel.

The noise level is too high, so I bought sound-reducing (headache-reducing) headphones.

I just had a 150-hp engine installed—wow! The next step is a Horton STOL conversion.

I have the auto-fuel STC. Now when I need gas I taxi across the road to the corner gas station and fill it up. Of course, I never did this before (wink).

They can really give you a rough ride on a bumpy day.

I used to take out the right seat and load up with watermelons, 300 or 400 pounds of them, then fly off from between the rows of melon plants. It's not hard to do if you're young and stupid.

The cabin is a little narrow for two big people.

If you're doing a lot of dirt strip work, get a set of improved wingtips like Deemers. They will allow you to touch down a little slower. Also, get protective material installed on the leading edge of the prop to protect it from little stones.

Most of the time I fly by myself, so this is a very economical (cheap) plane to fly and maintain. Not fast, but it gets there.

The visibility in a busy traffic pattern is poor, but that's the same for all high-wingers.

Love the big flaps. They can really save a poor approach.

I have a '64 model with manual flaps, and plan to keep it. I don't like the electric flaps; there's too much that can break on them.

I like the manual flaps, I have instant positive control of them, unlike the slow electric jobs.

I was going to build a homebuilt, but having a 150 is cheaper. Besides, if I ever want to sell it, I can. Try that with your homebuilt.

I want to put a STOL kit and larger engine on mine, then I can tackle the off-airport places here on the farm.

The 150 keeps you sharp in windy conditions. It's light, and blows around.

You have to pay attention to your speed on approaches, or you'll learn about stalls very quickly.

If you make your approach too fast, you'll pass right over the best part of the runway, still in the air.

The 150 is a two-finger airplane. You can fly it with the lightest of touches. Perhaps spritely would be more appropriate a phrase. It's not at all like the heavy-feeling Piper PA-28s. I feel there is a real connection between the pilot and the airplane. You order, and the plane responds. There is no pushing around the 150. Guess I just can't say enough good about how it handles. (**Note:** This is about as close to defining the true handling characteristics of a 150 as I have ever heard. I have to agree, the 150 is a two-finger airplane; however, this lightness can be a detriment in windy conditions.)

Owners

My old 150 was real good on maintenance; it didn't need much. Wish I had it back.

My last annual cost $375, and that's in the high-cost Washington, D.C., area. I'm real pleased with that.

The 12-volt batteries for the 150s are a lot cheaper than the 24-volt jobs needed for the 152.

The 152 uses more gas than the 150 I used to have, and I still have a lead fouling problem. I can't say that I am overjoyed with the 152, not for what it cost me compared to how I benefited.

The 150 is today's Model 'A' of the airplane world.

The only real problem I've had is nosewheel shimmy. Just keep the nosewheel light on rollout.

I wish the wingtips were made of something more durable than the junk plastic Cessna uses. Nothing seems to patch them except replacement.

The guy who put the key start in the 150s had a brother-in-law who manufactures starter parts, and I'm supporting him.

The 150 is a cheap plane to fly, about the cheapest around, unless you have an old Cub. But that'll cost you more to buy than a 150, and a lot more to maintain. You wash and polish aluminum; you replace fabric.

I like the straight-tail 150s, with pull starters and manual flaps. They don't cost as much to maintain. The mogas STCs are good; now we can do legally what we've been doing for many years. We never had a fuel tank here for airplanes, just for the tractor and mowing machine. I've often wondered if the fellow that delivered the gas ever wondered about all the gallons of fuel we used in the tractor.

Mechanics

There's not much that can go wrong with a Cessna high-wing that creates any mystery. They were built tough.

The new 150s with the key start can be a problem with the starter drive. Cessna should have left it simple with the pull handle; at least you could still start if the handle broke. The new Lycoming engine doesn't get on much better with 100LL fuel than the older Continentals. Guess that's the price of progress.

These planes are simple enough for the typical owner to care for with little supervision.

Any plane that can take the abuse a trainer gets and come back for more—that's thousands of hours or more—is okay by me.

Have the quick drain installed in the belly. It'll keep the water and debris out of the carb.

I wish all pilots—not just 150 and 152 drivers—would learn to properly lean. This simple procedure would add hundreds of hours to each engine's life, save lots of little pesky maintenance, and save fuel.

Probably the biggest complaint I hear is nosewheel shimmy. It's easy to fix—in fact, sometimes for free. Just keep the nose light when taking off and landing. You don't have to be doing 70 mph before you take it into the air.

Line service

Cessna 150s don't create much excitement 'round here, but they're cheap to fly. Can't say that about many other planes.

Used to be the only 150s coming here had a grinning student pilot inside with a logbook needing a signature. Recently, though, I've begun to see some that are privately owned, not just students passing through. Some of 'em are fixed up real fancy.

High wings are harder to fuel then low wings.

Wish all Cessnas had steps on the struts. They make refueling much easier, and eliminate the need for a stepladder.

All the old Cessna drivers were sure happy to see red (80/87 octane) fuel again.

Miniheavy iron, I call them. That's the highly modified 150s I've been seeing lately. Saw one the other day with a 180-hp engine and a constant-speed prop. He left the ground in about a hundred feet. It had big tundra wheels, even on the nose.

Some of the 150 drivers are refueling out of their cars. Guess it saves money for the owners, and they claim the auto gas runs better in their planes.

We sell mogas here, and the older 150s seem to run well on it; besides, it's cheaper than 100LL.

150s mean students on cross-country flights.

Sales

I like to sell 150s to novices because they can finish their learning in the plane, get their hours, and then get their investment back.

I've sold several to older couples who no longer have a need for a larger, more expensive plane.

Sometimes you will find a real bargain, if you are willing to overlook some minor appearance problems.

A 150 makes a good investment; if you take care of it, it will take care of you. You'll get most every penny back out of it that you put in . . . maybe even a profit.

Recently, I sold a 150 with a STOL kit on it to a couple who retired to Alaska. They sold their $140,000 Mooney, and went for the bush.

Insurance carriers

Cessna 150/152 airplanes are good business for us. Whether the plane is used for instructional or purely recreational flying, we feel confident in insuring them.

The 150 is a rugged plane, very easy to fly, yet has quirks that require the pilot to be proficient in his skills.

Mechanically, the little Cessnas are easy to put back together if they are broken. Parts are never the problem they can be on some other makes and models.

Cost-wise, insurance is expensive, no matter how you put it, but coverage cost for a 150 is low, even for a low-time pilot.

NTSB STATISTICS

The following tables of comparative accident data are a compilation of a study made by the National Transportation Safety Board. All figures are based upon the adjusted rate of 100,000 hours of flying time. It's interesting to note where the aircraft are placed on these charts: worst at the top, best at the bottom. If you are unsure of what some of the aircraft are, consult *The Illustrated Buyer's Guide to Used Airplanes—3rd edition* (TAB Book No. 4052).

Fatal accident rate comparison by manufacturer

Make/mean fatal accident rate (per 100,000 hours)

Bellanca	4.84
Grumman	4.13
Beech	2.54
Mooney	2.50
Piper	2.48
Cessna	1.65

Cessna 180	3.24
Cessna 170	2.88
Cessna 185	2.73
Cessna 150	2.48
Piper PA-28	2.37
Beech 33, 35, 36	2.22
Grumman AA-5	2.20
Cessna 182	2.08
Cessna 172	1.41

Engine failure rate (per 100,000 hours)

Globe GC-1	12.36
Stinson 108	10.65
Ercoupe	9.50
Grumman AA-1	8.71
Navion	7.84
Piper J-3	7.61
Luscombe 8	7.58
Cessna 120/140	6.73
Piper PA-12	6.54
Bellanca 14-19	5.98
Piper PA-22	5.67
Cessna 195	4.69
Piper PA-32	4.39
Cessna 210/205	4.25
Aeronca 7	4.23
Aeronca 11	4.10
Taylorcraft BC	3.81
Piper PA-24	3.61
Beech 23	3.58
Cessna 175	3.48
Mooney M-20	3.42
Piper PA-18	3.37
Cessna 177	3.33
Cessna 206	3.30

In-flight airframe failure rate (per 100,000 hours)

Bellanca 14-19	1.49
Globe GC-1	1.03
Ercoupe	0.97
Cessna 195	0.94
Navion	0.90
Aeronca 11	0.59
Beech 33, 35, 36	0.58
Luscombe 8	0.54
Piper PA-24	0.42
Cessna 170	0.36
Cessna 210/205	0.34
Cessna 180	0.31
Piper PA-22	0.30
Aeronca 7	0.27
Beech 23	0.27
Cessna 120/140	0.27
Piper PA-32	0.24
Taylorcraft BC	0.24
Piper J-3	0.23
Mooney M-20	0.18
Piper PA-28	0.16
Cessna 177	0.16
Cessna 182	0.12

In-flight airframe failure rate
(per 100,000 hours)

Cessna 206	0.11
Grumman AA-1	0.09
Cessna 172	0.03
Cessna 150	0.02

Stall rate
(per 100,000 hours)

Aeronca 7	22.47
Aeronca 11	8.21
Taylorcraft BC	6.44
Piper J-3	5.88
Luscombe 8	5.78
Piper PA-18	5.49
Globe GC-1	5.15
Cessna 170	4.38
Grumman AA-1	4.23
Piper PA-12	3.27
Cessna 120/140	2.51
Stinson 108	2.09
Navion	1.81
Piper PA-22	1.78
Cessna 177	1.77
Grumman AA-5	1.76
Cessna 185	1.47
Cessna 150	1.42
Beech 23	1.41
Ercoupe	1.29
Cessna 180	1.08
Piper PA-24	0.98
Beech 33, 35, 36	0.94
Cessna 175	0.83
Piper PA-28	0.80
Mooney M-20	0.80
Cessna 172	0.77
Cessna 210/205	0.71
Bellanca 14-19	0.60
Piper PA-32	0.57
Cessna 206	0.54
Cessna 195	0.47
Cessna 182	0.36

Hard landing rate
(per 100,000 hours)

Beech 23	3.50

Grumman AA-1	3.02
Ercoupe	2.90
Cessna 177	2.60
Globe GC-1	2.58
Luscombe 8	2.35
Cessna 182	2.17
Cessna 170	1.89
Beech 33, 35, 36	1.45
Cessna 150	1.37
Cessna 120/140	1.35
Cessna 206	1.30
Piper PA-24	1.29
Aeronca 7	1.20
Piper J-3	1.04
Grumman AA-5	1.03
Cessna 175	1.00
Cessna 180	0.93
Cessna 210/205	0.82
Piper PA-28	0.81
Cessna 172	0.71
Piper PA-22	0.69
Taylorcraft BC	0.48
Cessna 195	0.47
Piper PA-18	0.43
Piper PA-32	0.42
Cessna 185	0.42
Navion	0.36
Mooney M-20	0.31
Piper PA-12	0.23
Stinson 108	0.19

Ground loop rate
(per 100,000 hours)

Cessna 195	22.06
Stinson 108	13.50
Luscombe 8	13.00
Cessna 170	9.91
Cessna 120/140	8.99
Aeronca 11	7.86
Aeronca 7	7.48
Cessna 180	6.49
Cessna 185	4.72
Piper PA-12	4.67
Piper PA-18	3.90
Taylorcraft BC	3.58
Globe GC-1	3.09

Grumman AA-1	2.85
Piper PA-22	2.76
Ercoupe	2.74
Beech 23	2.33
Bellanca 14-19	2.10
Piper J-3	2.07
Cessna 206	1.73
Cessna 177	1.61
Grumman AA-5	1.47
Piper PA-32	1.42
Cessna 150	1.37
Piper PA-28	1.36
Piper PA-24	1.29
Cessna 210/205	1.08
Cessna 182	1.06
Cessna 172	1.00
Mooney M-20	0.65
Beech 33, 35, 36	0.55
Navion	0.36
Cessna 175	0.17

Landing undershoot rate (per 100,000 hours)

Ercoupe	2.41
Luscombe 8	1.62
Piper PA-12	1.40
Globe GC-1	1.03
Cessna 175	0.99
Grumman AA-1	0.95
Taylorcraft BC	0.95
Piper PA-22	0.83
Piper PA-32	0.70
Bellanca 14-19	0.60
Aeronca 11	0.59
Piper PA-28	0.59
Aeronca 7	0.59
Piper PA-24	0.57
Piper J-3	0.57
Stinson 108	0.57
Cessna 120/140	0.53
Cessna 195	0.47
Grumman AA-5	0.44
Piper PA-18	0.43
Beech 23	0.43
Cessna 185	0.41
Mooney M-20	0.37

Cessna 170	0.36
Navion	0.36
Cessna 150	0.35
Cessna 210/205	0.33
Cessna 206	0.32
Cessna 172	0.26
Cessna 182	0.24
Beech 33, 35, 36	0.21
Cessna 180	0.15
Cessna 177	0.10

Landing overshoot rate (per 100,000 hours)

Grumman AA-5	2.35
Cessna 195	2.34
Beech 23	1.95
Piper PA-24	1.61
Piper PA-22	1.33
Cessna 175	1.33
Stinson 108	1.33
Cessna 182	1.21
Aeronca 11	1.17
Luscombe 8	1.08
Piper PA-32	1.03
Globe GC-1	1.03
Mooney M-20	1.01
Cessna 172	1.00
Cessna 170	0.99
Grumman AA-1	0.95
Piper PA-12	0.93
Cessna 210/205	0.89
Cessna 177	0.88
Piper PA-18	0.81
Cessna 206	0.81
Piper PA-28	0.80
Cessna 120/140	0.71
Ercoupe	0.64
Bellanca 14-19	0.60
Cessna 180	0.56
Navion	0.54
Aeronca 7	0.48
Cessna 150	0.35
Piper J-3	0.34
Cessna 185	0.31
Beech 33, 35, 36	0.23

Appendix A

Advertising abbreviations

AD airworthiness directive
ADF automatic direction finder
AF airframe
AF&E airframe and engine
AI aircraft inspector
ALT altimeter
ANN annual inspection
AP autopilot
ASI airspeed indicator
A&E airframe and engine
A/P autopilot
BAT battery
CAT carburetor air temperature
CHT cylinder head temperature
COM communications radio
COMM communications radio
CS constant-speed propeller
C/S constant-speed propeller
C/W complied with
DBL double
DG directional gyro
FAC factory
FBO fixed-base operator
FGP full gyro panel
FWF firewall forward
G gravity
GAL gallons
GPH gallons per hour

GS glideslope
HD heavy duty
HP horsepower
IFR instrument flight rules
INSP inspection
INST instrument
KTS knots
L left
LDG landing
LED light emitting diode
LH left-hand
LIC license
LOC localizer
LTS lights
L&R left and right
MB marker beacon
MBR marker beacon receiver
MP manifold pressure
MPH miles per hour
MOD modification
NAV navigation
NAV/COM navigation/communication radio
NAV/COMM navigation/communication radio
NAVCOM navigation/communication radio
NDH no damage history
OAT outside air temperature
PMA parts manufacture approval
PROP propeller
R right
RC rate of climb
REMAN remanufactured
RH right-hand
RMFD remanufactured
RMFG remanufactured
ROC rate of climb
SAFOH since airframe overhaul
SCMOH since chrome major overhaul
SEL single engine land
SFACNEW since factory new
SFN since factory new
SFNE since factory new engine
SFREM since factory remanufacture
SFREMAN since factory remanufacture
SFRMFG since factory remanufacture
SMOH since major overhaul
SN serial number

SNEW   since new
SPOH   since propeller overhaul
STC   supplemental type certificate
STOH   since top overhaul
STOL   short takeoff and landing
TAS   true airspeed
TBO   time between overhaul
TC   turbocharged
TNSP   transponder
TNSPNDR   transponder
TSN   time since new
TSO   technical service order
TT   total time
TTAF   total time airframe
TTA&E   total time airframe and engine
TTE   total time engine
TTSN   total time since new
TXP   transponder
T&B   turn and bank
VAC   vacuum
VFR   visual flight rules
VHF   very high frequency
VOR   VHF omnidirectional range
XC   cross-country
XMTR   transmitter
XPDR   transponder
XPNDR   transponder

Appendix B

Telephone area codes

201 New Jersey north (Newark)
202 District of Columbia (Washington)
203 Connecticut
204 Manitoba, Canada
205 Alabama
206 Washington west (Seattle)
207 Maine
208 Idaho
209 California central (Fresno)
212 New York southeast (New York City)
213 California southwest (Los Angeles)
214 Texas northeast (Dallas)
215 Pennsylvania southeast (Philadelphia)
216 Ohio northeast (Cleveland)
217 Illinois central (Springfield)
218 Minnesota north (Duluth)
219 Indiana north (South Bend)

301 Maryland
302 Delaware
303 Colorado
304 West Virginia
305 Florida southeast (Miami)
306 Saskatchewan, Canada
307 Wyoming
308 Nebraska west (North Platte)
309 Illinois northwest (Peoria)
310 California southwest (Los Angeles)
312 Illinois northeast (Chicago)
313 Michigan southeast (Detroit)
314 Missouri east (St. Louis)

315 New York north central (Syracuse)
316 Kansas south (Wichita)
317 Indiana central (Indianapolis)
318 Louisiana northwest (Shreveport)
319 Iowa east (Dubuque)

401 Rhode Island
402 Nebraska east (Omaha)
403 Alberta, Canada
404 Georgia north (Atlanta)
405 Oklahoma west (Oklahoma City)
406 Montana
407 Florida east (Melbourne)
408 California northwest (San Jose)
409 Texas southeast (Galveston)
410 Maryland eastern shore
412 Pennsylvania southwest (Pittsburgh)
413 MA west (Springfield)
414 Wisconsin southeast (Milwaukee)
415 California central (San Francisco)
416 Ontario, Canada
417 Missouri southwest (Springfield)
418 Quebec, Canada
419 Ohio northwest (Toledo)

501 Arkansas
502 Kentucky west (Louisville)
503 Oregon
504 Louisiana southeast (New Orleans)
505 New Mexico
506 New Brunswick, Canada
507 Minnesota south (Rochester)
508 Massachusetts east (except Boston)
509 Washington east (Spokane)
510 California central (Oakland)
512 Texas south (San Antonio)
513 Ohio southwest (Cincinnati)
514 Quebec, Canada
515 Iowa central (Des Moines)
516 New York southeast (Long Island)
517 Michigan central (Lansing)
518 New York northeast (Albany)
519 Ontario, Canada

601 Mississippi
602 Arizona

603 New Hampshire
604 British Columbia, Canada
605 South Dakota
606 Kentucky east (Lexington)
607 New York south central (Binghamton)
608 Wisconsin southwest (Madison)
609 New Jersey south (Trenton)
612 Minnesota central (Minneapolis)
613 Ontario, Canada
614 Ohio southeast (Columbus)
615 Tennessee east (Nashville)
616 Michigan west (Grand Rapids)
617 Massachusetts east (Boston)
618 Illinois south (Centralia)
619 California south (San Diego)

701 North Dakota
702 Nevada
703 Virginia north and west (Arlington)
704 North Carolina west (Charlotte)
705 Ontario, Canada
707 California northwest (Santa Rosa)
708 Illinois north (Chicago)
709 Newfoundland, Canada
712 Iowa west (Council Bluffs)
713 Texas southeast (Houston)
714 California southwest (Orange)
715 Wisconsin north (Eau Claire)
716 New York west (Buffalo)
717 Pennsylvania central (Harrisburg)
718 New York southeast (Brooklyn)
719 Colorado south (Pueblo)

801 Utah
802 Vermont
803 South Carolina
804 Virginia southeast (Richmond)
805 California west central (Bakersfield)
806 Texas northwest (Amarillo)
807 Ontario, Canada
808 Hawaii
809 Bermuda, Puerto Rico, Virgin Islands, and other islands
812 Indiana south (Evansville)
813 Florida southwest (Tampa)
814 Pennsylvania northwest (Altoona)
815 Illinois northwest (Rockford)

816 Missouri northwest (Kansas City)
817 Texas north central (Fort Worth)
818 California southwest (Pasadena)
819 Quebec, Canada

901 Tennessee west (Memphis)
902 Nova Scotia, Canada
903 Mexico
904 Florida north (Jacksonville)
905 Mexico City, Mexico
906 Michigan northwest (Escanaba)
907 Alaska
908 New Jersey central
912 Georgia south (Savannah)
913 Kansas north (Topeka)
914 New York southeast (White Plains)
915 Texas southwest (San Angelo)
916 California northwest (Sacramento)
918 Oklahoma northeast (Tulsa)
919 North Carolina east (Raleigh)

Appendix C

Inspections

These are the general inspection requirements, as taken from the *Cessna 150 Service Manual*:

To avoid repetition throughout the inspection, general points to be checked are given below. In the inspection, only the items to be checked are listed; details as to how to check, or what to check for, are excluded. The inspection covers several different models. Some items may apply only to specific models, and some items are optional equipment that may or may not be found on a particular airplane. Check the FAA Airworthiness Directives and Cessna Service Letters for compliance at the time specified by them. Federal Aviation Regulations require that all civil aircraft have a periodic (annual) inspection as prescribed by the Administrator, and performed by a person designated by the Administrator. The Cessna Aircraft Company recommends a 100-hour periodic inspection for the airplane.

CHECK AS APPLICABLE

Movable parts: for lubrication, servicing, security of attachment, binding, excessive wear, safetying, proper operation, proper adjustment, correct travel, cracked fittings, security of hinges, defective bearings, cleanliness, corrosion, deformation, sealing, and tensions.

Fluid lines and hoses: for leaks, cracks, dents, kinks, chafing, proper radius, security, corrosion, deterioration, obstructions, and foreign matter.

Metal parts: for security of attachment, cracks, metal distortion, broken spotwelds, corrosion, condition of paint, and any other apparent damage.

Wiring: for security, chafing, burning, defective insulation, loose or broken terminals, heat deterioration, and corroded terminals.

Bolts in critical areas: for correct torque in accordance with proper torque values, when installed or when visual inspection indicates the need for a torque check.

Filters, screens, and fluids: for cleanliness, contamination and/or replacement at specified intervals.

AIRPLANE FILE

Miscellaneous data, information, and licenses are a part of the airplane file. Check that the following documents are up-to-date and in accordance with current FARs. Most of the items listed are required by the FARs. Because the regulations of other nations might require other documents and data, owners of exported aircraft should check with appropriate aviation officials to determine specific requirements.

To be displayed in the airplane at all times:

- Aircraft airworthiness certificate
- Aircraft registration certificate
- Aircraft radio license

To be carried in the airplane at all times:

- Weight and balance and associated papers
- Aircraft equipment list

To be made available upon request:

- Aircraft logbook and engine logbook

ENGINE RUN-UP

Before beginning the step-by-step inspection, start, run up, and shut down the engine in accordance with instructions in the owner's manual. During the run-up, observe the following, making note of any discrepancies or abnormalities:

- Engine temperatures or pressures
- Static rpm
- Magneto drop
- Engine response to changes in power
- Any unusual engine noises
- Fuel selector valve (Operate the engine on each position long enough to make sure the valve functions properly.)
- Idling speed and mixture; proper idle cutoff
- Alternator
- Suction gauge

After the inspection has been completed, if problems must be fixed, another engine run-up should be performed to ascertain that any discrepancies or abnormalities have been corrected.

PERIODIC INSPECTION

Continental engine. If the engine is equipped with an external oil filter, change the engine oil and filter element at 50-hour intervals. If the engine is not equipped with an external oil filter, change the engine oil and clean the oil screen every 25 hours.

Lycoming engine. If the engine is not equipped with an external oil filter, change the engine oil and clean the oil screens at 50-hour intervals. If the engine is equipped with an external oil filter, the engine oil change intervals may be extended to 100-hour intervals, providing the external filter element is changed at 50-hour intervals.

The 50-hour inspection includes:

- A visual check of the engine, propeller, and aircraft exterior for any apparent damage or defects
- An engine oil change as required above
- Accomplishment of lubrication and servicing requirements
- Removal of the propeller spinner and engine cowling, and replacement after the inspection has been completed

The 100-hour or annual inspection includes everything in the 50-hour inspection. Loosen or remove fuselage, wing, empennage, and upholstery inspection doors, plates, and fairings only as necessary to perform a thorough, searching inspection of the aircraft. Replace after the inspection has been completed.

Note: Any inspection and related maintenance should be conducted in accordance with FARs and applicable aircraft service requirements.

Time intervals in the following charts indicate the hours between inspections and servicing.

Propeller

	Time
1. Spinner and spinner bulkhead	50
2. Blades	50
3. Hub	50
4. Bolts and/or nuts	50

Engine compartment

Check for evidence of oil and fuel leaks, then clean the entire engine and compartment, if needed, prior to inspection.

	Time
1. Engine oil, screen, filler cap, dipstick, drain plug, and filter	50
2. Oil Cooler	50
3. Induction air filter	50
4. Induction airbox, air valves, doors, and controls	50
5. Cold and hot air hoses	50
6. Engine baffles	50
7. Cylinders, rocker box covers, and push rod housings	50
8. Crankcase, oil sump, accessory section, and front crankshaft seal	50
9. All lines and hoses	50

Engine compartment

	Time
10. Intake and exhaust systems	50
11. Ignition harness	50
12. Spark plugs and compression	100
13. Crankcase and vacuum system breather lines	50
14. Electrical wiring	50
15. Vacuum pump, oil separator, and relief valve	50
16. Vacuum relief valve filter	100
17. Engine controls and linkage	50
18. Engine shock mounts, engine mount structure, and ground straps	50
19. Cabin heater valves, doors, and controls	50
20. Starter, solenoid, and electrical connections	50
21. Starter brushes, brush leads, and commutator	200
22. Alternator and electrical connections	50
23. Alternator brushes, brush leads, and commutator/slip ring	500
24. Voltage regulator mounting and electrical leads	50
25. Magnetos (externally) and electrical connections	50
26. Slick magneto timing	100
27. Carburetor	50
28. Firewall	100
29. Engine cowling	50
30. Carburetor drain plug for security	50

Fuel system

	Time
1. Fuel strainer, drain valve, and control	50
2. Fuel strainer screen and bowl	100
3. Fuel tanks, fuel lines, drains, filler caps, and placards	100
4. Drain fuel and check tank interior, attachment, and outlet screens	1000
5. Fuel vents and vent valves	100
6. Fuel selector valve and placards	100
7. Engine primer	100

Landing gear

	Time
1. Brake fluid, lines and hoses, linings, discs, brake assemblies, and master cylinders	100
2. Main gear wheels, wheel bearings, step and spring strut, tires, and fairings	100
3. Main gear and nose gear wheel bearings and lubrication	500
4. Torque link lubrication	50
5. Nose gear strut servicing	100
6. Nose gear shimmy damper service	100
7. Nose gear wheel, wheel bearings, strut, steering system, shimmy damper, tire, fairing, and torque links	100
8. Parking brake system	100

Airframe

	Time
1. Aircraft exterior	50
2. Aircraft structure	100
3. Windows, windshield, and doors	50
4. Seats, rails and stops, upholstery, structure, and seat mounting	50
5. Safety belts and attaching brackets	50
6. Control "U" bearings, sprockets, pulleys, cables, chains, and turnbuckles	100
7. Control lock, control wheel, and control "U" mechanism	100
8. Instruments and markings	100
9. Gyros, central air filter	100
10. Magnetic compass compensation	1000
11. Instrument wiring and plumbing	100
12. Instrument panel, shock mounts, ground straps, cover, and decals/labeling	100
13. Defrosting, heating, ventilating systems, and controls	100
14. Cabin upholstery, trim, sun visors, and ashtrays	100
15. Area beneath floor, lines, hoses, wires, and control cables	100
16. Lights, switches, breakers/fuses, and spare fuses	50
17. Exterior lights	50
18. Pitot and static system	100
19. Stall warning sensing unit, pitot warning heater	100
20. Radio and radio controls	100
21. Radio antennas	100
22. Battery, battery box, and battery cables	100
23. Battery electrolyte level	50

Control systems

In addition to the items listed below, always check for correct direction of movement, correct travel, and correct cable tension.

	Time
1. Cables, terminals, pulleys, brackets, cable guards, turnbuckles, and fairleads	100
2. Chains, terminals, sprockets, and chain guards	100
3. Trim control wheel, indicators, and actuator	100
4. Travel stops	100
5. All decals and labeling	100
6. Flap control switch (or lever), flap rollers and tracks, flap transmitter and linkage, and flap position indicator flap electric motor and transmission	100
7. Elevator trim	100
8. Rudder pedal assemblies and linkage	100
9. Skin and structure of control surface and trim tabs	100
10. Balance weight attachment	100

Appendix D

FAA office locations

Whenever you need a question answered, you can always turn to the Federal Aviation Administration. The FAA has many offices spread around the country with experts to serve the public. Remember, FAA employees are government employees, there to serve, and paid with tax dollars. In the many years that I have been associated with general aviation, I have never been disappointed with the help I received from the FAA. When a problem arises, contact them.

Alabama

FSDO 09
6500 43rd Avenue North, Birmingham, AL 35206
(205) 731-1393

Alaska

FSDO 01
6348 Old Airport Way, Fairbanks, AK 99709
(907) 474-0276

FSDO 03
4510 West Int'l Airport Road, Suite 302, Anchorage, AK 99502-1088
(907) 243-1902

FSDO 05
1910 Alex Holden Way, Suite A, Juneau, AK 99801
(907) 789-0231

Arizona

FSDO
15041 North Airport Drive, Scottsdale, AZ 85260
(602) 640-2561

Arkansas

FSDO 11
1701 Bond Street, Little Rock, AR 72202
(501) 324-5565

California

LAX FSDO
5885 West Imperial Hwy, Los Angeles, CA 90045
(310) 215-2150

FSDO
831 Mitten Rd., Rm 105, Burlingame, CA 94010
(415) 876-2771

FSDO
16501 Sherman Way, Suite 330, Van Nuys, CA 91406
(818) 904-6291

FSDO
1250 Aviation Ave., Suite 295, San Jose, CA 95110-1130
(408) 291-7681

FSDO
8525 Gibbs Drive, Suite 120, San Diego, CA 92123
(619) 557-5281

FSDO
Fresno Air Terminal
4955 East Anderson, Suite 110, Fresno, CA 93727-1521
(209) 487-5306

FSDO
6961 Flight Road, Riverside, CA 92504
(714) 276-6701

FSDO
6650 Belleau Wood Lane, Sacramento, CA 95822
(916) 551-1721

FSDO
P.O. Box 2397, Airport Station, Oakland, CA 94614
(510) 273-7155

FSDO
2815 East Spring Street, Long Beach, CA 90806
(310) 426-7134

Colorado

FSDO
5440 Roslyn St., Suite 201, Denver, CO 80216
(303) 286-5400

Connecticut

FSDO 03
Building 85-214 1st Flr, Bradley International Airport, Windsor Locks, CT 06096
(203) 654-1000

Florida

FSDO
FAA Building, Craig Municipal Airport, 855 Saint John's Bluff Road
Jacksonville, FL 32225
(904) 641-7311

FSDO 15
9677 Tradport Dr., Suite 100, Orlando, FL 32827
(407) 648-6840

FSDO 17
286 South West 34th St., Ft. Lauderdale, FL 33315
(305) 463-4841

FSDO 19
P.O. Box 592015, Miami, FL 33159
(305) 526-2572

Georgia

FSDO 11
1680 Phoenix Pkwy., Second Flr, College Park, GA 30349
(404) 994-5276

Hawaii

FSDO
90 Nakolo Place, Room 215, Honolulu, HI 96819
(808) 836-0615

Illinois

FSDO 03
Post Office Box H, DuPage County Airport, West Chicago, IL 60185
(708) 377-4500

FSDO 19
Capitol Airport, #3 North Airport Dr., Springfield, IL 62708
(217) 492-4238

FSDO 31
9950 West Lawrence Ave., Suite 400, Schiller Park, IL 60176
(312) 353-7787

Indiana
FSDO 11
6801 Pierson Drive, Indianapolis, IN 46241
(317) 247-2491

FSDO 17
1843 Commerce Drive, South Bend, IN 46628
(219) 236-8480

Iowa
FSDO 01
3021 Army Post Road, Des Moines, IA 50321
(515) 285-9895

Kansas
FSDO 64
Mid-Continent Airport, 1801 Airport Rd., Rm 103,Wichita, KS 67209
(316) 941-1200

Kentucky
FSDO
Kaden Building, 5th Flr, 6100 Dutchmans Lane, Louisville, KY 40205-3284
(502) 582-5941

Louisiana
FSDO
Ryan Airport
9191 Plank Rd., Baton Rouge, LA 70811
(504) 356-5701

Maine
FSDO 05
2 Al McKay Ave., Portland, ME 04102
(207) 780-3263

Maryland
FSDO 07
P.O. Box 8747, BWI Airport, MD 21240
(410) 787-0040

Massachusetts

FSDO 01
Civil Air Terminal Bldg., 2nd Flr., Hanscom Field, Bedford, MA 01730
(617) 274-7130

Michigan

FSDO 09
Kent County International Airport, P.O. Box 888879, Grand Rapids, MI 49588-8879
(616) 456-2427

FSDO 23
Willow Run Airport (east side), 8800 Beck Road, Belleville, MI 48111
(313) 487-7222

Minnesota

FSDO 15
6020 28th Ave. South, Rm 201, Minneapolis, MN 55450
(612) 725-4211

Mississippi

FSDO 07
120 North Hangar Drive, Suite C, Jackson Municipal Airport, Jackson, MS 39208
(601) 965-4633

Missouri

FSDO 03
FAA Bldg, 10801 Pear Tree Ln., Suite 200, St. Ann, MO 63074
(314) 429-1006

FSDO 05
Kansas City International Airport, 525 Mexico City Ave., Kansas City, MO 64153
(816) 243-3800

Montana

FSDO
FAA Building, Room 3, Helena Airport, Helena, MT 59601
(406) 449-5270

Nebraska

FSDO 09
General Aviation Building, Lincoln Municipal Airport, Lincoln, NE 68524
(402) 437-5485

Nevada

FSDO
210 South Rock Blvd., Reno, NV 89502
(702) 784-5321

FSDO
6020 South Spencer, Suite A7, Las Vegas, NV 89119
(702) 388-6482

New Jersey

FSDO 25
150 Fred Wehran Drive, Room 1, Teterboro Airport, Teterboro, NJ 07608
(201) 288-1745

New Mexico

FSDO
1601 Randolph Road, SE Suite 200N, Albuquerque, NM 87106
(505) 247-0156

New York

FSDO 01
Albany County Airport, Albany, NY 12211
(518) 869-8482

FSDO 11
Administration Building, Suite #235 RTE 110, Republic Airport
Farmingdale, NY 11735
(516) 694-5530

FSDO 15
181 South Franklin Ave, 4th Flr, Valley Stream, NY 11581
(718) 917-1848

FSDO 23
1 Airport Way, Suite 110, Rochester, NY 14624
(716) 263-5880

North Carolina

FSDO 05
8025 North Point Blvd., Suite 250, Winston-Salem, NC 27106
(919) 631-5147

FSDO 06
2000 Aerial Center Pkwy., Suite 120, Morrisville, NC 27263
(919) 840-5510

FSDO 08
FAA Building, 5318 Morris Field Drive, Charlotte, NC 28208
(704) 359-8471

North Dakota

FSDO 21
1801 23rd Ave. N., Fargo, ND 58102
(701) 232-8949

Ohio

CVG FSDO
4242 Airport Road, Lunken Executive Building, Cincinnati, OH 45226
(513) 533-8110

FSDO 07
3939 International Gateway, 2nd Flr., Port Columbus International Airport
Columbus, OH 43219
(614) 469-7476

FSDO
Federal Facilities Building, Cleveland Hopkins International Airport
Cleveland, OH 44135
(216) 265-1345

Oklahoma

FSDO
1300 South Meridian, Suite 601, Bethany, OK 73108
(405) 231-4196

Oregon

FSDO
Portland/Hillsboro Airport, 3355 NE Cornell Road, Hillsboro, OR 97124
(503) 326-2104

Pennsylvania

FSDO 03
Allegheny County Airport, Terminal Bldg., Rm 213, West Mifflin, PA 15122
(412) 462-5507

FSDO 05
3405 Airport Rd. North, Allentown, PA 18103
(215) 264-2888

FSDO 13
400 Airport Dr., Rm 101, New Cumberland, PA 17070
(717) 774-8271

FSDO 17
Scott Plaza 2, 2nd Flr., Philadelphia, PA 19113
(215) 596-0673

FSDO 19
One Thorn Run Center, Suite 200, 1187 Thorn Run Ext., Corapolis, PA 15108
(412) 644-5406

South Carolina

FSDO 13
103 Trade Zone Dr., West Columbia, SC 29169
(803) 765-5931

South Dakota

FSDO
Rapid City Regional Airport, Route 2 Box 4750, Rapid City, SD 57701
(605) 393-1359

Tennessee

FSDO 03
2 International Plaza Dr., Suite 700, Nashville, TN 37217
(615) 781-5437

FSDO 04
3385 Airways Blvd., Suite 115, Memphis, TN 38116
(901) 544-3820

Texas

FSDO
7701 North Stemmons Fwy Suite 300, Lock Box 5, Dallas, TX 75247
(214) 767-5850

FSDO
Dallas-Fort Worth Regional Airport, P.O. Box 619020
Dallas-Ft. Worth Airport, TX 75261
(214) 574-2150

FSDO
8800 Paul B. Koonce Drive, Room 152, Houston, TX 77061-5190
(713) 640-4400

FSDO
Route 3, Box 51, Lubbock, TX 79401
(806) 762-0335

FSDO
10100 Reunion Place, Suite 200, San Antonio, TX 78216
(512) 341-4371

Utah

FSDO
116 North 2400 West, Salt Lake City, UT 84116
(801) 524-4247

Virginia

FSDO 21
Richmond International Airport, Executive Terminal, 2nd Flr.
Sandstone, VA 23150-2594
(804) 222-7494

FSDO 27
GT Building, Suite 112, Box 17325, Dulles International Airport
Washington, D.C. 20041
(703) 557-5360

Washington
FSDO
1601 Lind Ave., SW, Renton, WA 98055-4046
(206) 227-2810

West Virginia
FSDO 09
Yeager Airport, 301 Eagle Mountain Road, Room 144, Charleston, WV 25311
(304) 343-4689

Wisconsin
FSDO 13
4915 South Howell Avenue, 4th Flr., Milwaukee, WI 53207
(414) 747-5531

Appendix E

Cessna 150/152 price guide

The prices for used Cessna 150/152 airplanes are based upon average asking and selling prices. Price accounts for typical avionics and middle time on the engine. Middle time on the engine is the middle one-third of the TBO (an 1800-hour TBO engine would have 600–1200 hours SMOH). Add $1500 for the Aerobat A150 model and add $3000 for the Aerobat A152 model.

Year	Model	Asking price	Year	Model	Asking price
1959	150	$ 9,600	1973	150	13,900
1960	150	9,600	1974	150	14,300
1961	150	9,800	1975	150	14,500
1962	150	9,900	1976	150	14,900
1963	150	10,300	1977	150	15,300
1964	150	10,500	1978	152	21,500
1965	150	10,700	1979	152	23,500
1966	150	11,100	1980	152	25,000
1967	150	11,700	1981	152	25,500
1968	150	11,800	1982	152	26,500
1969	150	12,000	1983	152	30,500
1970	150	12,200	1984	152	34,500
1971	150	12,500	1985	152	41,000
1972	150	13,500			

Appendix F

Cessna 150/152 prepurchase checklist

The prepurchase checklist is intended to provide a means of comparing airplanes you have considered for purchase. It is a means of remembering specific details about each airplane that you have looked at.

Cessna 150/152 Pre–Purchase Check List

Year _____ Model _____ Color _____ N–number_____

The plane is located at _____

It was advertised in _____

INTERVIEW (by telephone or in person)
Why selling _____
General appearance/condition of the plane (1–10)_____
How many total hours on the airframe _____
How many hours on the engine since new _____
How many hours since the last overhaul _____
What type of overhaul was done _____
Who did the overhaul _____
Is there any damage history yes/no _____
What is the asking price _____

VISUAL INSPECTION
CABIN
Appearance (1–10) _____
Overall condition (1–10) _____
Upholstry (1–10) _____
Carpet (1–10) _____
Headliner (1–10) _____
Door panels (1–10) _____
Windshield condition (1–10) _____
Side and rear window condition (1–10) _____
Door operation (1–10) _____
Seat track condition (1–10) _____
Instrument panel appearance (1–10) _____
Condition of instruments (1–10) _____
List of avionics _____

Age of instruments/avionics _____
IFR or VFR _____
Workability (1–10) _____
Remarks _____

AIRFRAME
Appearance (1–10) _____
Overall condition (1–10) _____
Paint (1–10) _____
Visible corrosion _____
Visible rust _____
Dents, wrinkles, or tears in skin _____
Fuel leaks yes/no _____
Landing gear (1–10) _____
Tires (1–10) _____
Oleo strut (1–10) _____
Control surface movement _____
Control surface alignment _____
Control surface damage _____

ENGINE
Signs of oil leaks _____
Condition of hoses and lines (1–10) _____
Linkage or cable damage _____
Battery box condition (1–10) _____
Condition of Propeller (1–10) _____
Propeller damage _____
Exhaust system (1–10) _____
Color of exhaust pipe residue _____
Exhaust stains on the belly _____

LOGBOOKS
Required paperwork:
    Airworthiness Certificate _____
    Aircraft Registration Certificate _____
    FCC Station License _____
    Flight manual or operating limitations _____
    Logbooks (airframe, engine and propeller) _____
    Current equipment list _____
    Weight & balance chart _____
Airframe Logbook
    List of ADs and dates of compliance _____
    Total time since new _____
    Minor repairs noted _____
    Major repairs noted _____
    Total time and date of last inspection _____
    Modifications _____
    Form 337s _____
Engine Logbook
    Original engine yes/no _____
    List of ADs and dates of compliance _____
    Total time since new _____
    Total time since overhaul _____
    Who did the overhaul _____
    Minor repairs noted _____
    Major repairs noted _____
    Total time and date of last inspection _____
    Compression check report _____
    Modifications _____
    Form 337s _____
    Time between oil changes _____
    Oil analysis _____

REMARKS

Shopping for an airplane can become confusing when the details of several airplanes start to run together. This prepurchase checklist helps a buyer acquire specific information for later comparison shopping.

THE TEST FLIGHT

Airplane insured by _____

Pilot's name _____

Pilot's ratings and medical status _____

Engine start _____
Gauge action _____
Run–up _____
Control action _____
Ventilation/heat _____
Turns _____
Stalls _____
Level flight _____
Hands–off trim _____
Brake operation _____
Wheel shimmy _____
Avionics comments _____
_____

REMARKS

MECHANIC'S INSPECTION

Mechanic's name _____

Ratings and certificate number _____

Cost of inspection _____

Outstanding ADs _____

Compression check _____

Borescope inspection _____

REMARKS

NOTES AND COMMENTS

CURRENT OWNER INFORMATION

Name _____

Address _____

Phone number _____

REMARKS

Index

windows/windscreens
   Omni-Vision windshields in-
      troduced, 5, 20, 29
   side window replacement,
      162
wings
   conical cambered tips of-
      fered, 22
   gap seal modifications, 181
   short takeoff/landing (STOL)
      modifications, 176-178
   wingtip modifications, 179-180
wiring, inspection, 223
World War II Cessnas, 3

X

XL-19B turboprop Cessna, 4
XT-37A jet Cessna, 4